CRITICAL THINKING ACTIVITIES

IN PATTERNS, IMAGERY, LOGIC

Dale Seymour

Ed Beardslee

DALE SEYMOUR PUBLICATIONS

Approximately half the activities in this book were originally designed by the Dale Seymour Publications staff as ancillary materials for Silver Burdett Mathematics, copyright 1987 by Silver Burdett and Ginn. Development was done with the understanding that the two companies share joint ownership of the activities, and that each company has the right to publish the activities in its own format. Dale Seymour Publications gratefully acknowledges the support of Silver Burdett and Ginn in the development and production of the initial phase of this project. The following pages are copyright 1987 by Silver Burdett and Ginn: 2, 3, 6, 7, 8, 9, 10, 11, 12, 13, 17, 18, 19, 20, 21, 22, 24, 25, 33, 34, 36, 37, 52, 53, 54, 55, 56, 57, 60, 61, 63, 64, 69, 70, 71, 72, 73, 74, 78, 79, 88, 89, 90, 91, 92, 93, 104, 105, 106, 107, 108, 109, 110, 111, 112, 113, 114, 115, 118, 119, 120, 121, 122, 123, 132, 133, 135, 136, 138, 139.

ISBN 0-86651-471-6
Printed in the United States of America
25 26 V031 13

Dale Seymour Publications
Pearson Learning Group

1-800-321-3106
www.pearsonlearning.com

CONTENTS

INTRODUCTION

Thinking skills and problem solving are currently given high priority in curriculum development and inservice programs. Although each area of the curriculum defines and approaches thinking skills and problem solving somewhat differently, the basic emphasis on teaching students how to think and how to learn has strong support from most people concerned with the education of youngsters.

Too often, thinking skills have been overlooked or considered extra, something above and beyond the basics that must be taught. Teachers need to recognize that thinking skills *are* basic. The term *critical thinking skills* is a good one because the word *critical* has a number of different meanings. It means *analytical,* and it means *evaluative* or *judgmental,* but it also means *indispensable, vital, essential.* Indeed, critical thinking activities should be considered indispensable to the education of every child.

This book presents activities to help students develop their thinking and problem-solving skills. Mathematics curriculum specialists have identified from ten to fifteen strategies that can help students solve nonroutine math problems. Often students may need to use more than one such strategy to arrive at the solution for a given problem. Some of these strategies require that students use skills such as thinking visually, recognizing patterns, using logical reasoning, and doing organized counting—all of which are elements of critical thinking in mathematics.

There are a number of different ways to categorize thinking skills. No two authors would choose the same list or prioritize the importance of each skill in the same way. This book concentrates on three specific types of thinking skills: *patterns, imagery,* and *logic.* If students are to become successful problem solvers, they need to become good critical thinkers at the same time.

How to Use This Book

As a supplement to a regular textbook this book provides materials that can be used in a variety of ways to introduce, reinforce, and elaborate on specific critical thinking skills.

Reproducible Pages

The pages in this book are designed to be photocopied for distribution to students as individual worksheets or problem cards. Preparing a transparency of any page (using a photocopy machine and transparency acetate) makes it possible to present a lesson to a group or to the entire class by using an overhead projector. Note that with very young students (such as kindergartners or first graders) teachers may have to help them read the directions on the worksheets. In this case, presenting the lesson to a group may work better than having students complete the sheets on their own.

Sequence

In general, there is no recommended sequence for presenting the topics or the activities within a single topic. Teachers may choose and order the activities in whatever way they believe will best meet their instructional goals. Activities within a topic are generally ordered from simpler to more difficult, as indicated by their one-triangle, two-triangle, or three-triangle rating.

Class Discussion

Students develop their thinking skills by observing how other people think. For this reason, class discussion of the activities for every topic is invaluable. Teachers are advised to spend class time discussing different ways to formulate problems and brainstorming possible approaches to their solution. Students need help in overcoming the misconception that in math there is always one exact answer and only one way to solve the problem. Teachers need to encourage and reward creativity and divergent thinking in these activities.

Teaching Suggestions by Topic

Part 1: Patterns

Mathematics is often defined as the *study of patterns.* Making students conscious of patterns can help them to see important relationships in mathematics. Number patterns are a nonthreatening way to help students learn about special number properties. Students should be encouraged to create their own patterns—both visual and numerical.

Organized counting dovetails nicely with pattern recognition. A student soon learns that multiplication is a shortcut to counting or adding. Breaking a problem into smaller parts may be easier than approaching it as a whole. Students should talk about the advantages and disadvantages of approaching a problem through the organized counting of patterns.

For exercises in which students are asked to continue a given pattern, there may be more than one solution. Teachers should not be too quick to assume that a student's answer is wrong just because it is different; examining that pattern may show that the student has discovered a perfectly good pattern of his or her own.

Part 2: Imagery

The ability to visualize is extremely helpful in solving problems. In the regular curriculum, students rarely have an opportunity to develop visual-thinking skills. In addition to providing much-needed practice, these lessons may serve as models for teachers who wish to create similar activities for further work in imagery and visual thinking.

Many of the activities in this section lend themselves to elaboration. Students should be encouraged to look for geometric shapes and visual patterns in their environment. They might bring in clippings from magazines and newspapers to illustrate such concepts as symmetry, congruence, and similarity. Most students enjoy creating their own designs that allow them to explore geometric relationships.

Part 3: Logic

For many students, the worksheets on logic will be more difficult than others in this book. Consequently, teachers are advised to take the additional time needed to explain the conventions of Venn diagrams and to provide model solutions. Students should be shown how to formulate their own questions, for this can enhance their understanding of the principles and structure of logic problems. Logic problems that seem overwhelmingly complex can often be simplified by breaking the problem into smaller problems. Students who do this will discover that taking one small step at a time can lead them to a solution.

You may need to give special attention to the terminology of Venn diagrams. Some students may be especially confused by the terms *both, and, either, or,* and *only.* For example, *in A and B* means "within the sections where A and B meet"; *either* means "in A or in B or in the section where A and B meet"; *in A only* means "in the portion of A that is not shared by any other shape." Examples are given in the text to clarify these terms.

Making Successful Thinkers and Problem Solvers

Students will see themselves as good problem solvers if they experience repeated success. Thus, when first introducing new critical thinking activities in any topic, it is better to err in selecting pages that are too easy than to have students struggle and conclude that they are unable to solve nonroutine problems. Through class discussion and work within small groups, students will have the chance to observe the thinking strategies of their peers. Eventually, they will muster the confidence to explore possible solution strategies on their own. At this point, they will be well on their way to becoming proficient critical thinkers in all their mathematics work.

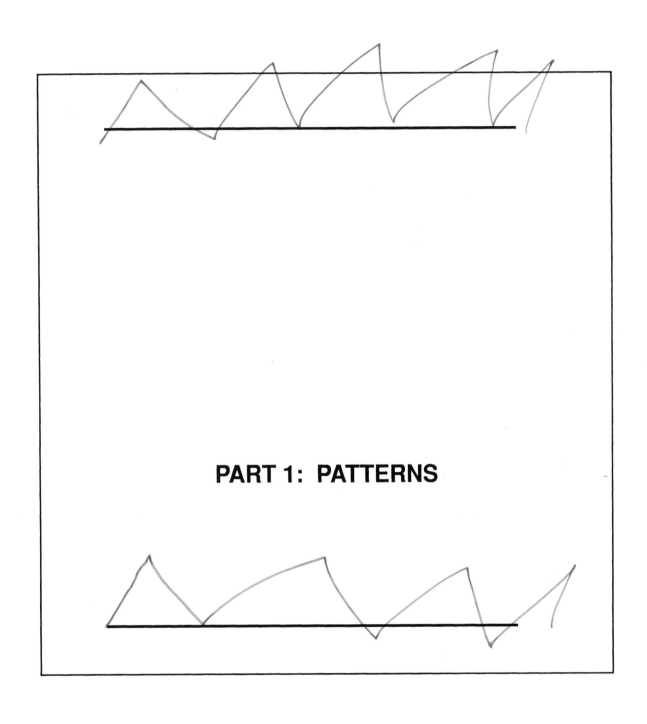

PART 1: PATTERNS

PATTERN TRAINS (I)

Each row has a pattern. Write numbers in the blank spaces to match the pattern.

1
2

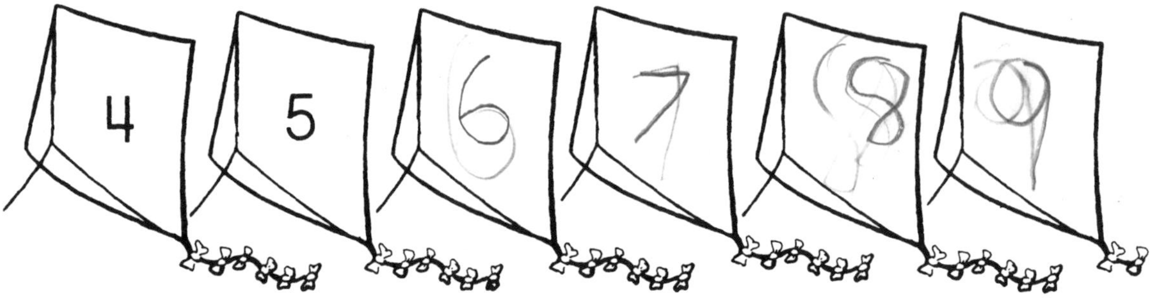
4
5

1
3
5
7

5
2
1

PATTERN MATCH

Copy each pattern.

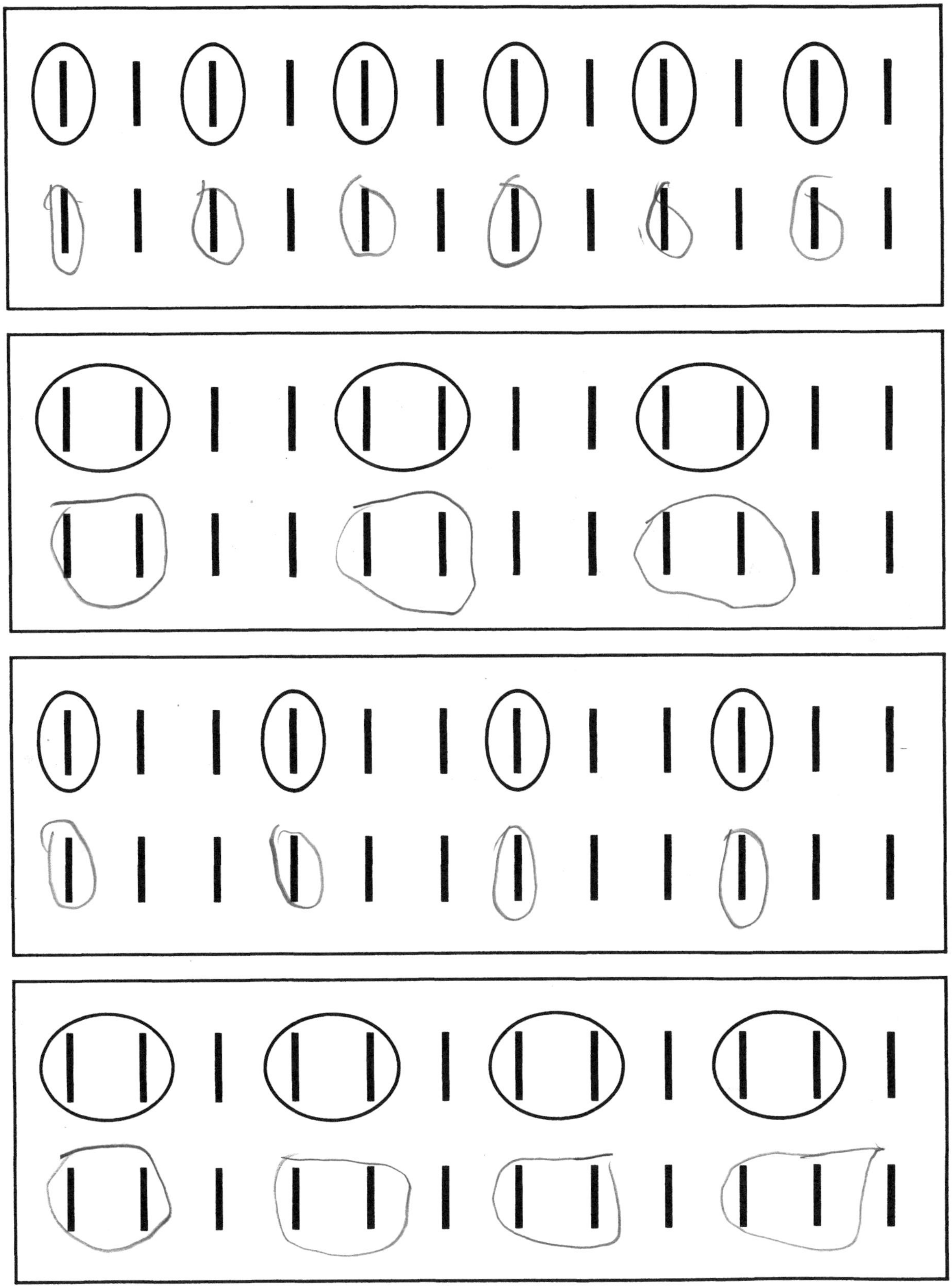

ONE HUNDRED APPLES

Look for patterns in the hundreds chart. Write the missing numbers in the apples.

1	2	3	4	5	6	7	8	9	10
11	12	13	14	15	16	17	18	19	20
21	22	23	24	25	26	26	28	29	30
31	32	33	34	35	36	37	38	39	40
41	42	43	44	45	46	47	48	49	50
51	52	53	54	55	56	57	58	59	60
61	62	63	64	65	66	67	68	69	70
71	72	73	74	75	76	77	78	79	80
81	82	83	84	85	86	87	88	89	90
91	92	93	94	95	96	97	98	99	100

COUNTING CIRCLES (I)

Write the numbers as far as you can.
How many circles are there?

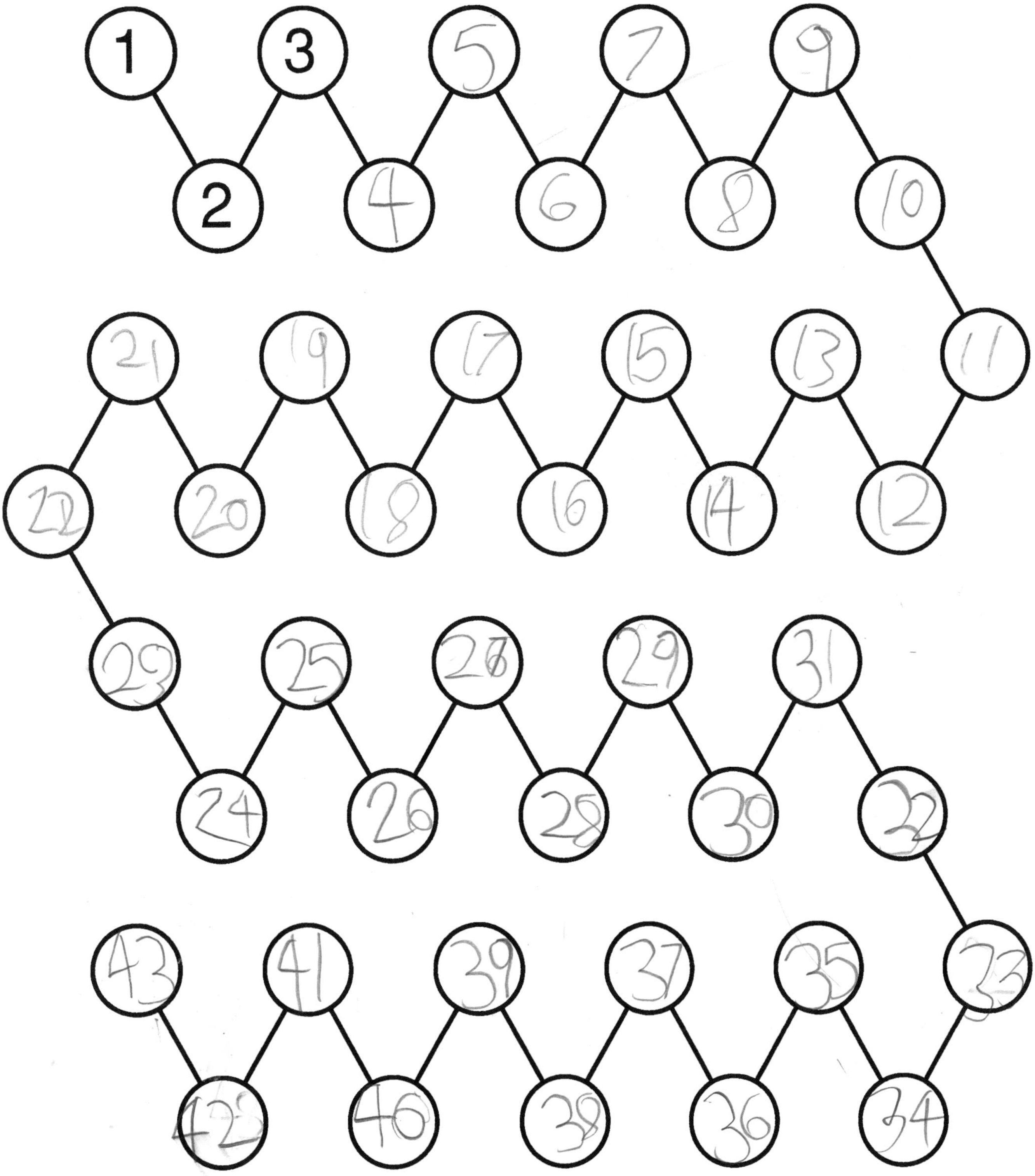
1
3
2

LINE PATTERNS

Continue each pattern.

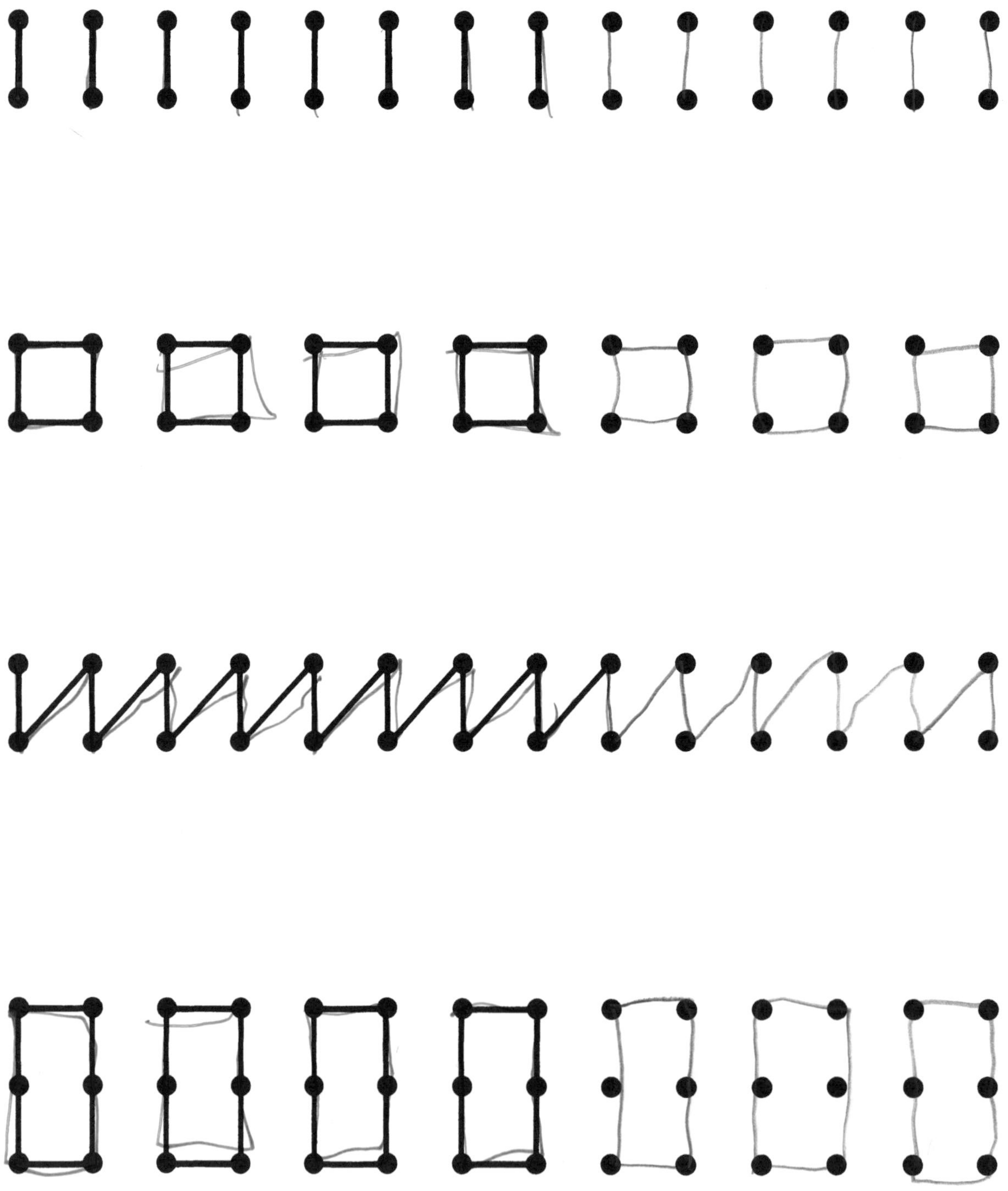

MORE LINE PATTERNS

Continue each pattern.

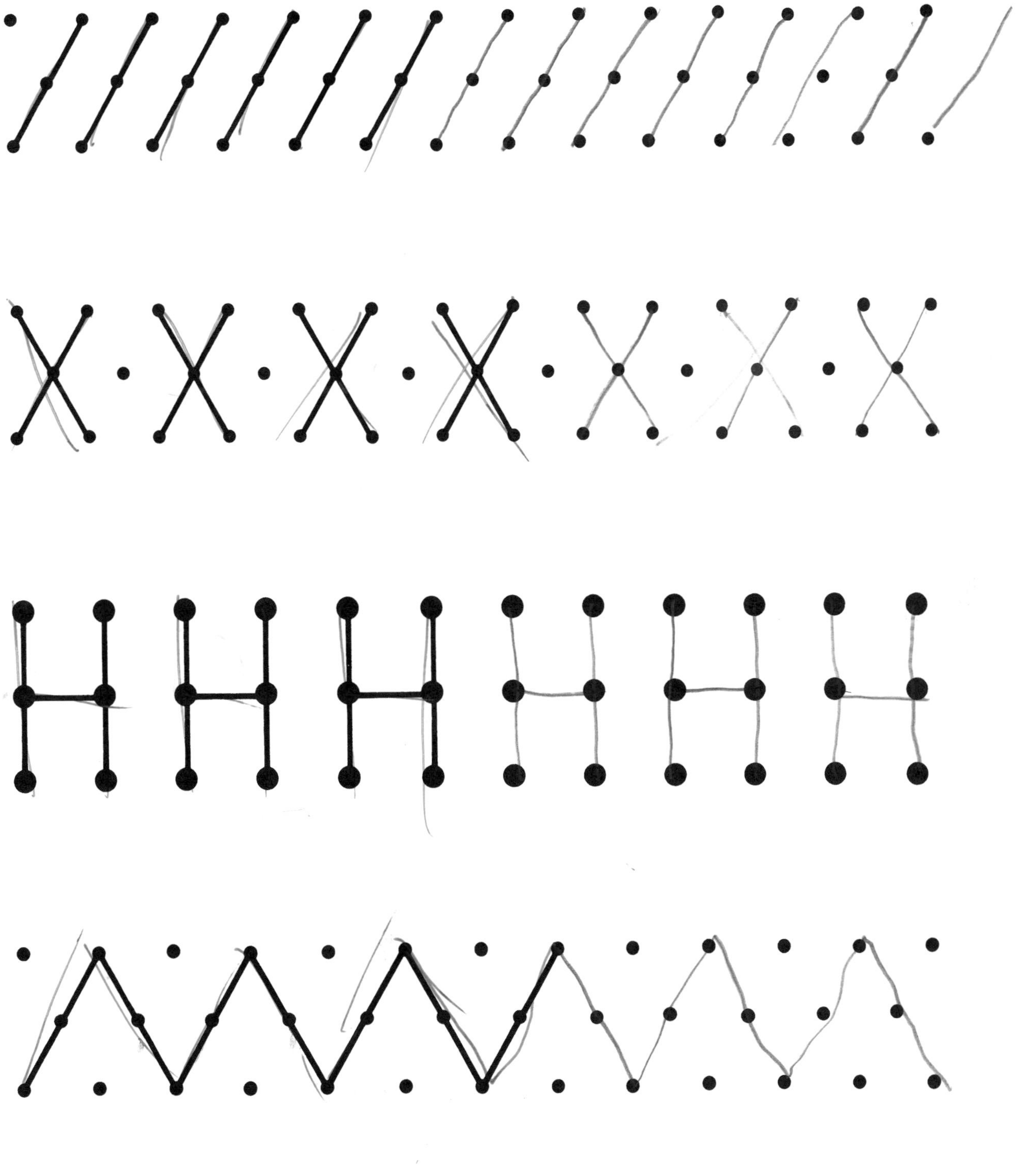

MAKE A MATCH

Continue each pattern.

1. 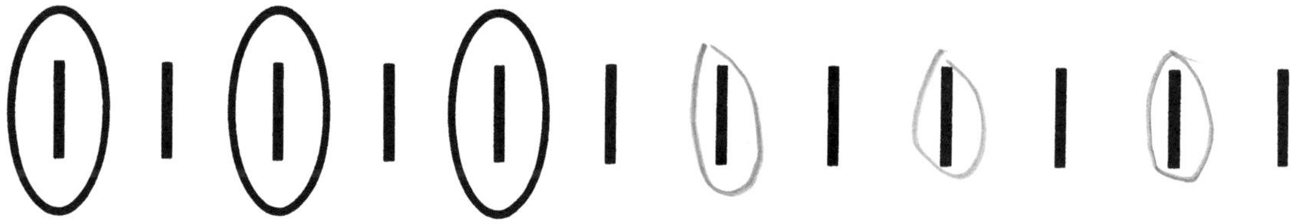

2. 

3. 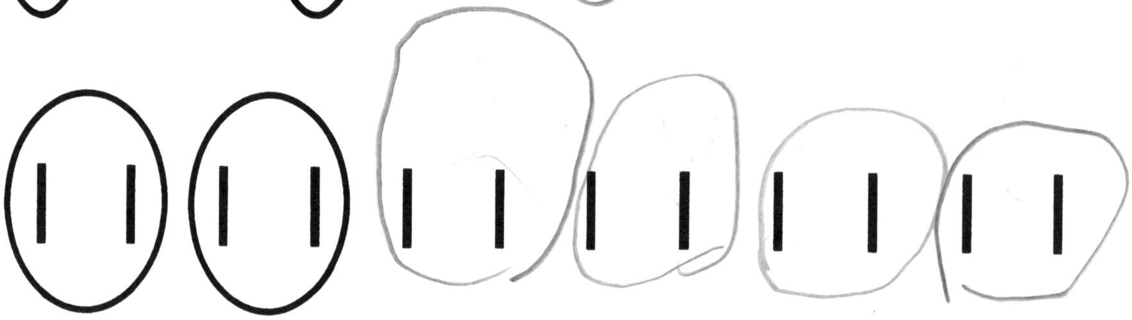

4. 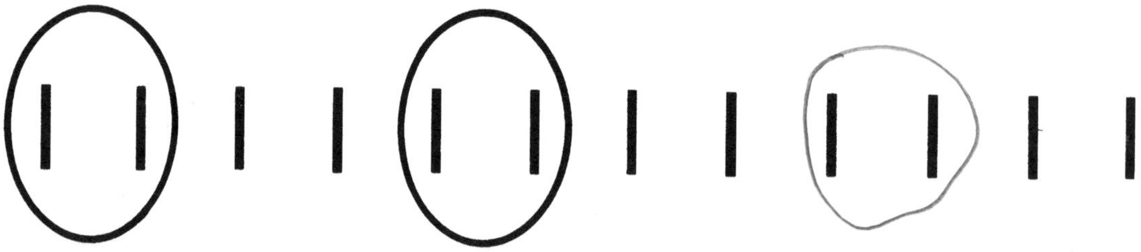

5. 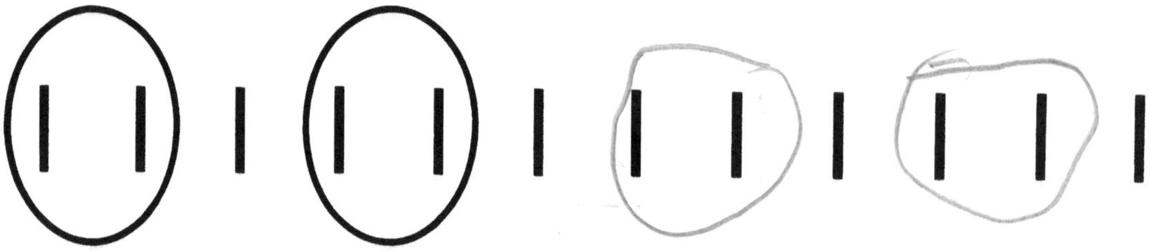

6. 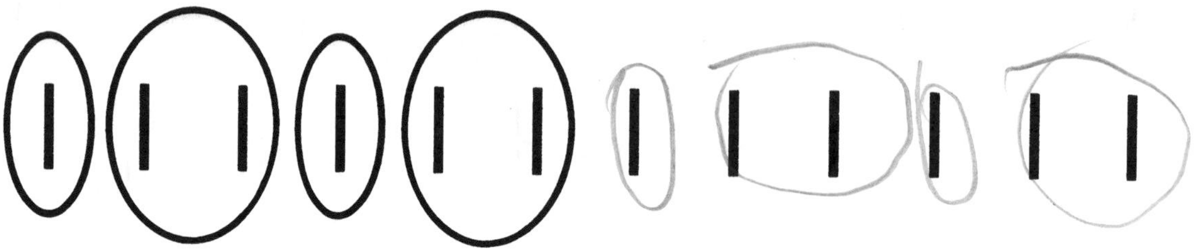

TEDDY'S CHART

Each chart has a pattern. Fill in the charts to match the patterns.

Hi!
My name is Teddy.

1.

1	2	3	4	5	6	7	8	9	10
11	12	13	14	15	16	17	18	19	20
21	22	23	24	25	26	27	28	29	30
31	32	33	34	35	36	37	38	39	40
41	42	43	44	45	46	47	48	49	50

2.

51	52	53	54	55	56	57	58	59	60
61	62	63	64	65	66	67	68	69	70
71	72	73	74	75	76	77	78	79	80
81	82	83	84	85	86	87	88	89	90
91	92	93	94	95	96	97	98	99	100

LINES AND SHAPES (I)

Continue each pattern.

1. 

2. 

3. 

4. 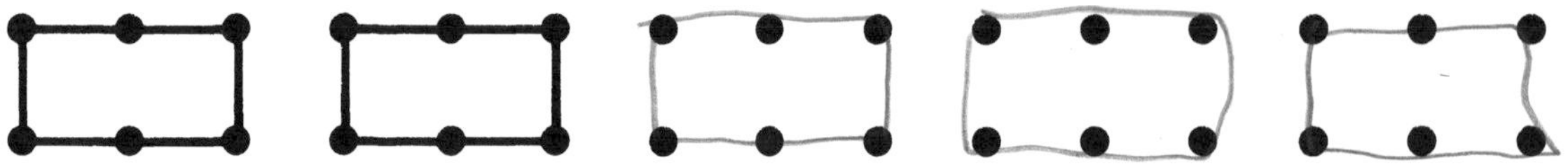

5. 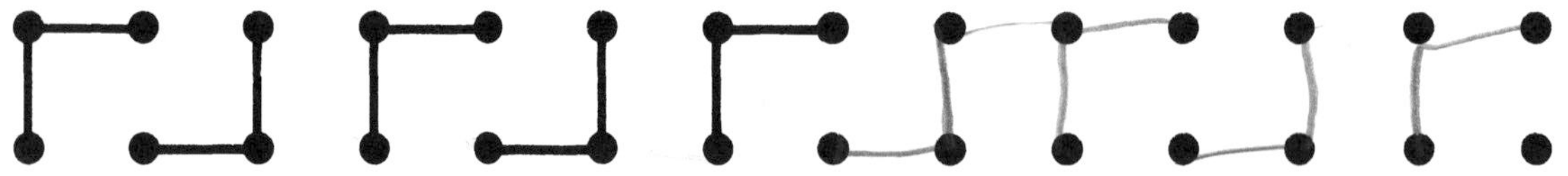

MORE LINES AND SHAPES (I)

Continue each pattern.

1.

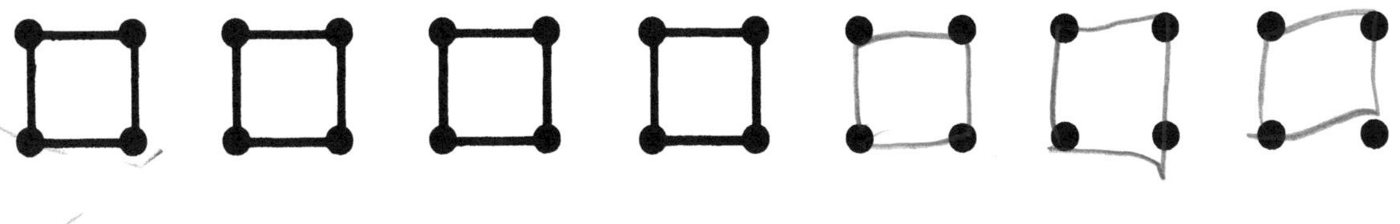

2.

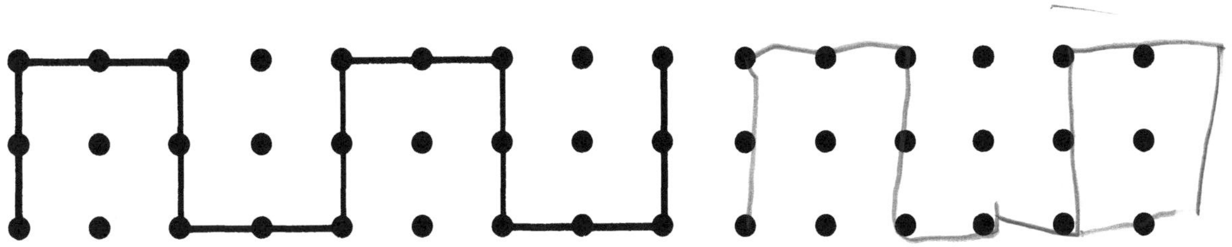

3.

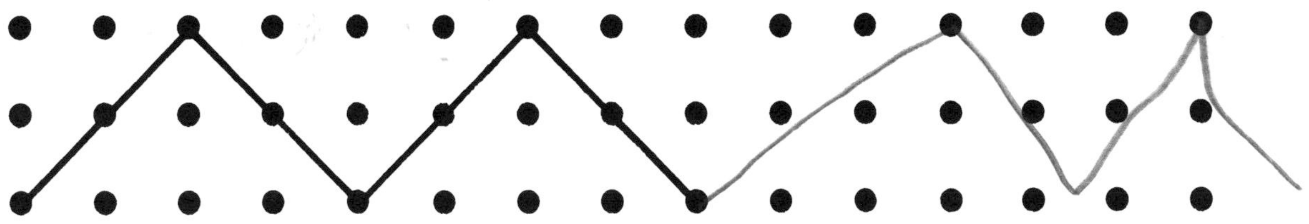

4.

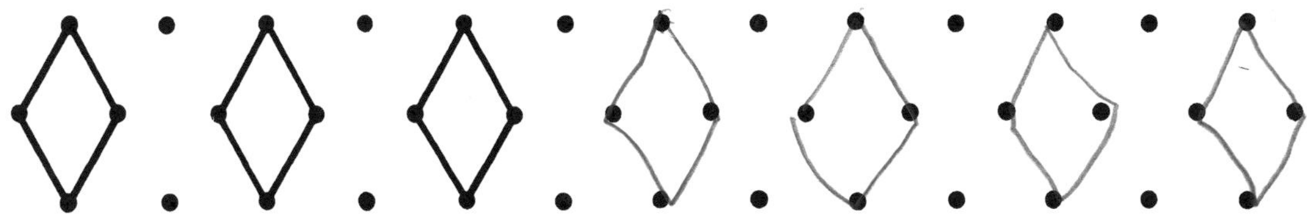

5.

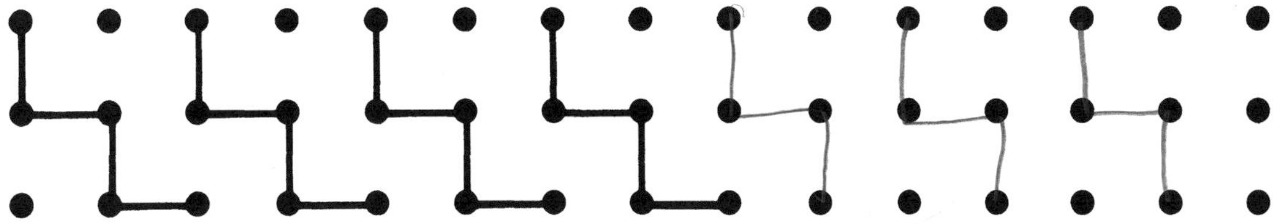

COMMON NUMBERS (I) ▼

Look at the numbers in each shape. What do the numbers have in common?

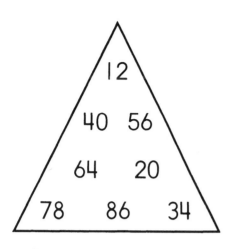

12
40 56
64 20
78 86 34

11	55	99
66	77	22
88	44	33

1. Even
These are all even

2. Each 2 digit
number are the same

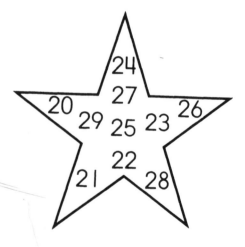

25 65 15 95 45 75 35 85 55

24 27 26 23 25 29 20 22 28 21

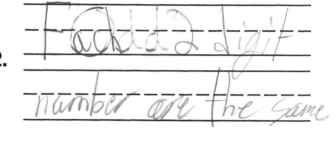

3. The 2nd digit
in each number is five

4. The 1st digit in
each number is 2

REPEAT THE PATTERN (I)

▼

Continue each pattern.

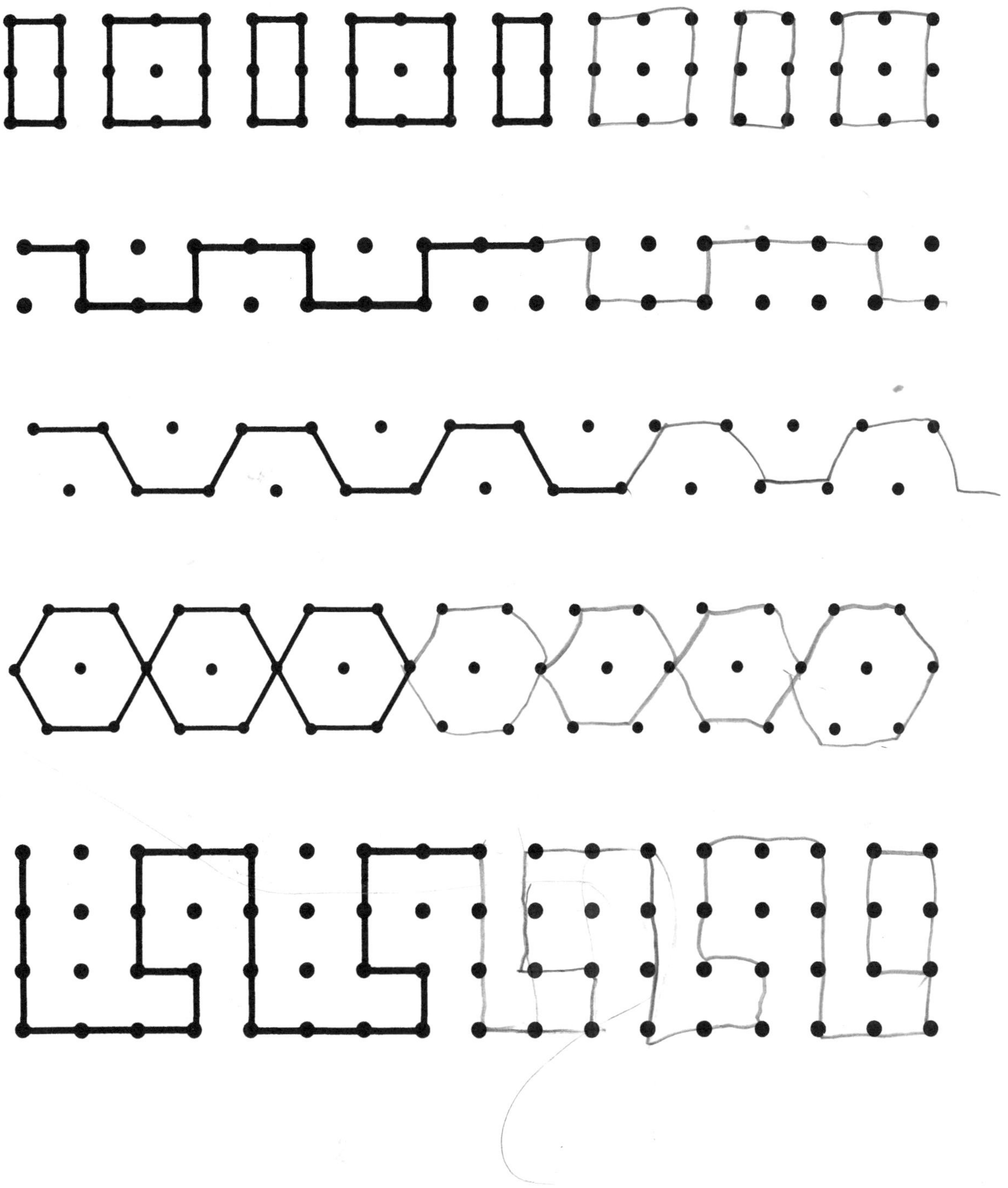

DRAW THE PATTERNS (I)

Continue each pattern.

1. 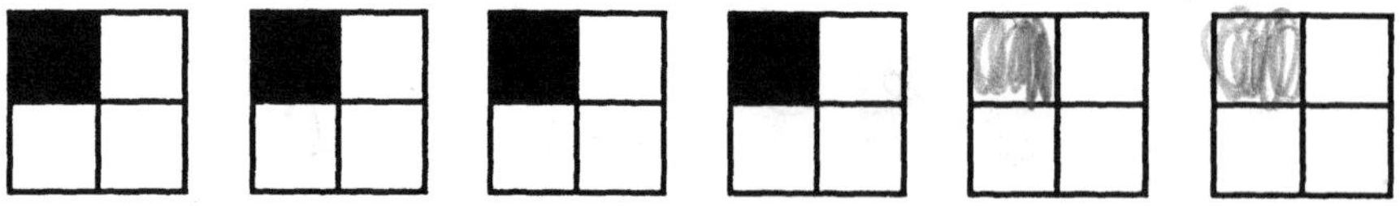

2. 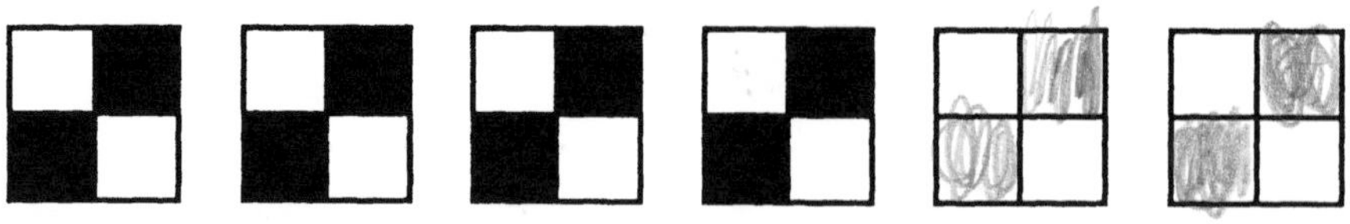

3. 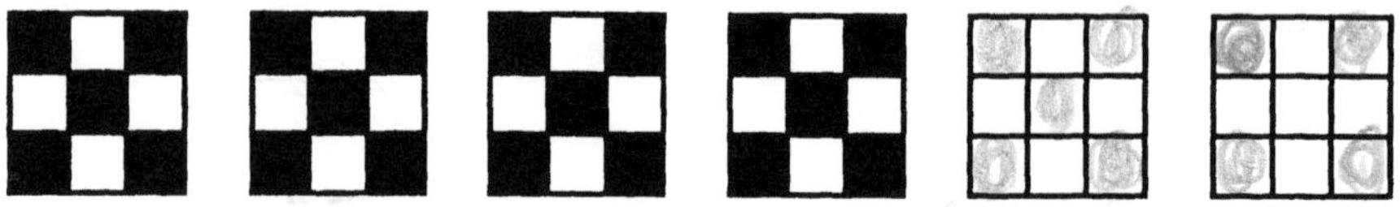

4. 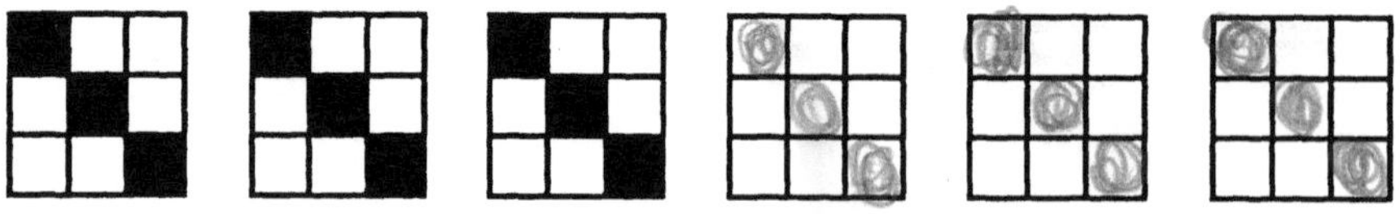

5. 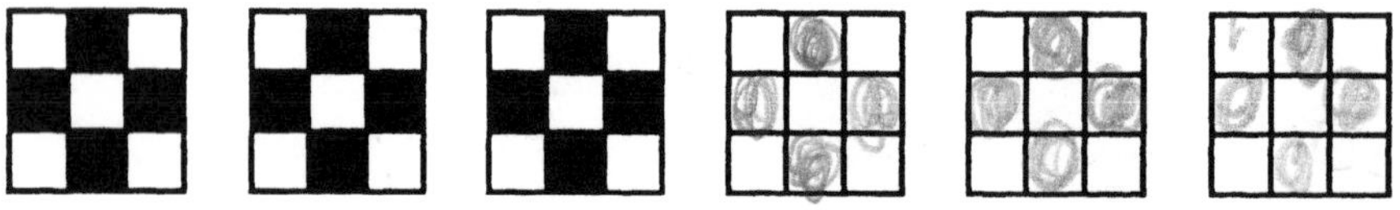

6. 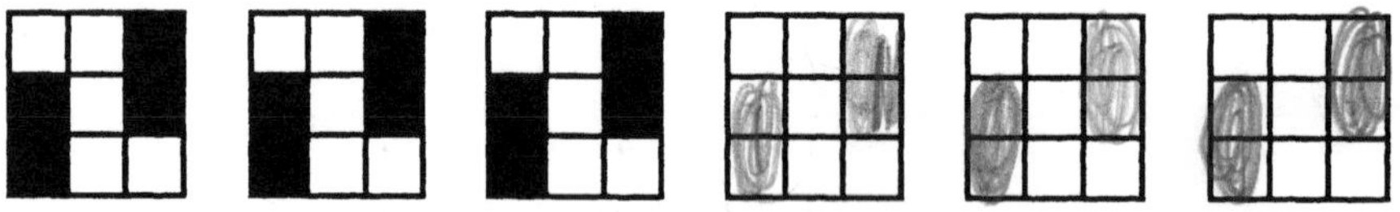

7. 

8. 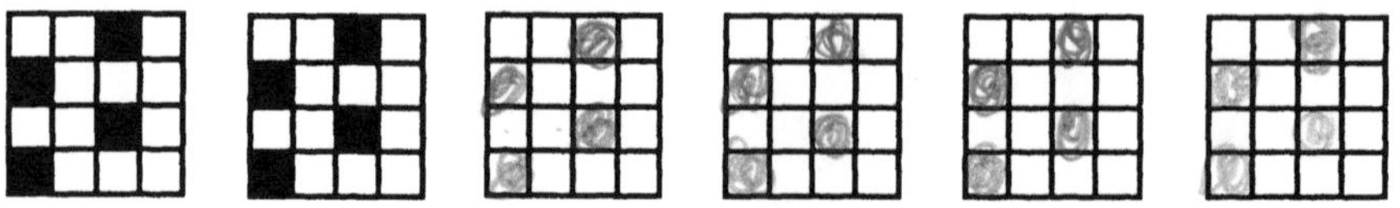

DRAW YOUR PATTERN (I)

Draw your own pattern on the squares below.

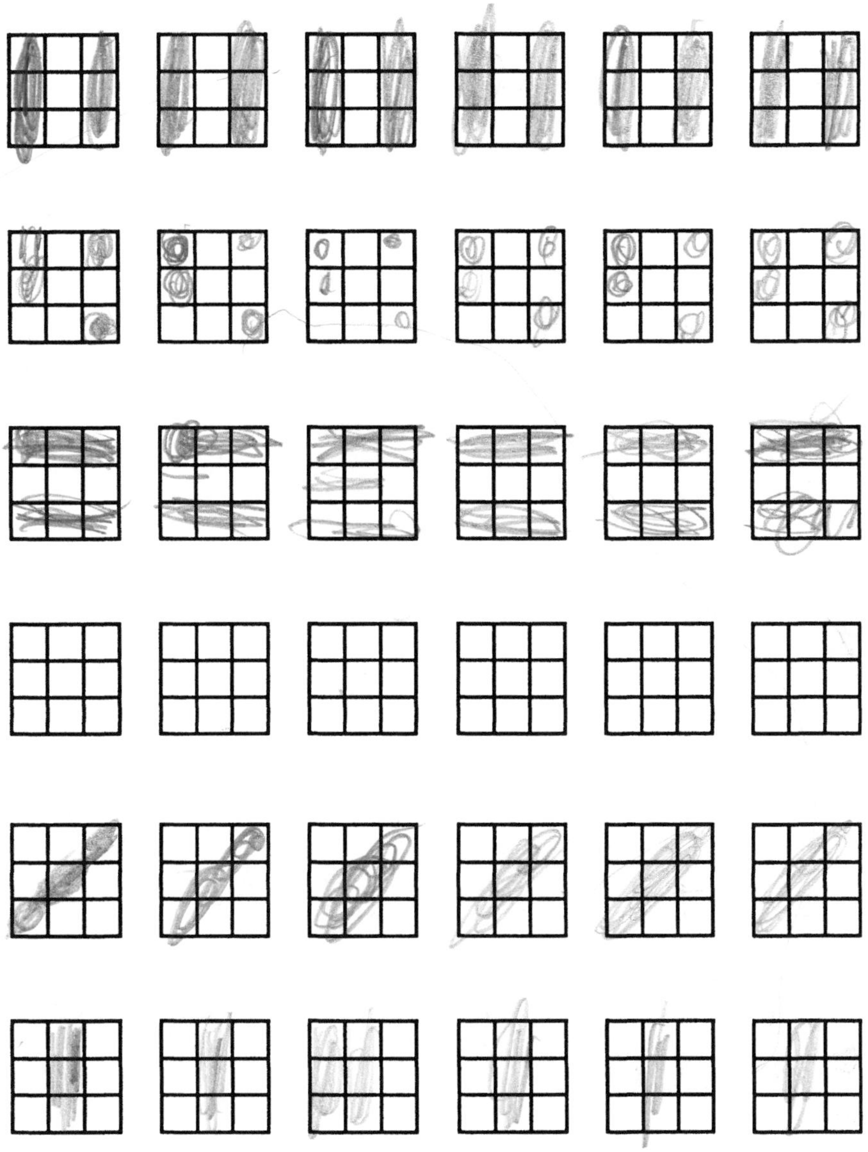

ONE HUNDRED HEARTS

Look for patterns in the hundreds chart. Write the missing numbers in the hearts.

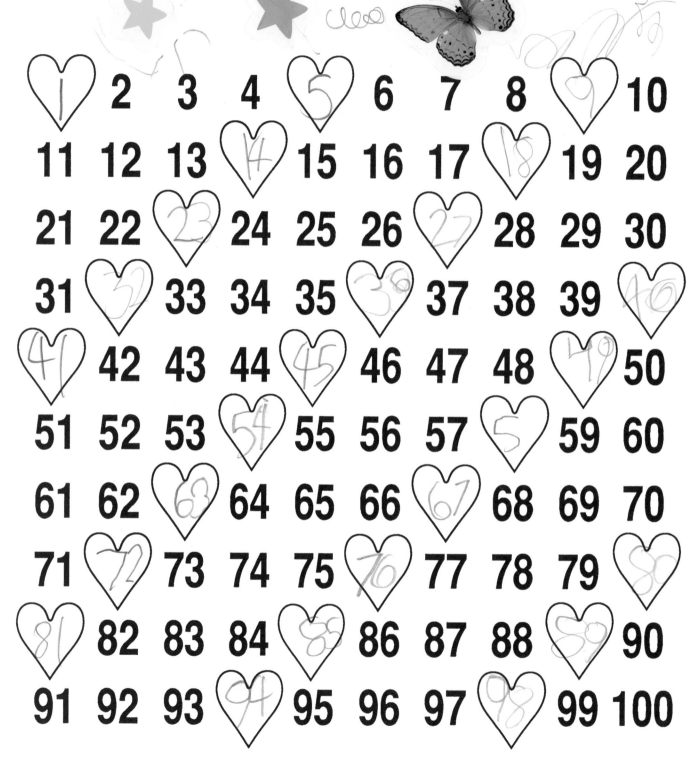

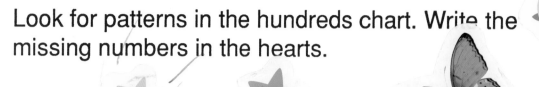

	2	3	4		6	7	8		10
11	12	13		15	16	17		19	20
21	22		24	25	26		28	29	30
31		33	34	35		37	38	39	
	42	43	44		46	47	48		50
51	52	53		55	56	57		59	60
61	62		64	65	66		68	69	70
71		73	74	75		77	78	79	
	82	83	84		86	87	88		90
91	92	93		95	96	97		99	100

16 • PATTERNS

CRITICAL THINKING ACTIVITIES IN PATTERNS, IMAGERY, LOGIC (K–3)

© Dale Seymour Publications

PATTERN TRAINS (II)

Each train has a pattern. Write numbers in the blank spaces to match the pattern.

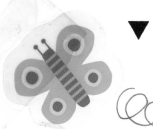

1.

1
2
3
4
5

2.

5
4
3
2
1

3.

10
11
12
13
14

4.

2
4
6
8
10

5.

5
10
15
20
25

LINES AND SHAPES (II) ▼▼

Continue each pattern.

1. 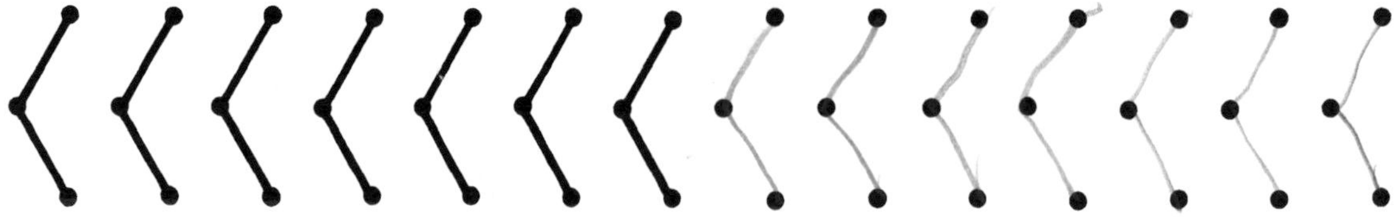

2. 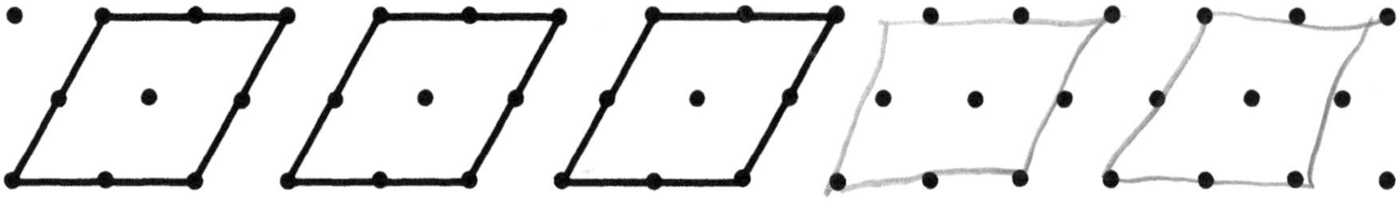

3. 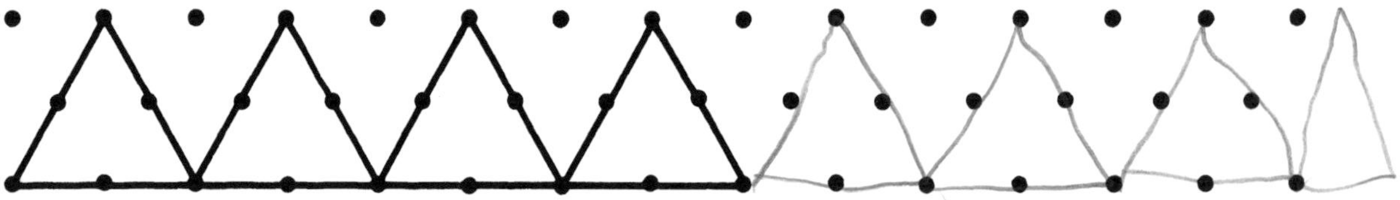

4. 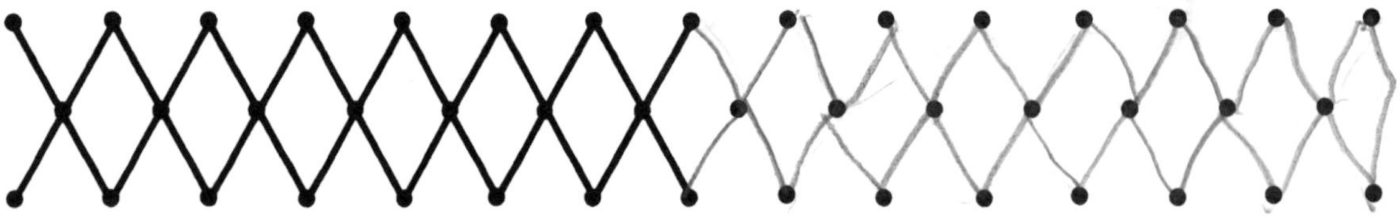

5. 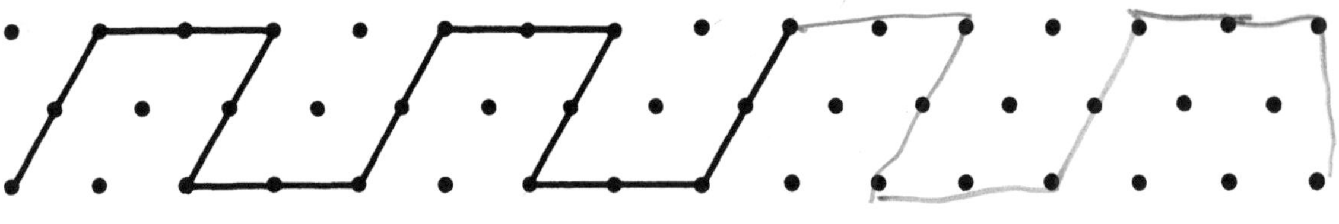

MIX AND MATCH

Continue each pattern.

1. 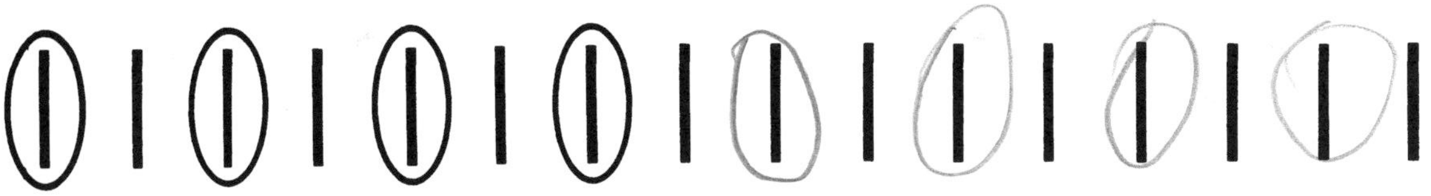

2. 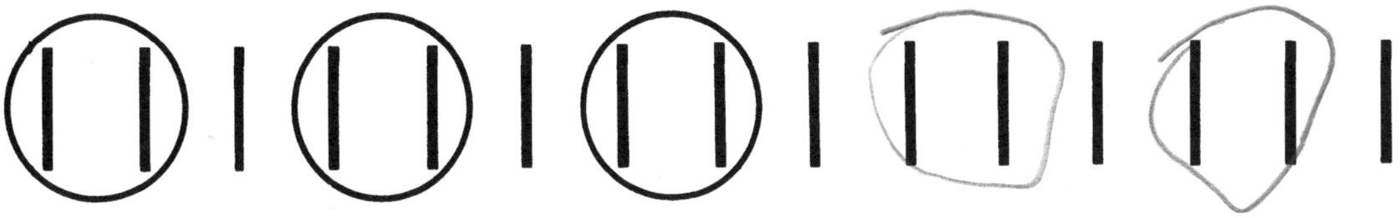

3. 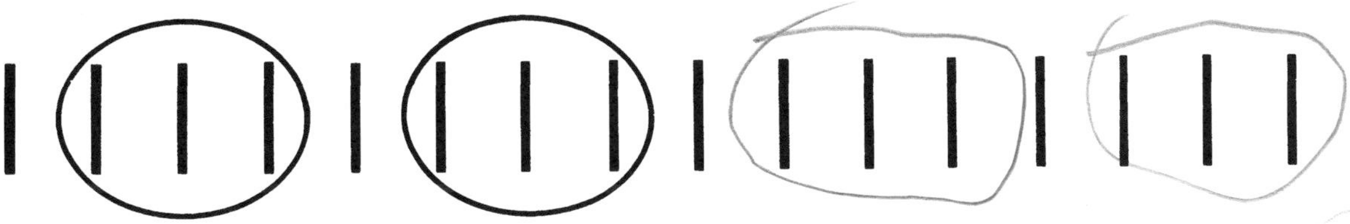

4. 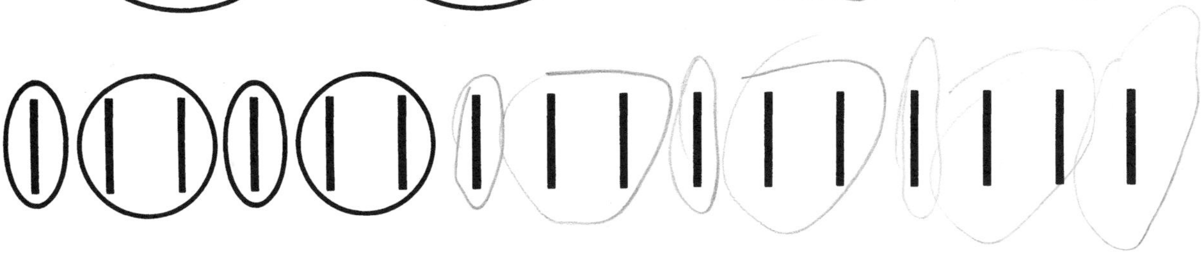

5. 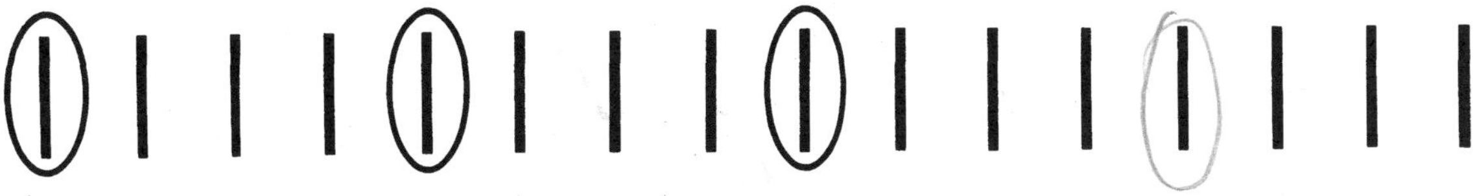

6. 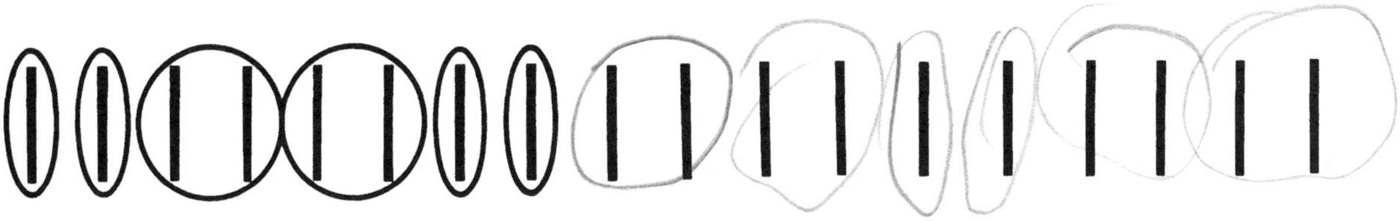

7. 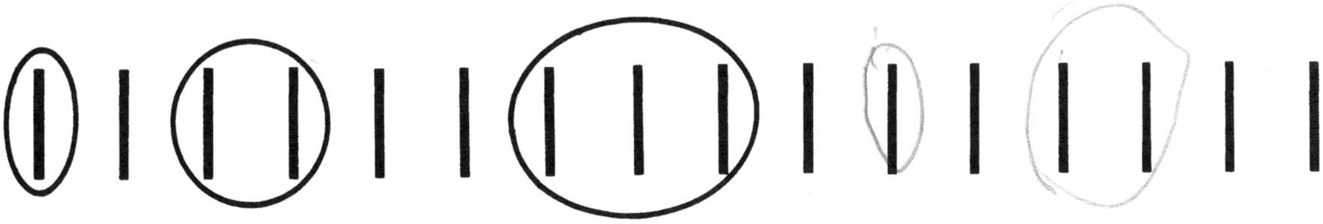

8. 

FREDDY'S CHART

Fill in the missing numbers.
What is the pattern of the missing numbers in each chart?

Hi, I'm Freddy! Can you find my patterns?

1.

1	2	3	4	5	6	7	8	9	10
11	12	13	14	15	16	17	18	19	20
21	22	23	24	25	26	27	28	29	30
31	32	33	34	35	36	37	38	39	40
41	42	43	44	45	46	47	48	49	50

This is counting by 5

2.

1	2	3	4	5	6	7	8	9	10
11	12	13	14	15	16	17	18	19	20
21	22	23	24	25	26	27	28	29	30
31	32	33	34	35	36	37	38	39	40
41	42	43	44	45	46	47	48	49	50

This is counting by 2

MORE LINES AND SHAPES (II)

Continue each pattern.

1. 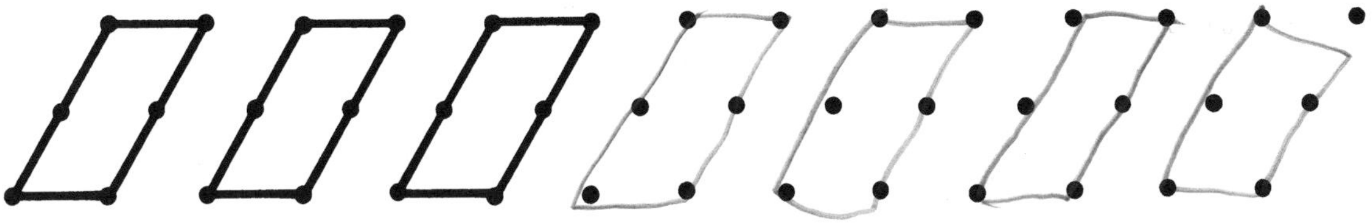

2. 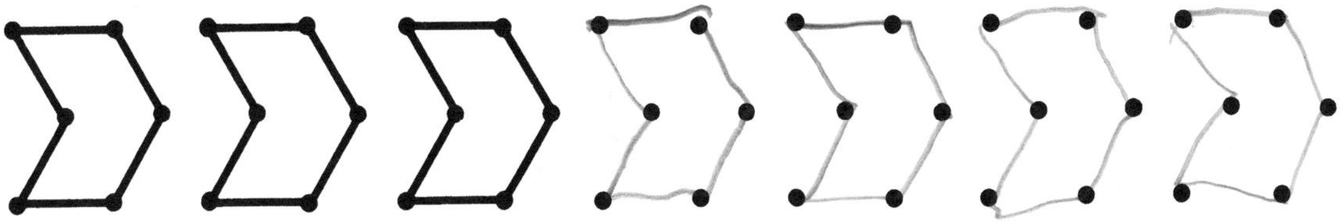

3. 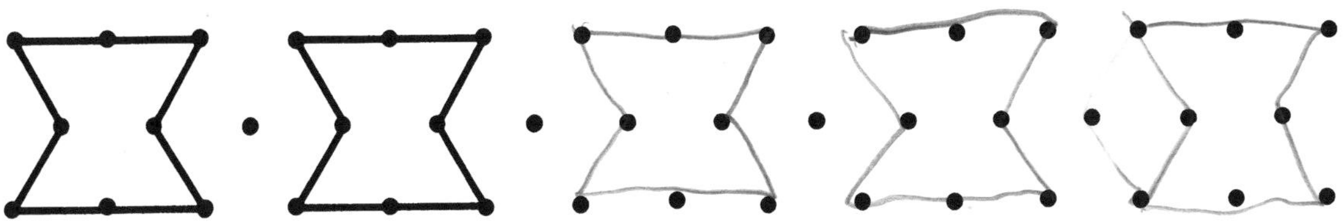

4. 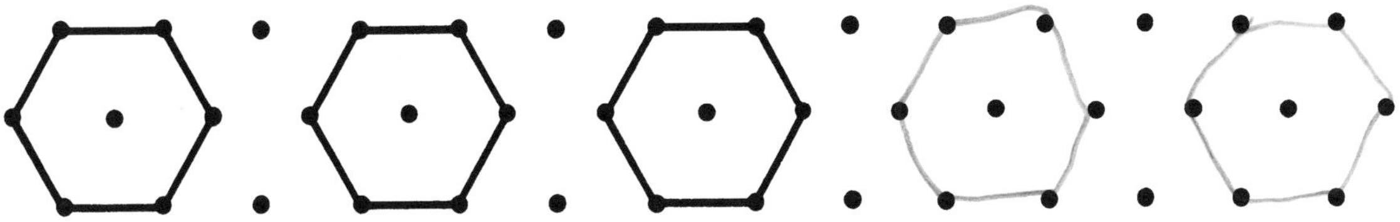

5. 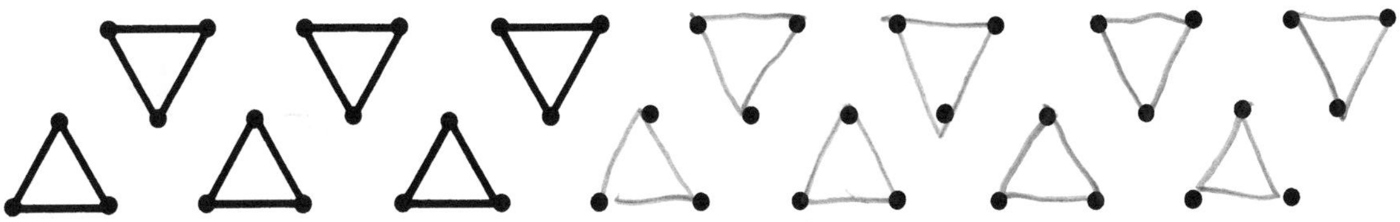

TRAINS AND CHAINS (I)

▼▼

Each row has a pattern. Write numbers in the blank spaces to match the pattern.

1.

1
3
5
7

2.

10
9
8

3.

10
20
30
40

4.

11
12
14
16

5.

16
12
8
4

6.

5
15
20
35

COUNTING CIRCLES (II)

Fill in the missing numbers.

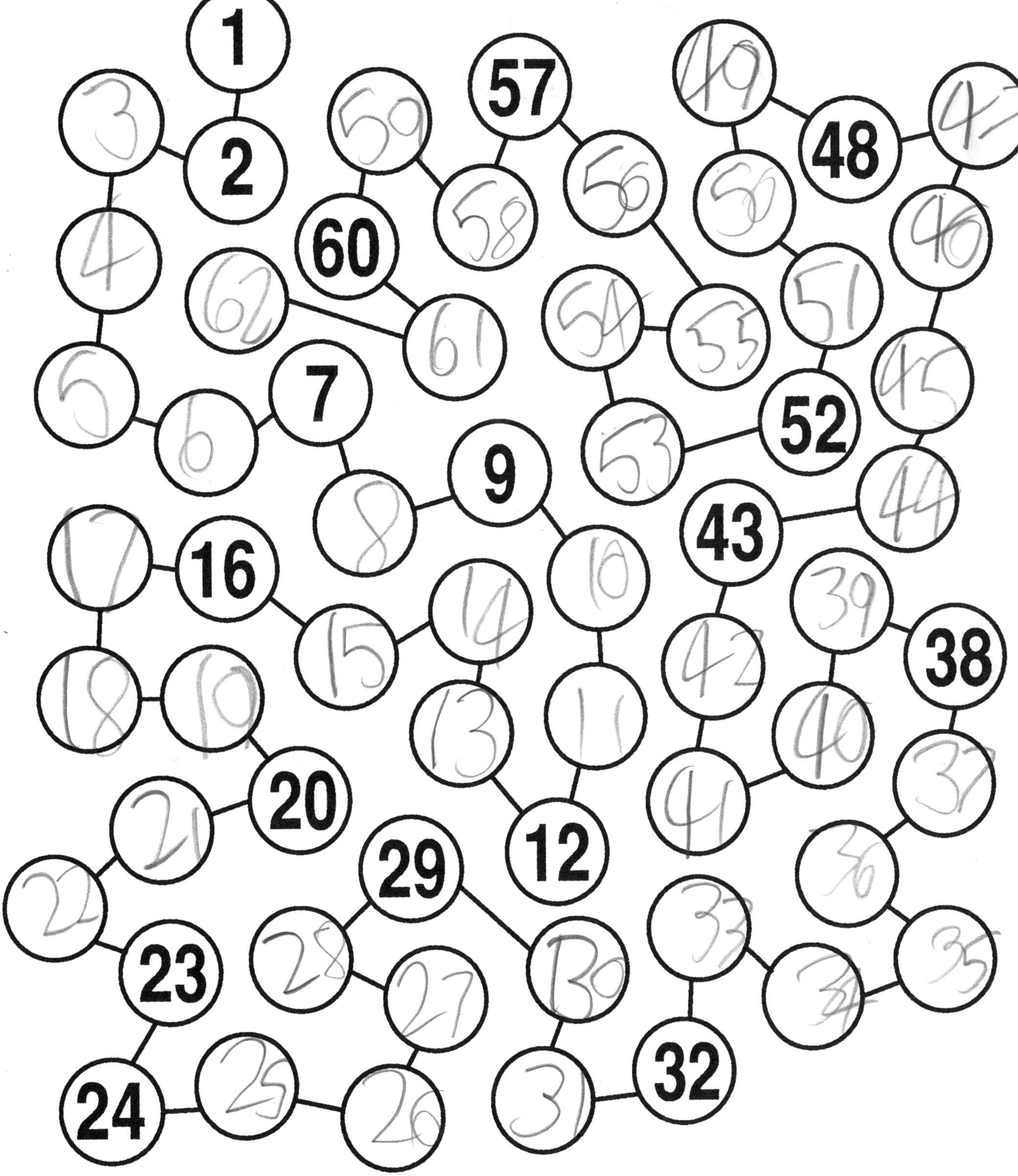
1
2
57
48
60
7
52
9
43
16
38
20
29
12
23
32
24

REPEAT THE PATTERN (II)

▼▼

Continue each pattern.

1. 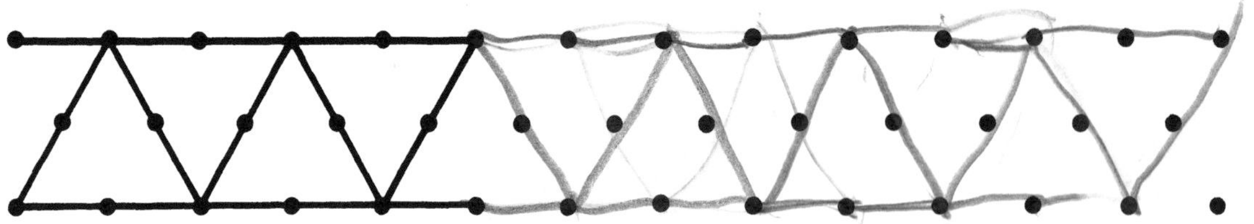

2. 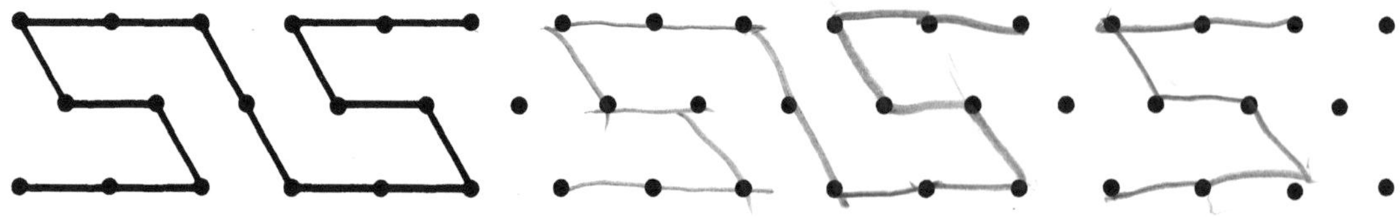

3. 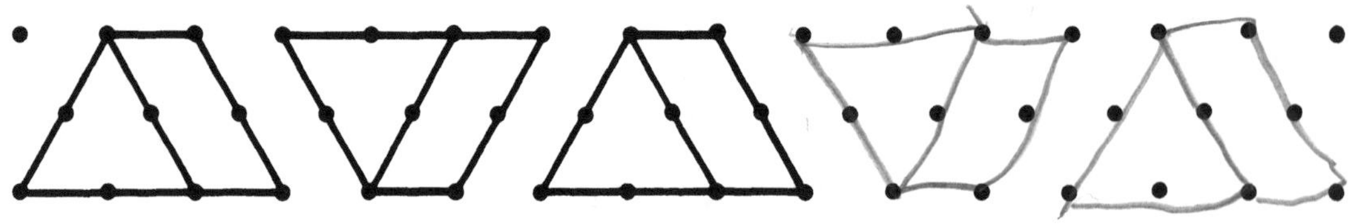

4. 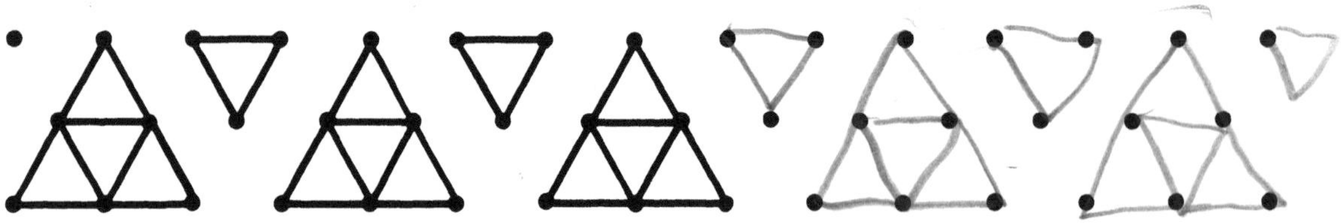

REPEAT THE PATTERN (III)

Continue each pattern.

1. 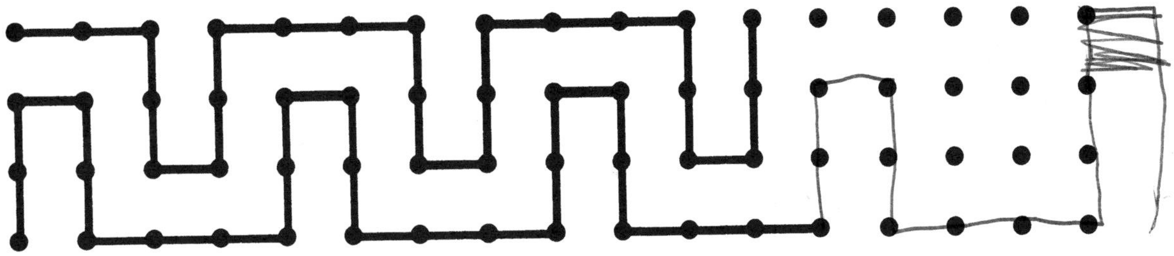

2. 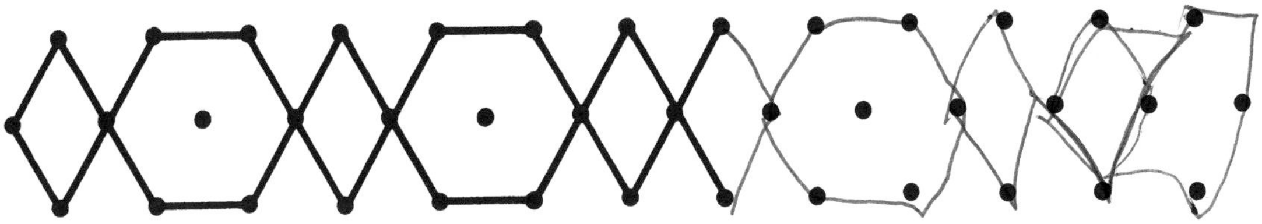

3. 

4. 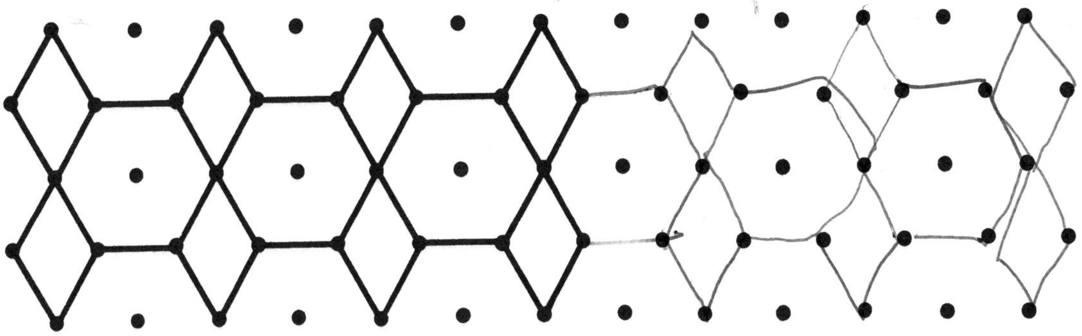

TRIANGLE WINDOWS

Study the number chart. Use it to fill in a number in each blank triangle below.

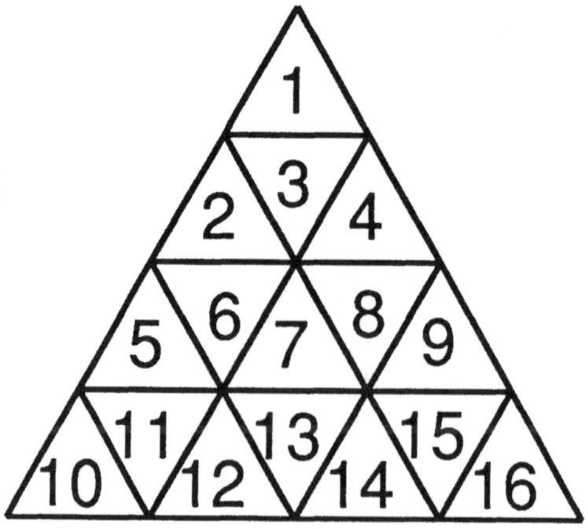
1
2 3 4
5 6 7 8 9
10 11 12 13 14 15 16

Number Chart

1.

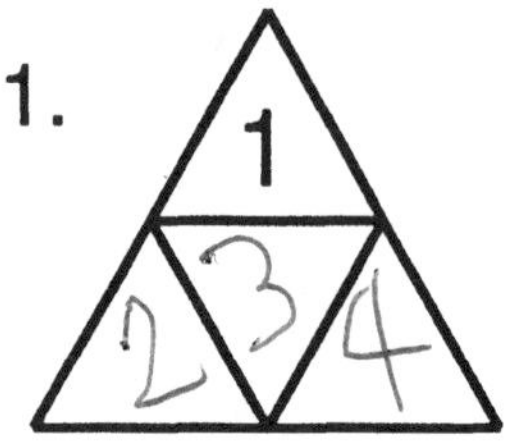
1

2.

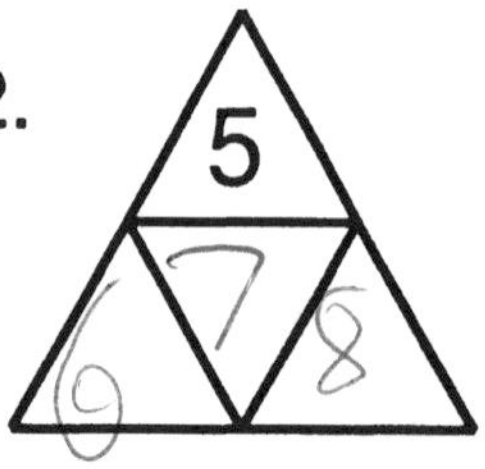
5

3.

4

4.

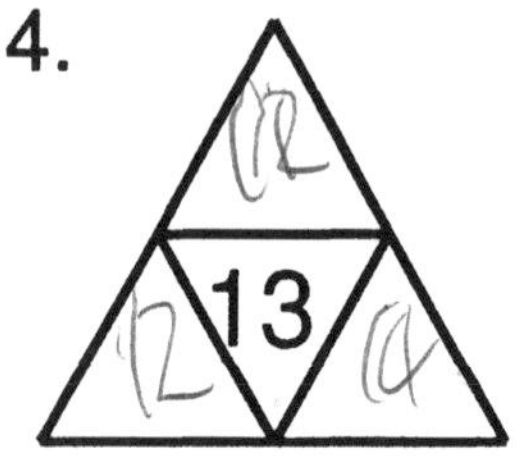
13

5.

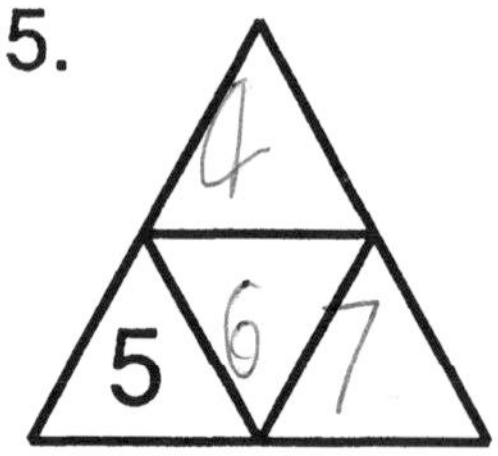
5

6.

7

7.

14

8.

3

9.

14

10.

7

TWO AT A TIME

In each pattern, add two numbers to get the next number.

1. 1 1 2 3 5 8 13 21

2. 2 2 4 6 ~~10~~ 10 ~~16~~ 16 ~~26~~ 26 42

3. 1 3 4 7 11 18 29 47

4. 1 4 5 9 14 23 37 60

5. 2 3 5 8 13 21 34 55

6. 2 5 7 12 19 31 50 81

7. 2 4 6 10 16 26 42 68

8. 1 2 3 5 8 13 21 34

9. 0 5 10 15 25 40 65 105

10. Make up your own problem:

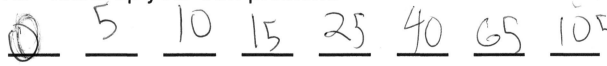

0 5 10 15 25 40 65 105

DICE PATTERNS

Find the pattern in each row. Fill in the dots on the blank dice.

1. 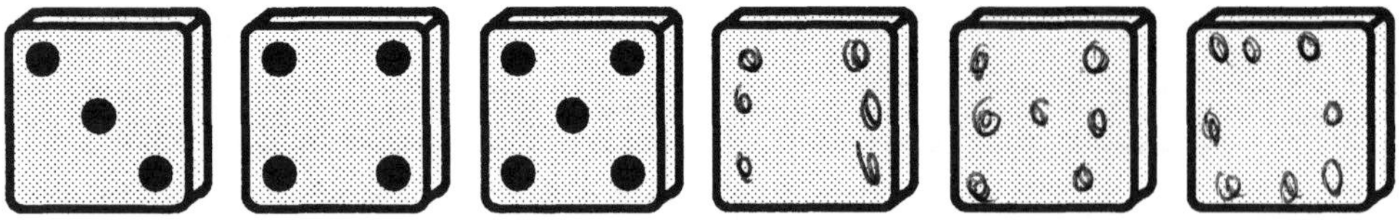

2. 

3. 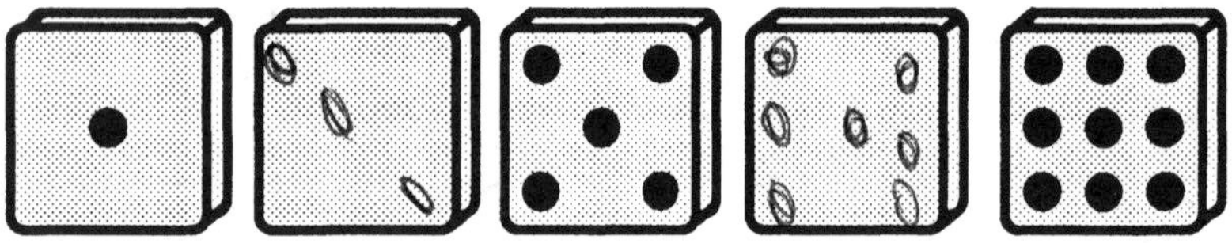

4. 

5. 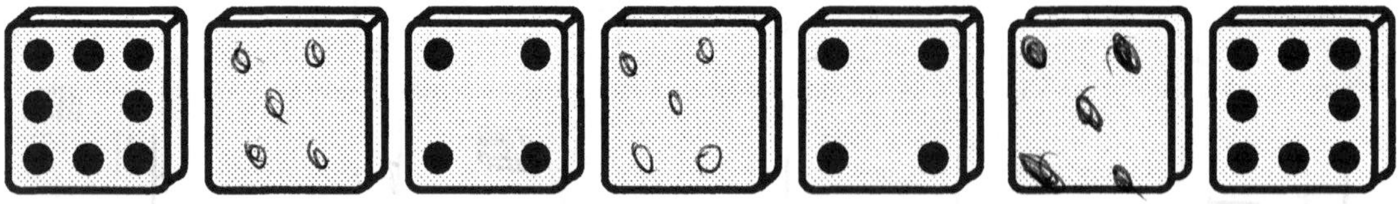

6. Make up your own pattern. Fill in the dots:

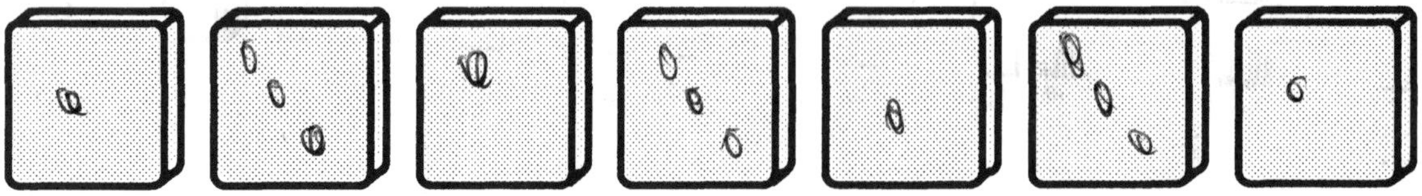

DRAW THE PATTERNS (II)

Continue each pattern.

1. 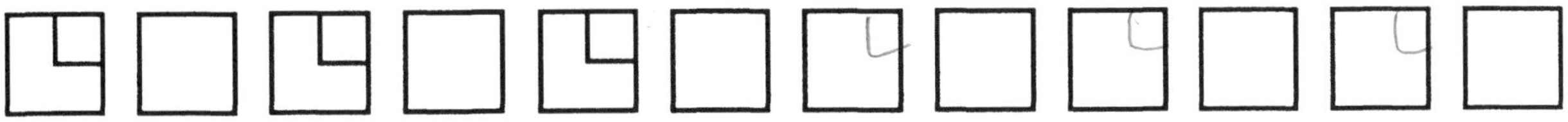

2. 

3. 

4. 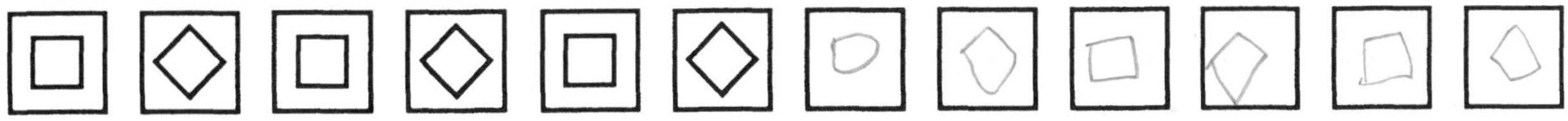

5. 

6. 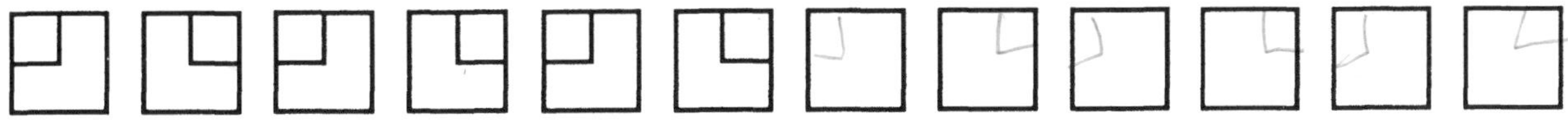

7. 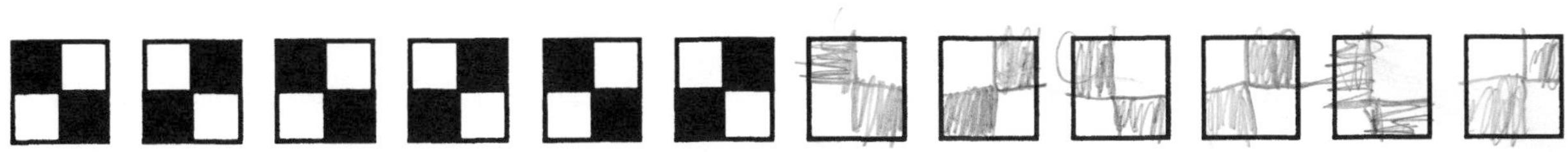

8. 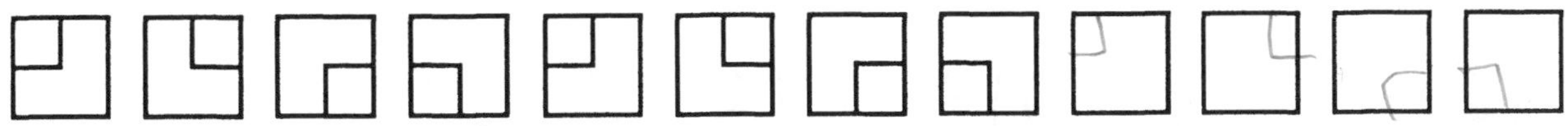

9. 

10. 

PATTERN BLOCK

Complete the pattern.

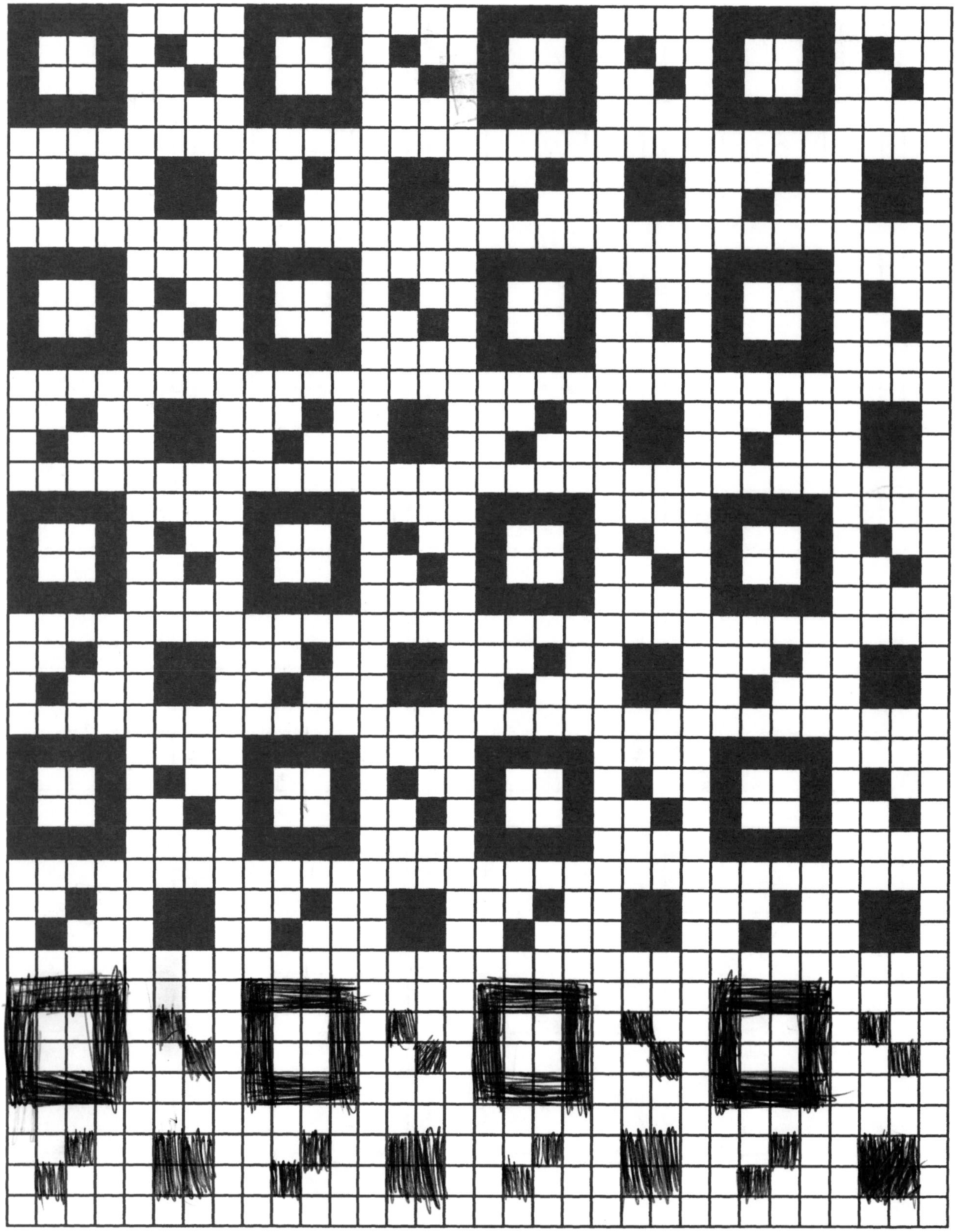

DRAW YOUR PATTERN (II)

Draw your own pattern on the grid below.

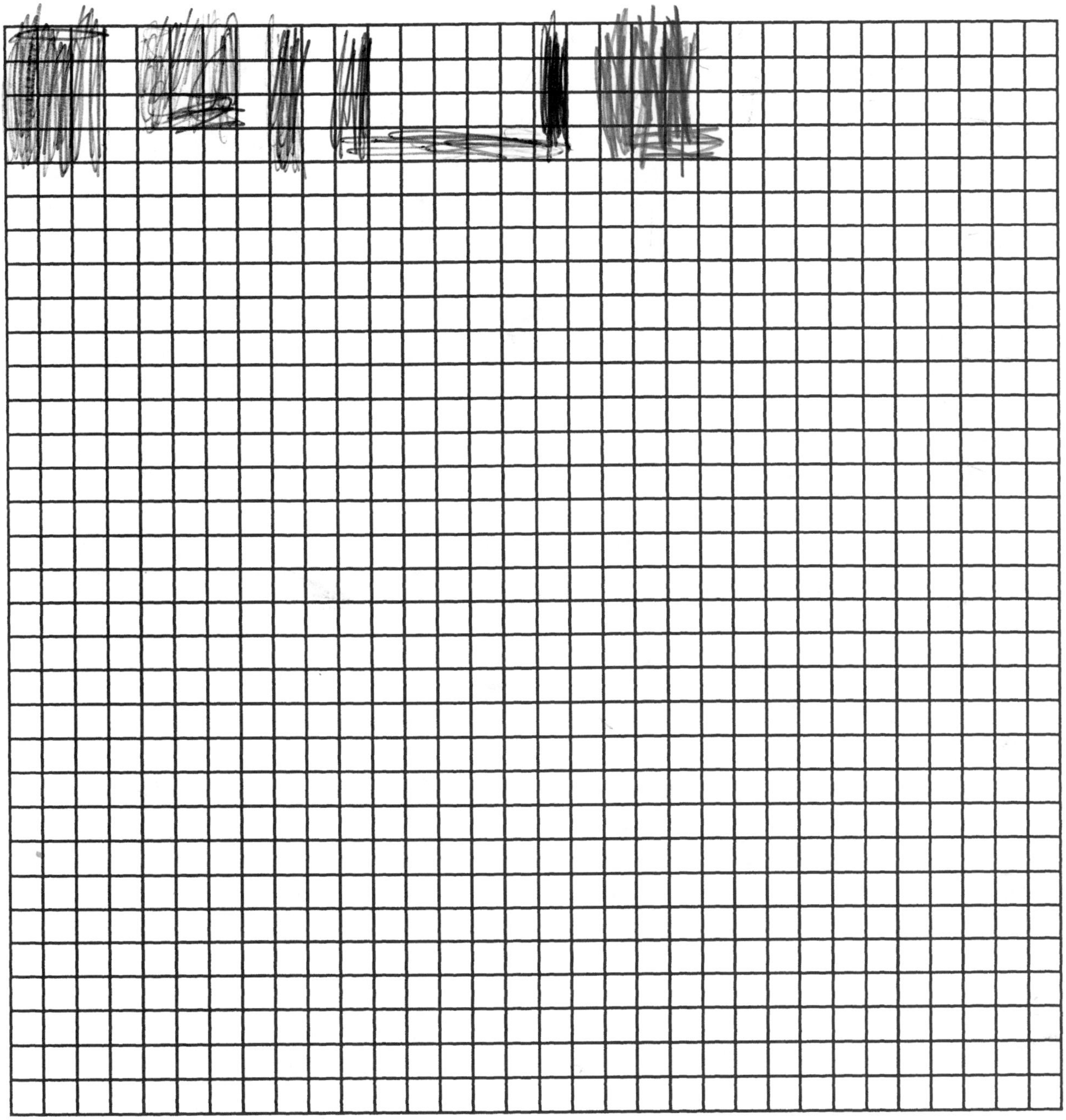

ONE HUNDRED SUNS

▼▼▼

Look for patterns in the hundreds chart. Write the missing numbers in the suns.

1	2	3	4	5	6	7	8	9	10
11	12	13	14	15	16	17	18	19	20
21	22	23	24	25	26	27	28	29	30
31	32	33	34	35	36	37	38	39	40
41	42	43	44	45	46	47	48	49	50
51	52	53	54	55	56	57	58	59	60
61	62	63	64	65	66	67	68	69	70
71	72	73	74	75	76	77	78	79	80
81	82	83	84	85	86	87	88	89	90
91	92	93	94	95	96	97	98	99	100

Explain the patterns you notice:

each number that goes down from the same row, the ones place is same

ZEDDY'S CHART

Fill in the missing numbers in each chart.

Hey, I'm Zeddy the Pattern Teddy!

1.

1	2	3	4	5	6	7	8	9	10
11	12	13	14	15	16	17	18	19	20
21	22	23	24	25	26	27	28	29	30
31	32	33	34	35	36	37	38	39	40
41	42	43	44	45	46	47	48	49	50

2.

1	2	3	4	5	6	7	8	9	10
11	12	13	14	15	16	17	18	19	20
21	22	23	24	25	26	27	28	29	30
31	32	33	34	35	36	37	38	39	40
41	42	43	44	45	46	47	48	49	50

What is the pattern of the missing numbers in chart 2?

They're skipping by twos.

TRAINS AND CHAINS (II)

Each row has a pattern. Write numbers in the blank spaces to match the pattern.

1.

23
24
26
29

2.

73
75
77

3.

3
6
9

4.

1
1
2
2
3

5.

12
22
32
42

6.

10
30
50

NUMBER CHAIN

▼▼▼

Make a number chain. Connect the numbers from one to twenty.

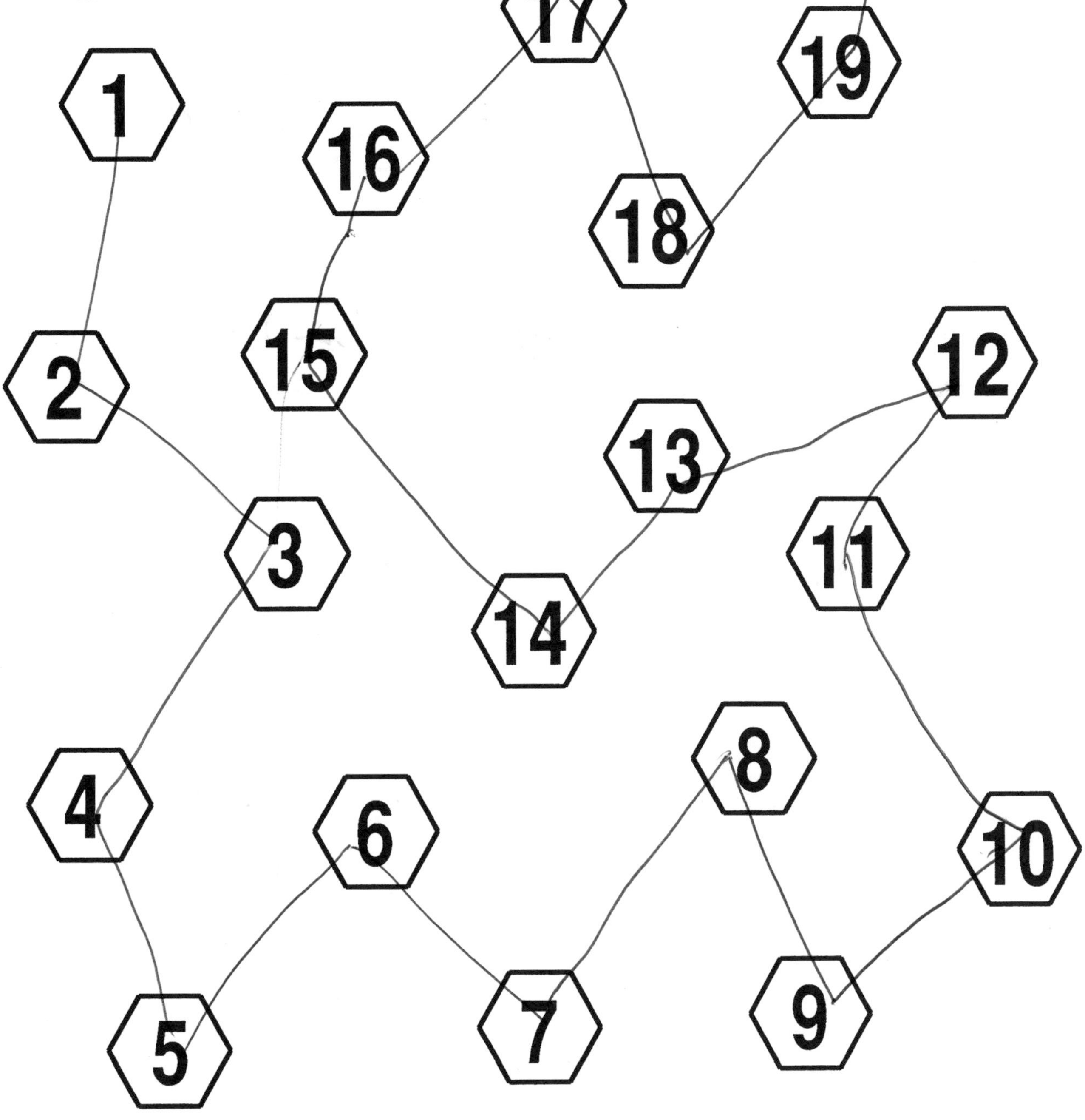
20
17
19
1
16
18
2
15
12
13
3
11
14
4
6
8
10
5
7
9

NUMBER PATTERNS

Continue each pattern.

1. 1 2 3 4 5 6

2. 1 2 3 4 5

3. 1 2 3 4 5 6 7 8

4. 1 2 3 4 5 6 7 8

5.

1
1 2
2 3
1 2 3
1 3 4 5
2 3 6
5

6.

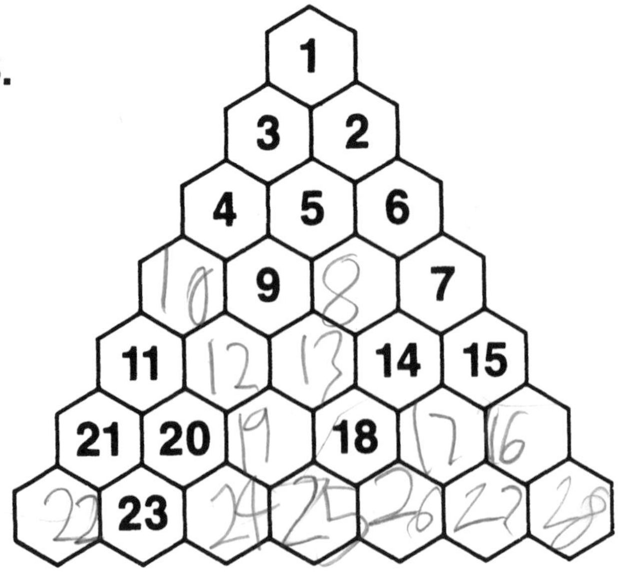

1
3 2
4 5 6
9 7
11 14 15
21 20 18
23

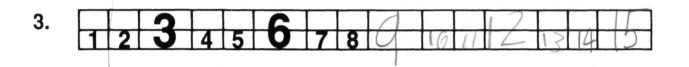

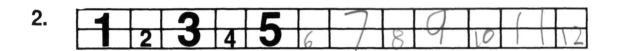

COMMON NUMBERS (II)

▼▼▼

Look at the numbers in each shape. What do the numbers have in common?

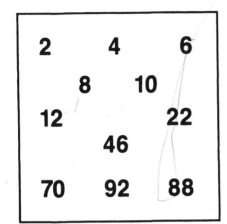

2 4 6
8 10
12 22
46
70 92 88

67
7 23
21 11
83 35
49

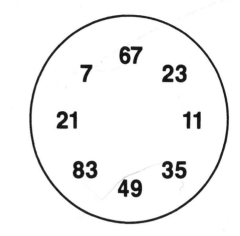

1. They're all even

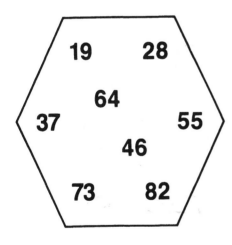

2. ______________________

19 28
64
37 55
46
73 82

21 42
63 84

3. ______________________

4. ______________________

SHAPE PATTERNS

▼▼▼

Find the pattern in each row. Draw shapes that continue the pattern.

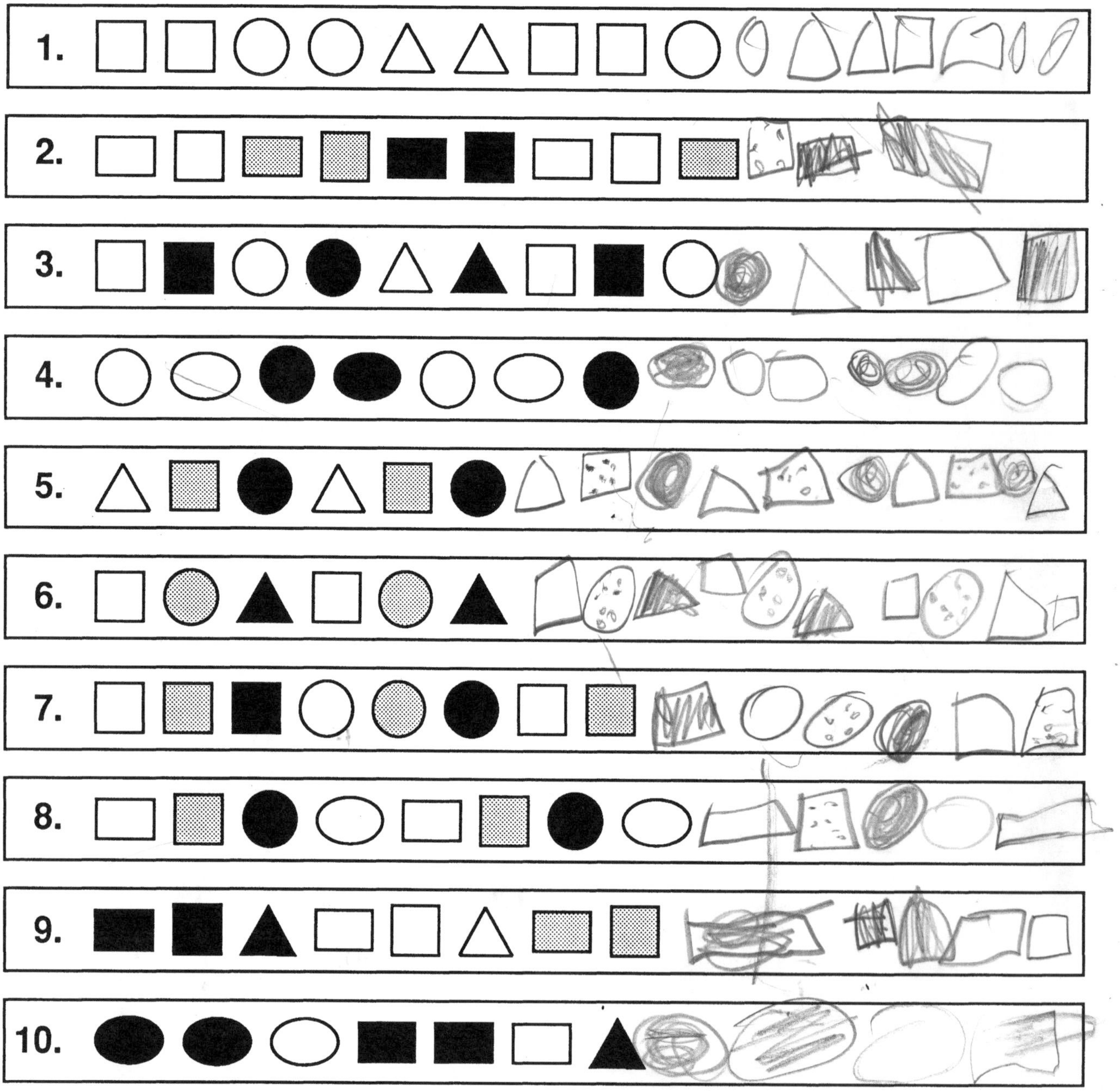
1.
2.
3.
4.
5.
6.
7.
8.
9.
10.

Explain one of the patterns here:

They're doing two of the same

NUMBER TRIANGLES

▼▼▼

Fill in the missing numbers in the triangles. Each missing number is the sum of the two numbers above it.

Example:

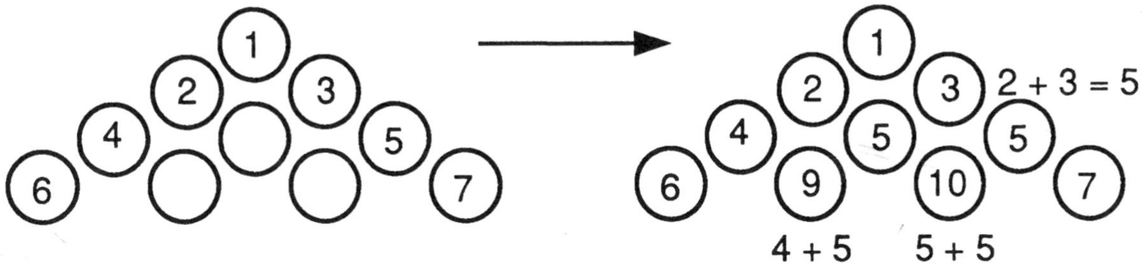

1
2 3
4 5
6 7
1
2 3
4 5 5
6 9 10 7
2 + 3 = 5
4 + 5
5 + 5

1.

1
2 2
3 4 3
1 7 7 1

2.

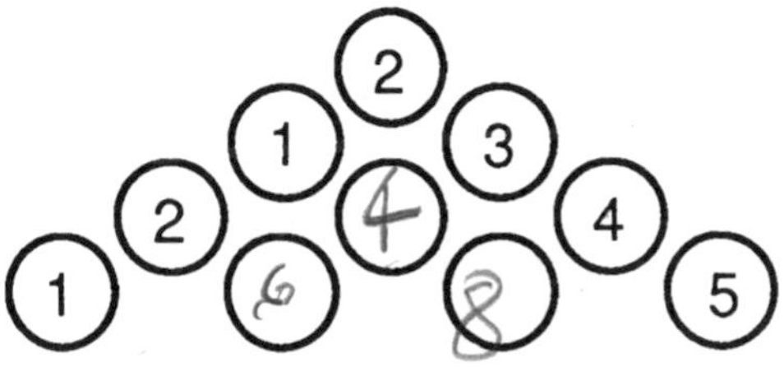

2
1 3
2 4 4
1 6 8 5

3.

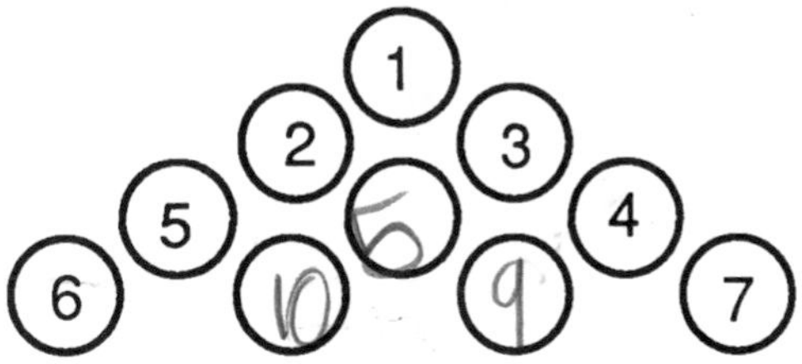

1
2 3
5 5 4
6 10 9 7

4.

1
2 6
7 2 4
6 4 12 5

5.

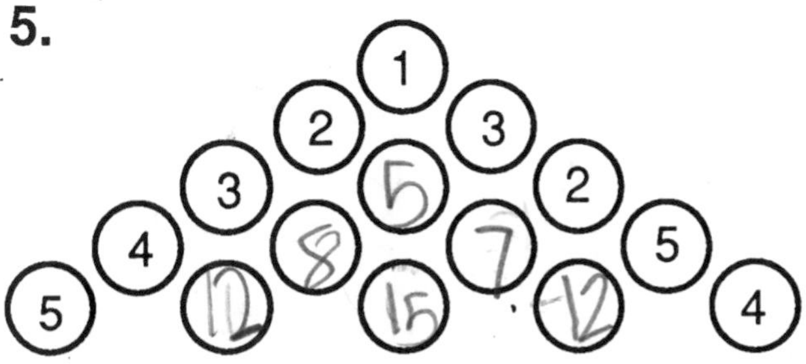

1
2 3
3 5 2
4 8 7 5
5 12 15 12 4

6.

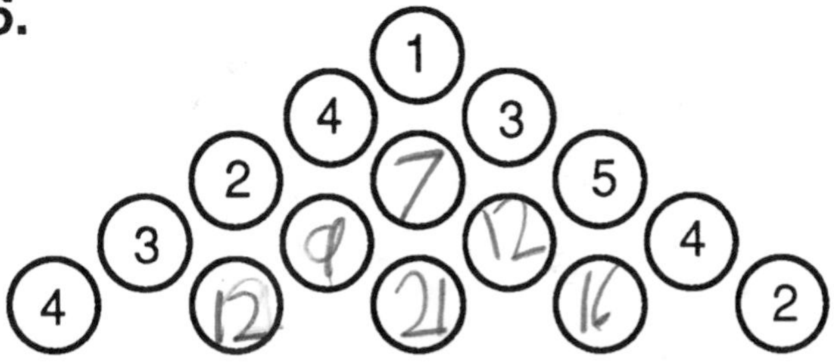

1
4 3
2 7 5
3 9 12 4
4 12 21 16 2

7. Design your own number triangle.

MAILBOX PATTERNS

▼▼▼

The numbers on each row of mailboxes make a pattern. Fill in the missing digits on each mailbox.

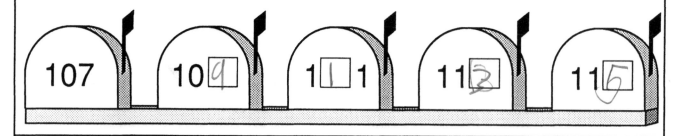

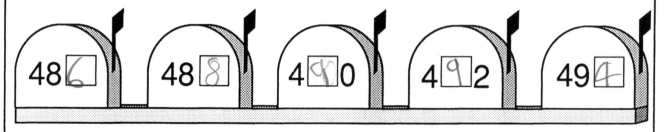

243	245	24[7]	24[9]	2[5]1
814	816	8[1]8	82[0]	82[2]
139	1[4]1	14[3]	14[5]	147
107	10[9]	1[1]1	11[3]	11[5]
48[6]	48[8]	4[9]0	4[9]2	49[4]

SQUARE WINDOWS

▼▼▼

Study the number chart. Use it to fill in a number in each blank square below.

1	2	3	4	5
6	7	8	9	10
11	12	13	14	15
16	17	18	19	20
21	22	23	24	25

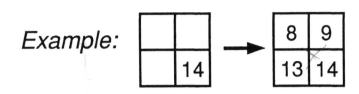

Number Chart

Example:

	14

→

8	9
13	14

1.

6	7
11	12

2.

13	14
18	19

3.

17	18
22	23

4.

19	20
24	25

5.

12	13
17	18

6.

9	10
14	15

7.

1	2	3
6	7	8

8.

8	9
13	14
18	19

9.

11	12
16	17
21	22

10.

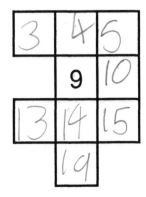

3	4	5
	9	10
13	14	15
	19	

COUNT AND CHECK

▼▼▼

Find a pattern, then continue it. Any pattern is fine—if you can explain it.

1.
1 2 3 1 2 3 1 2 3 1 2 3 1 2 3 1 2 3 1

2.
1 2 1 1 2 1 1 1 2 1 1 1 1 2 1 2 1 1 2 1

3.
5 1 5 5 1 5 5 5 1 5 5 5 5 1 5 5 5 5

4.
3 6 4 5 3 6 4 5 3 6 4 5 3 6 4 5 3 6 4 5

5.
0 1 0 0 2 0 0 0 3 0 0 0 0 4 0 0 0 0 0 5

6.
3 9 3 3 8 3 3 3 7 3 3 3 3 6 3 3 3 3 3

7.
1 2 3 1 3 4 1 4 5 1 5 6 1 6 7 1 7 8 1 8

8.
0 9 1 1 8 2 2 2 7 3 3 3 3 6 4 4 4 4 4

9.
9 0 8 8 1 7 7 7 2 6 6 6 6 3 5 5 5 5 4

10.
1 1 2 1 2 3 1 2 3 4 5 2 3 4 5 1 2 3 4

THE SAME DIFFERENCE

▼▼▼

Step 1: Write the first number to the right in each row.

Step 2: Find the difference of each pair.

Repeat steps 1 and 2 until the numbers are the same.

Example:

8 4 2 6

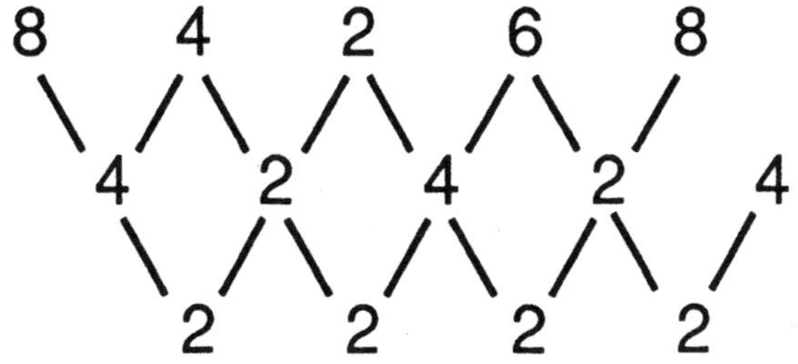
8 4 2 6 8
4 2 4 2 4
2 2 2 2

1. 9 4 8 2	**2.** 8 1 6 3
3. 3 5 6 8	**4.** 3 5 9 2
5. 4 7 9 1	**6.** 5 2 7 4

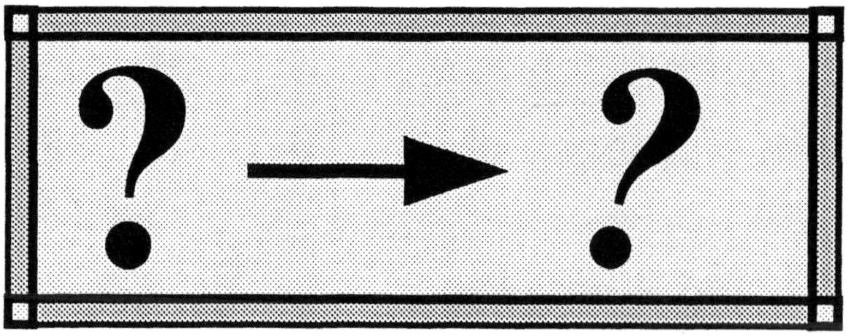

Find the pattern in each row.
Write numbers in the boxes to match the pattern.

1. 23 → 5 61 → 7 54 → □ 35 → □ 49 → □

2. 101 → 2 234 → 9 142 → □ 315 → □ 514 → □

3. 93 → 6 81 → 7 52 → □ 73 → □ 60 → □

4. 23 → 6 42 → 8 71 → □ 82 → □ 39 → □

5. 223 → 12 234 → 24 632 → □ 254 → □ 526 → □

6. 825 → 5 934 → 8 713 → □ 654 → □ 798 → □

Make up your own pattern.
See if a friend can figure it out.

7. ____ → □ ____ → □ ____ → □ ____ → □

FOLLOW THE ARROWS

▼▼▼

Start at the △. Write numbers in the boxes that match the pattern of the arrows. You must use the numbers 1, 2, 3, 4, 5, 6, 7, 8, and 9 in order.

Example:

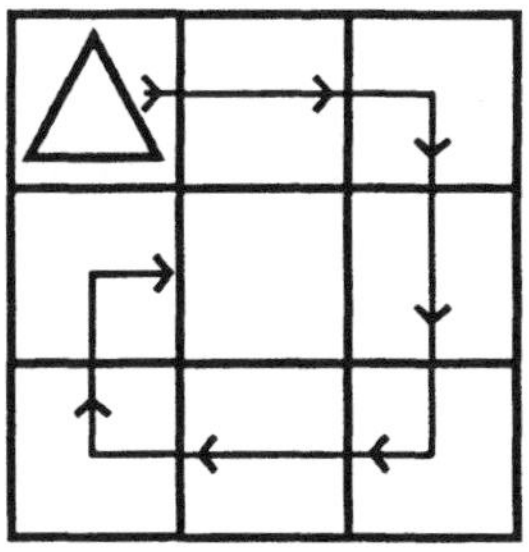

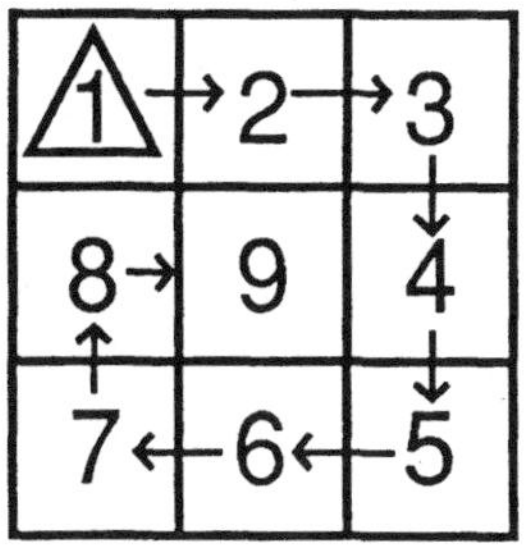
1 2 3
8 9 4
7 6 5

1.

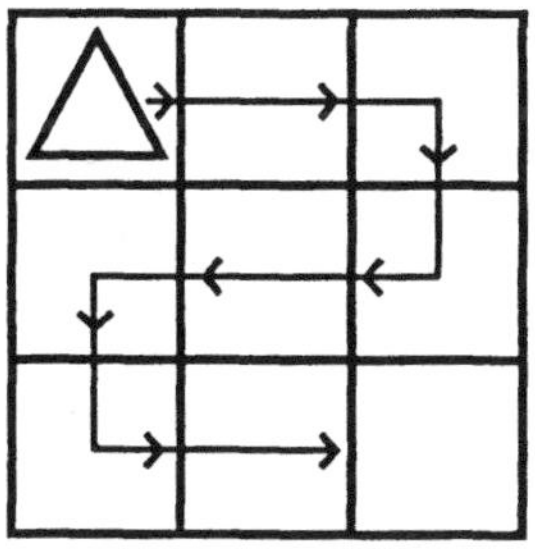

2.

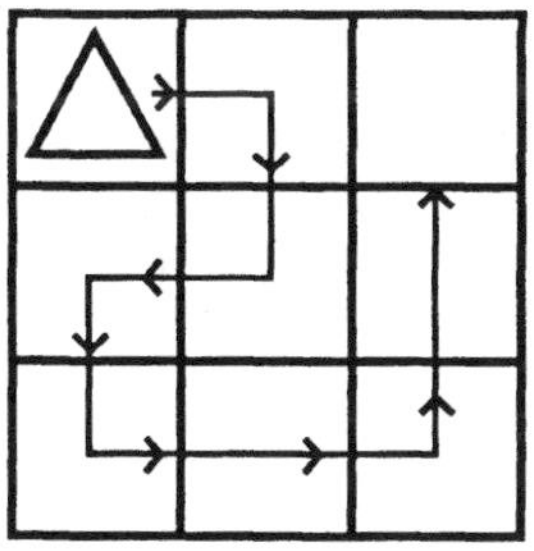

3.

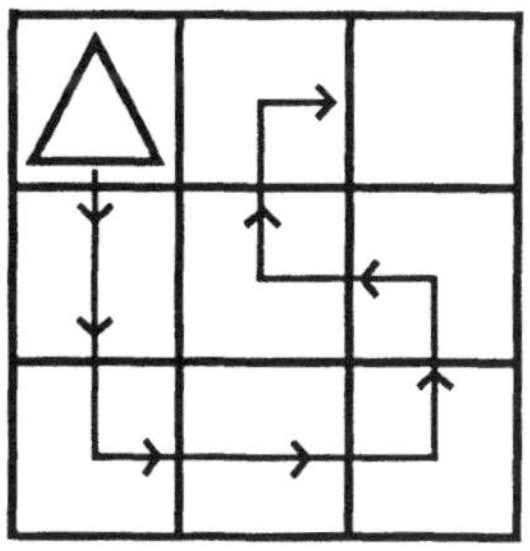

4.

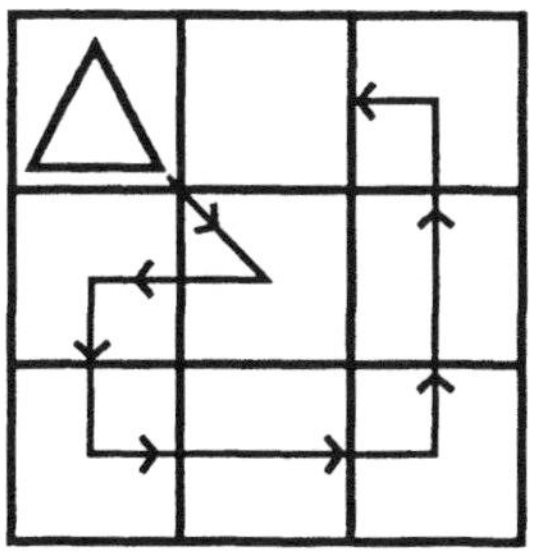

5.

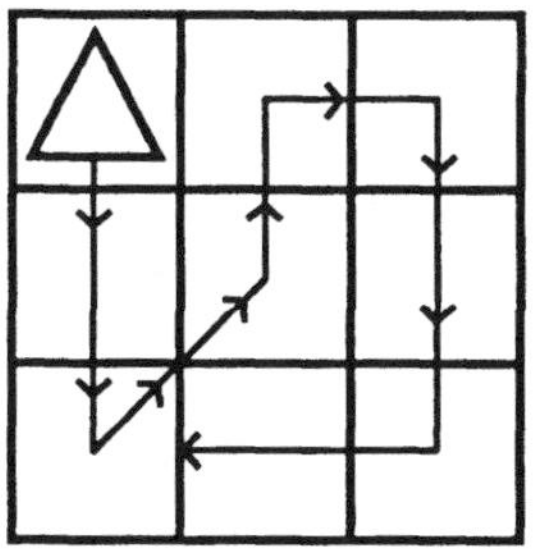

6.

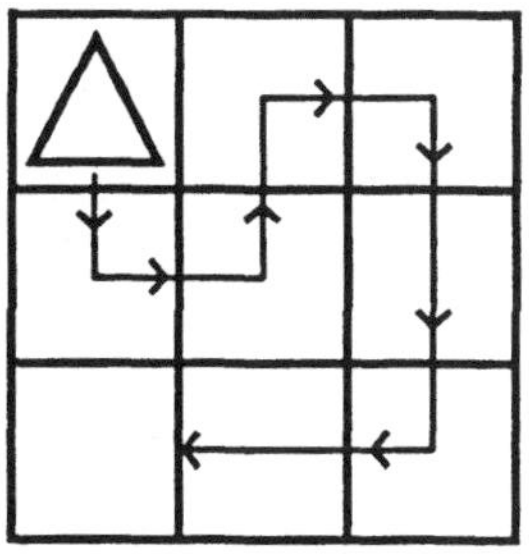

7.

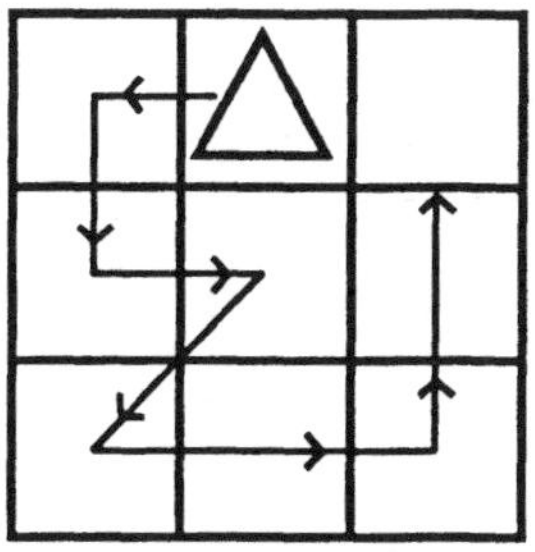

8.

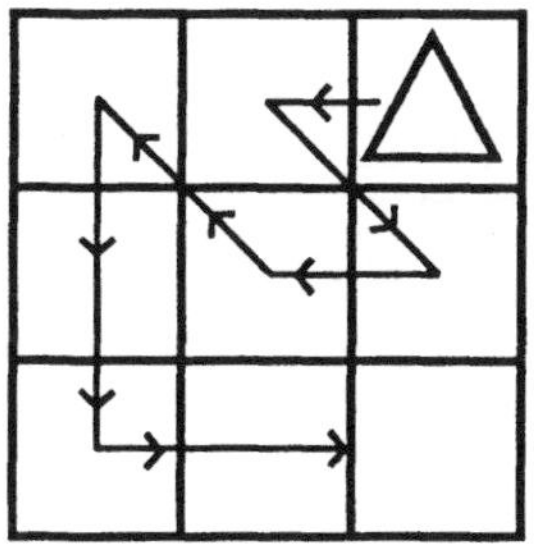

9.

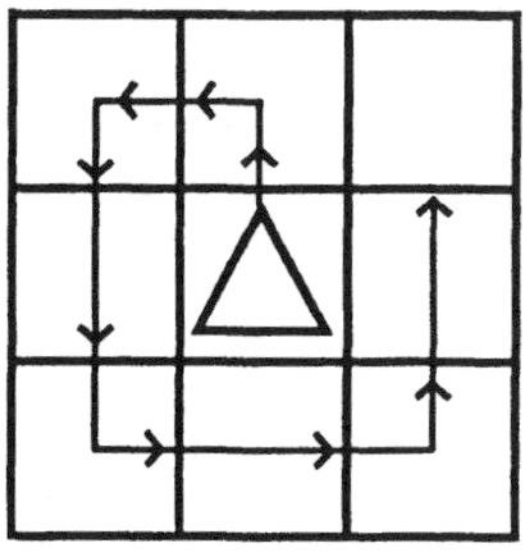

SAME SUM? ▼▼▼

MAGIC BOX
WOW!

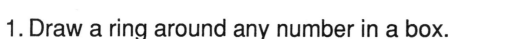

1. Draw a ring around any number in a box.
2. Cross out the rest of that number's row and column.
3. Draw a ring around another uncrossed-out number in that box
4. Cross out the rest of that number's row and column.
5. Draw a ring around any other uncrossed-out numbers.
6. Add the three numbers with rings around them.
7. Look for a pattern with the sums.

Example: 3 + 4 + 8 = 15

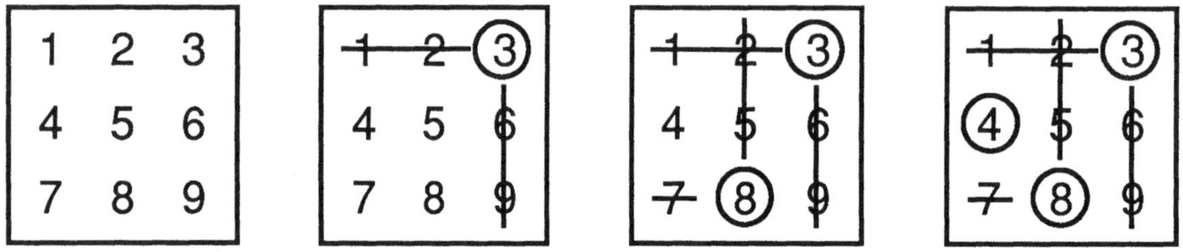

Sum = 15

1.

4	5	6
7	8	9
10	11	12

Sum = ____

2.

4	5	6
7	8	9
10	11	12

Sum = ____

3.

4	5	6
7	8	9
10	11	12

Sum = ____

4.

3	5	7
9	11	13
15	17	19

Sum = ____

5.

3	5	7
9	11	13
15	17	19

Sum = ____

6.

3	5	7
9	11	13
15	17	19

Sum = ____

7.

7	8	9
12	13	14
17	18	19

Sum = ____

8.

7	8	9
12	13	14
17	18	19

Sum = ____

9.

7	8	9
12	13	14
17	18	19

Sum = ____

DRAW THE PATTERNS (III)

Continue each pattern.

1. 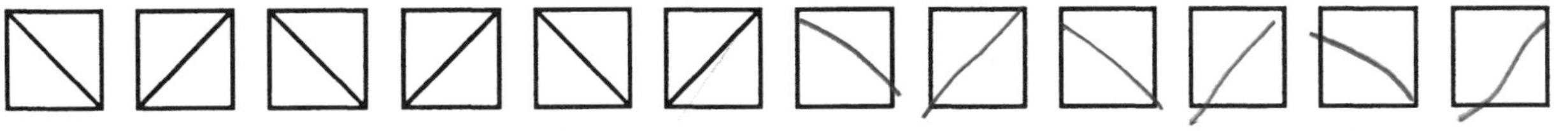

2. 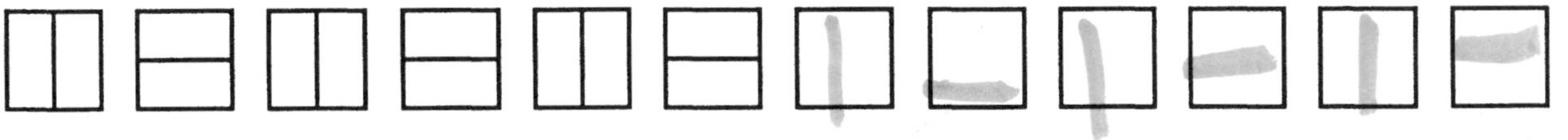

3. 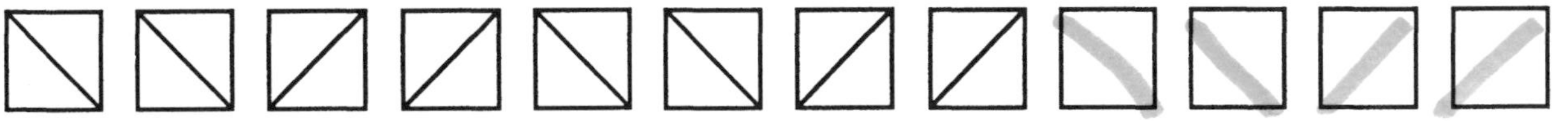

4. 

5. 

6. 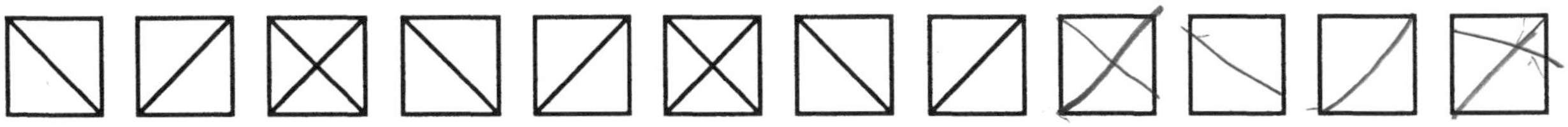

7. 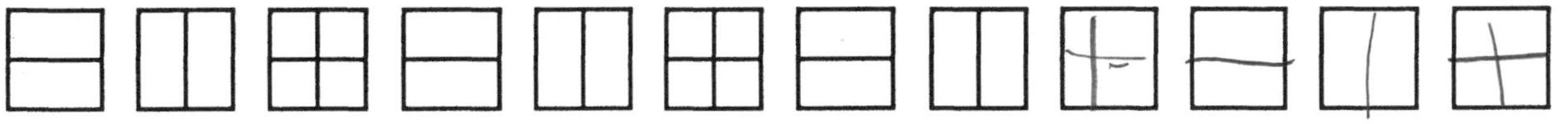

8. 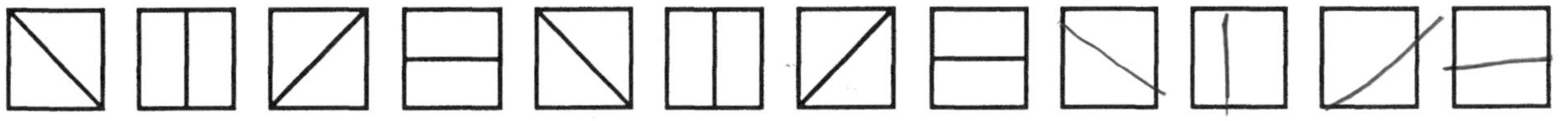

9. 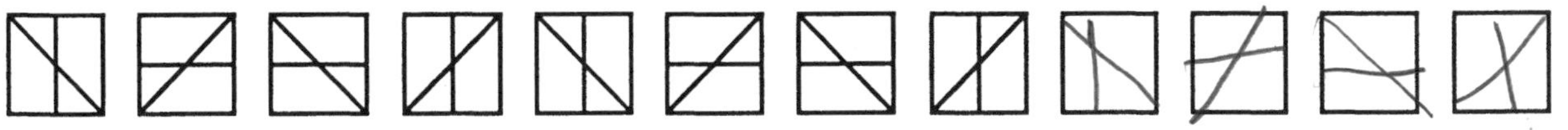

10. 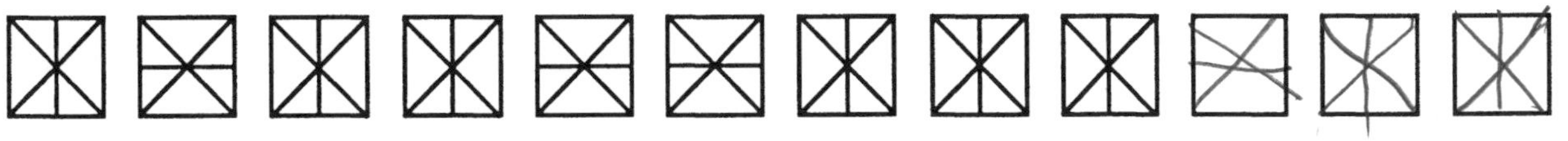

DRAW YOUR PATTERN (III)

▼▼▼

Draw your own pattern on each row of squares below.

1.
2.
3.
4.
5.
6.
7.
8.
9.
10.

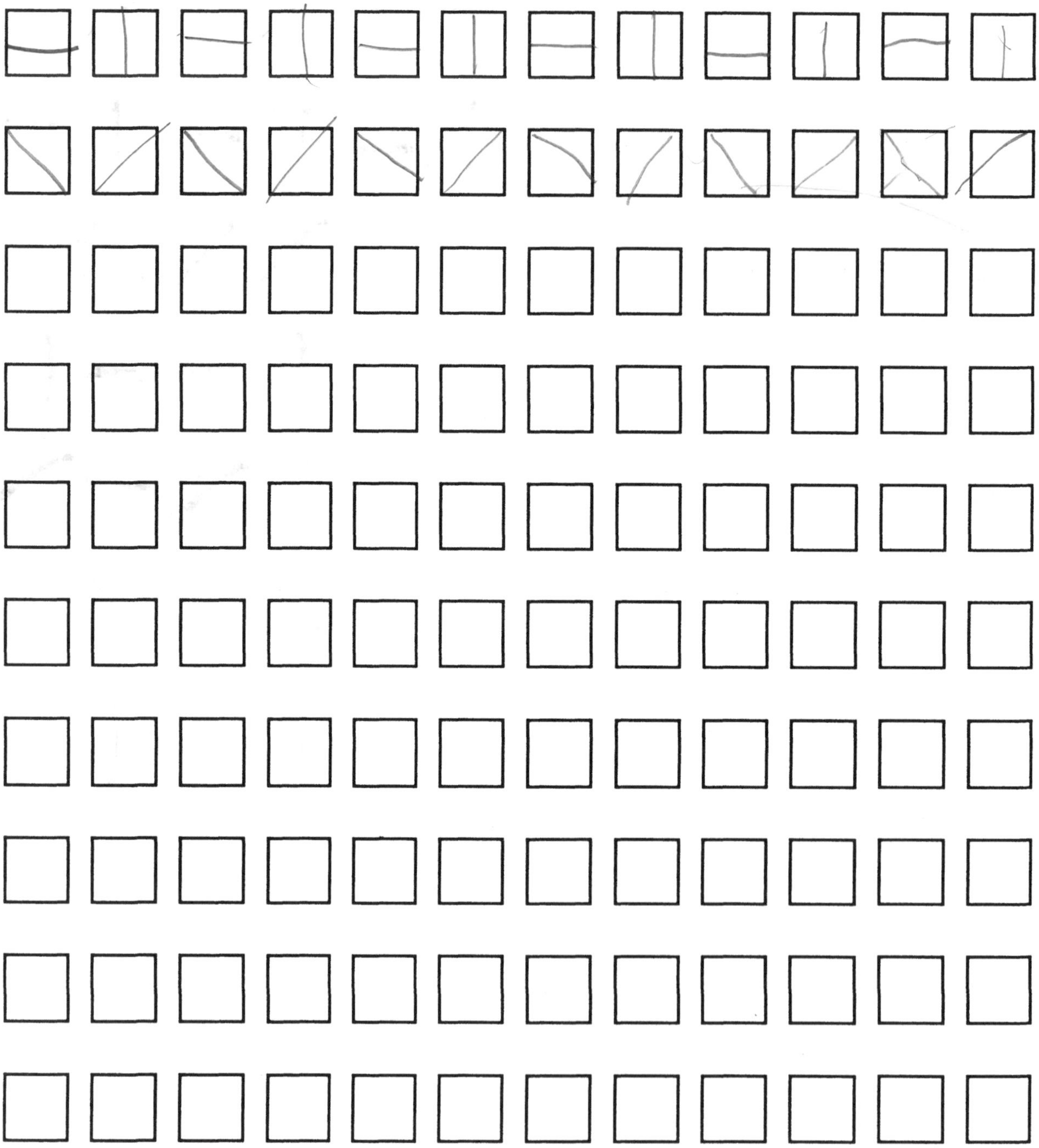

ADDITION TABLE

PATTERN
RESOURCE

+	1	2	3	4	5	6	7	8	9
1	2	3	4	5	6	7	8	9	10
2	3	4	5	6	7	8	9	10	11
3	4	5	6	7	8	9	10	11	12
4	5	6	7	8	9	10	11	12	13
5	6	7	8	9	10	11	12	13	14
6	7	8	9	10	11	12	13	14	15
7	8	9	10	11	12	13	14	15	16
8	9	10	11	12	13	14	15	16	17
9	10	11	12	13	14	15	16	17	18

HUNDREDS CHART

PATTERN
RESOURCE

1	2	3	4	5	6	7	8	9	10
11	12	13	14	15	16	17	18	19	20
21	22	23	24	25	26	27	28	29	30
31	32	33	34	35	36	37	38	39	40
41	42	43	44	45	46	47	48	49	50
51	52	53	54	55	56	57	58	59	60
61	62	63	64	65	66	67	68	69	70
71	72	73	74	75	76	77	78	79	80
81	82	83	84	85	86	87	88	89	90
91	92	93	94	95	96	97	98	99	100

Avery

PART 2: IMAGERY

SAME SHAPES

Find two shapes that are the same in each row.
Draw a ring around them.

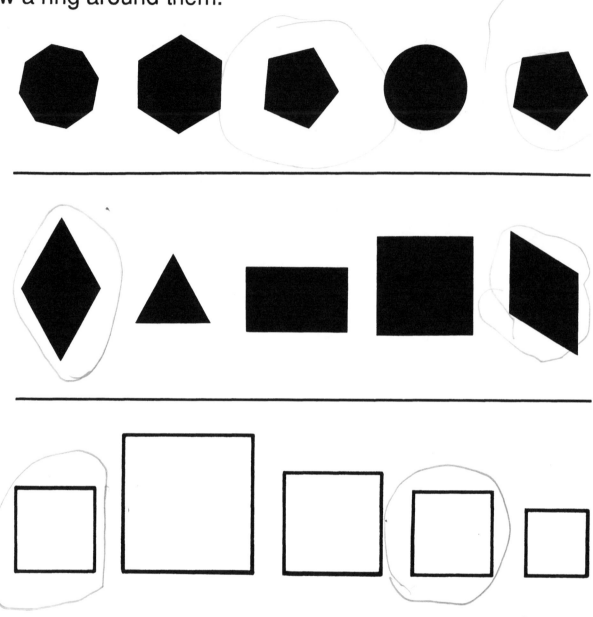

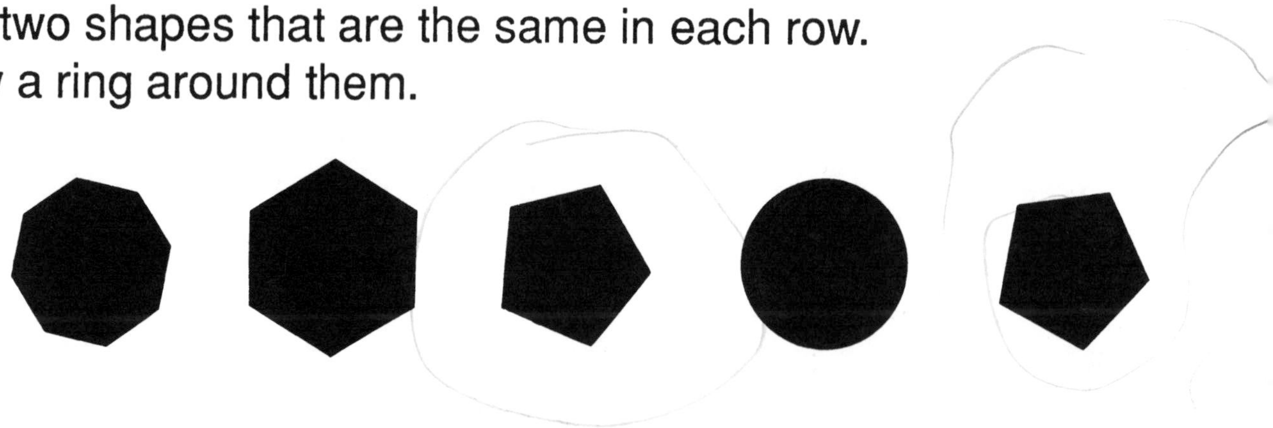

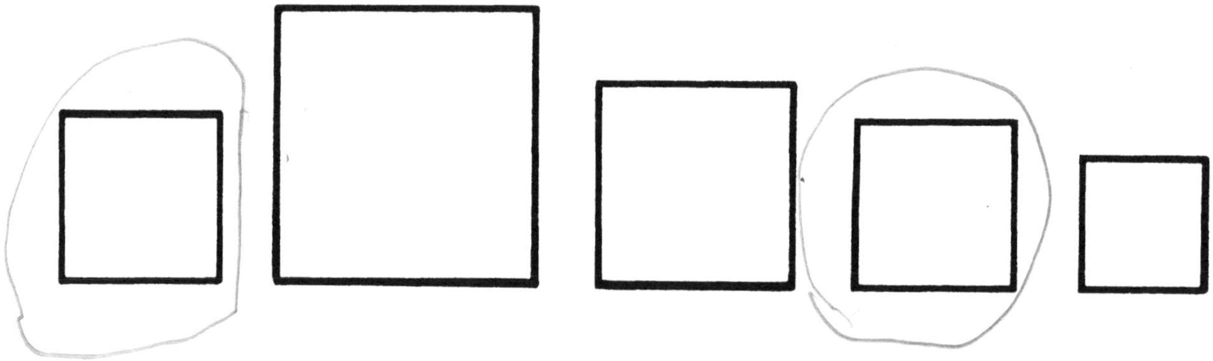

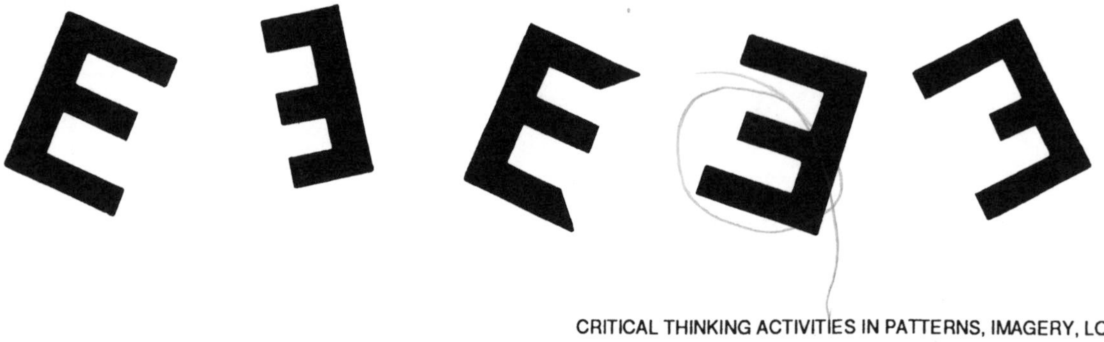

DIFFERENT SHAPES

Draw a ring around the shape in each row that is different.

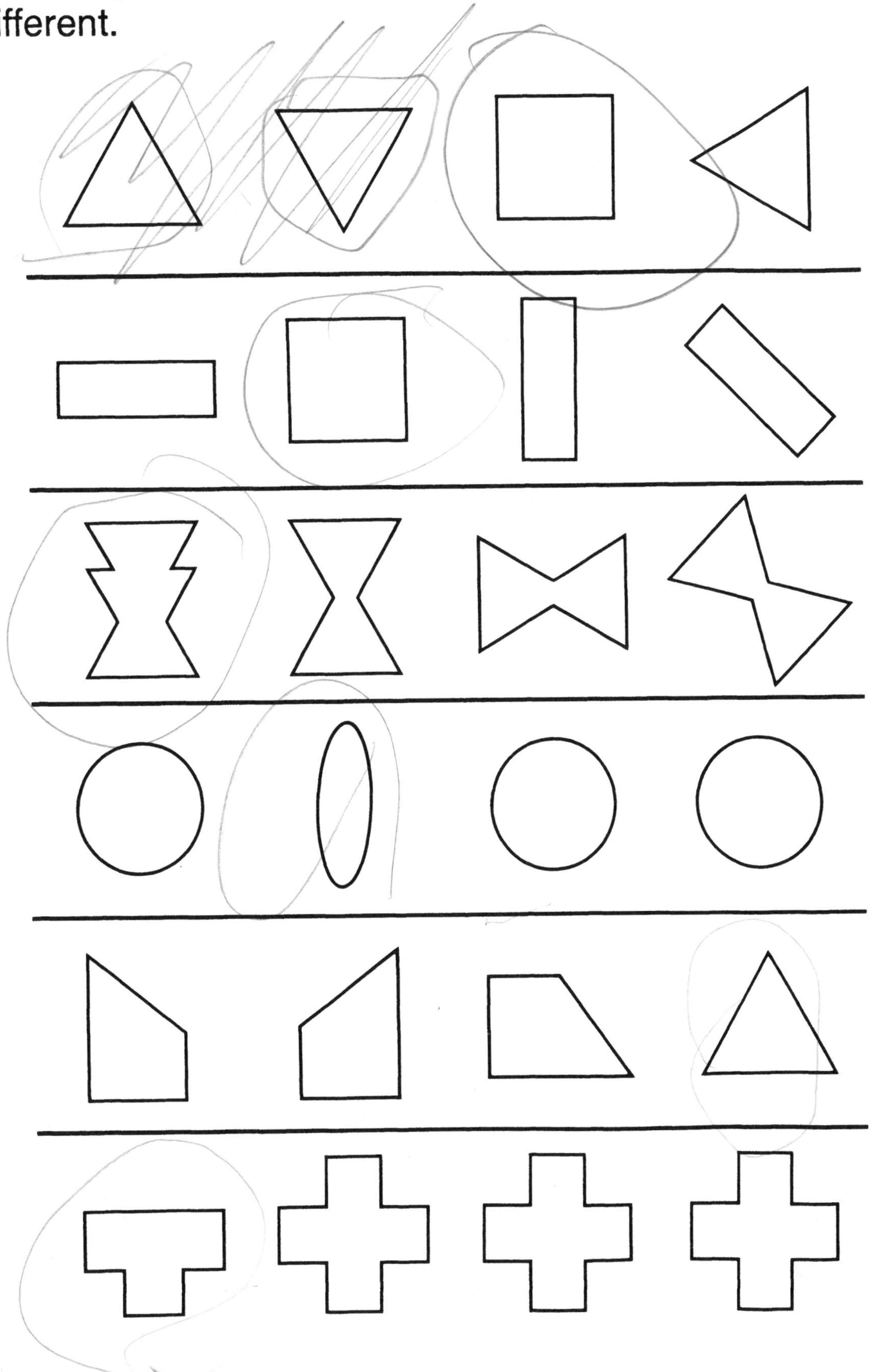

CAT MATCH

Draw a line between each of the cats that match.

DOT DESIGN (I)

Copy each design.

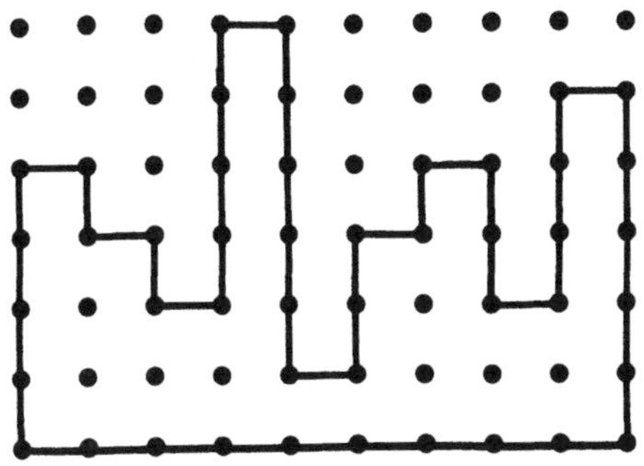

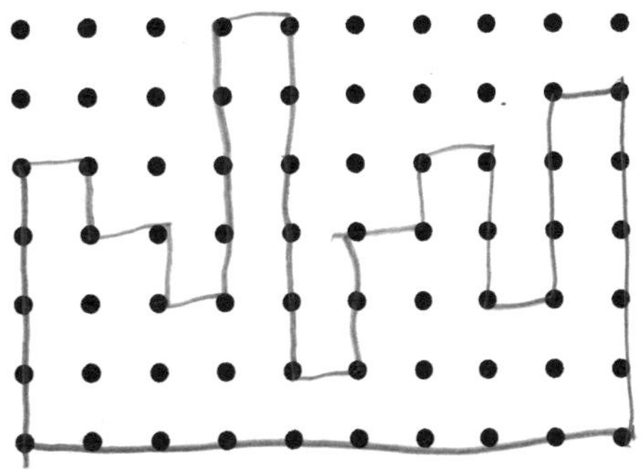

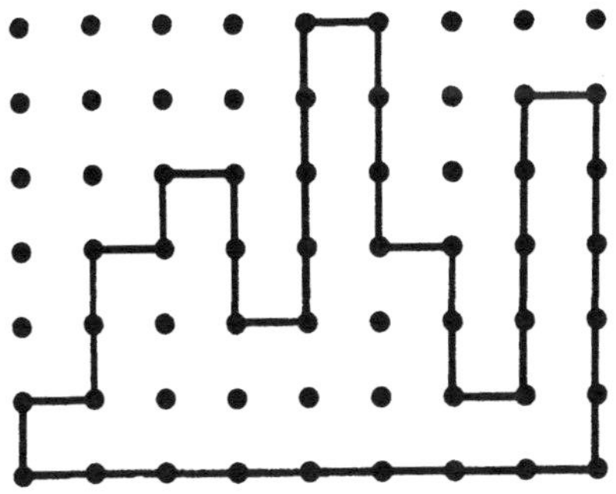

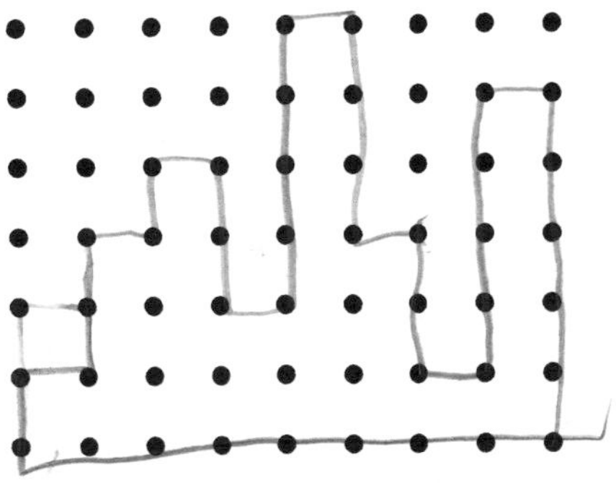

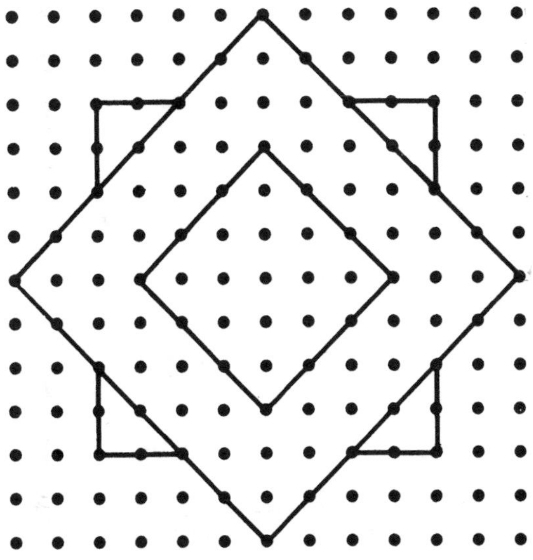

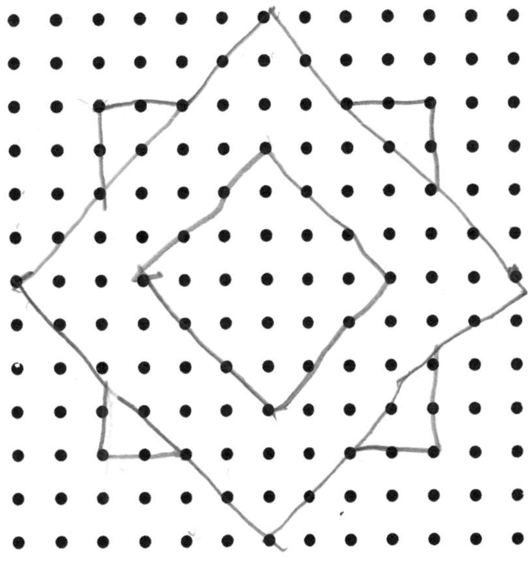

DOTS RIGHT

Color the dots for each number below.

1 2 3 4 5 6 7 8 9

2 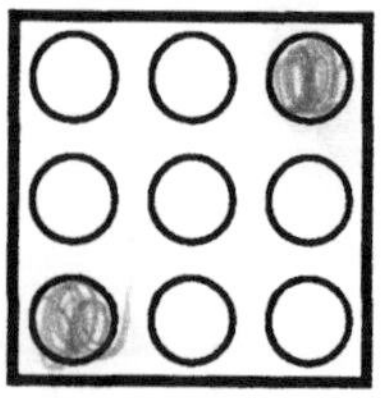

5 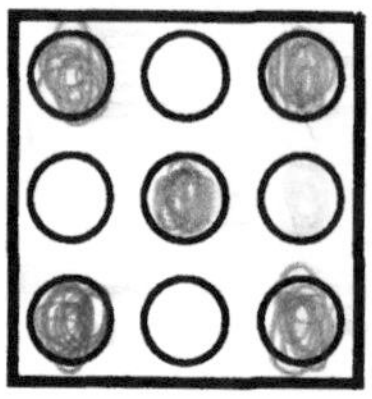

4 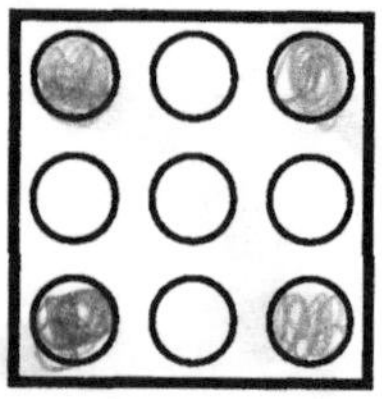

1 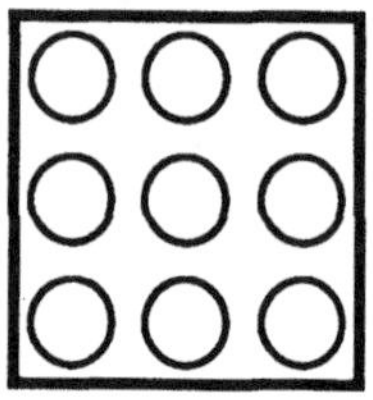

7 

9 

8 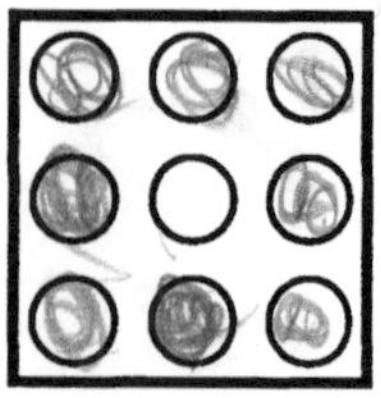

3 

6 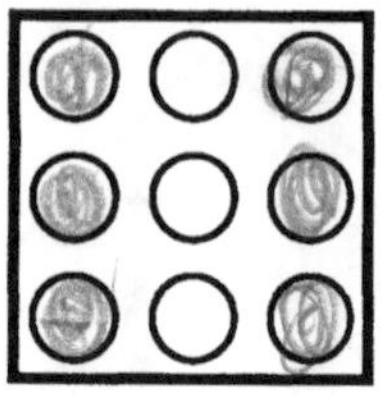

COLOR THE SHAPES (I)

Color the same shapes with the same color.

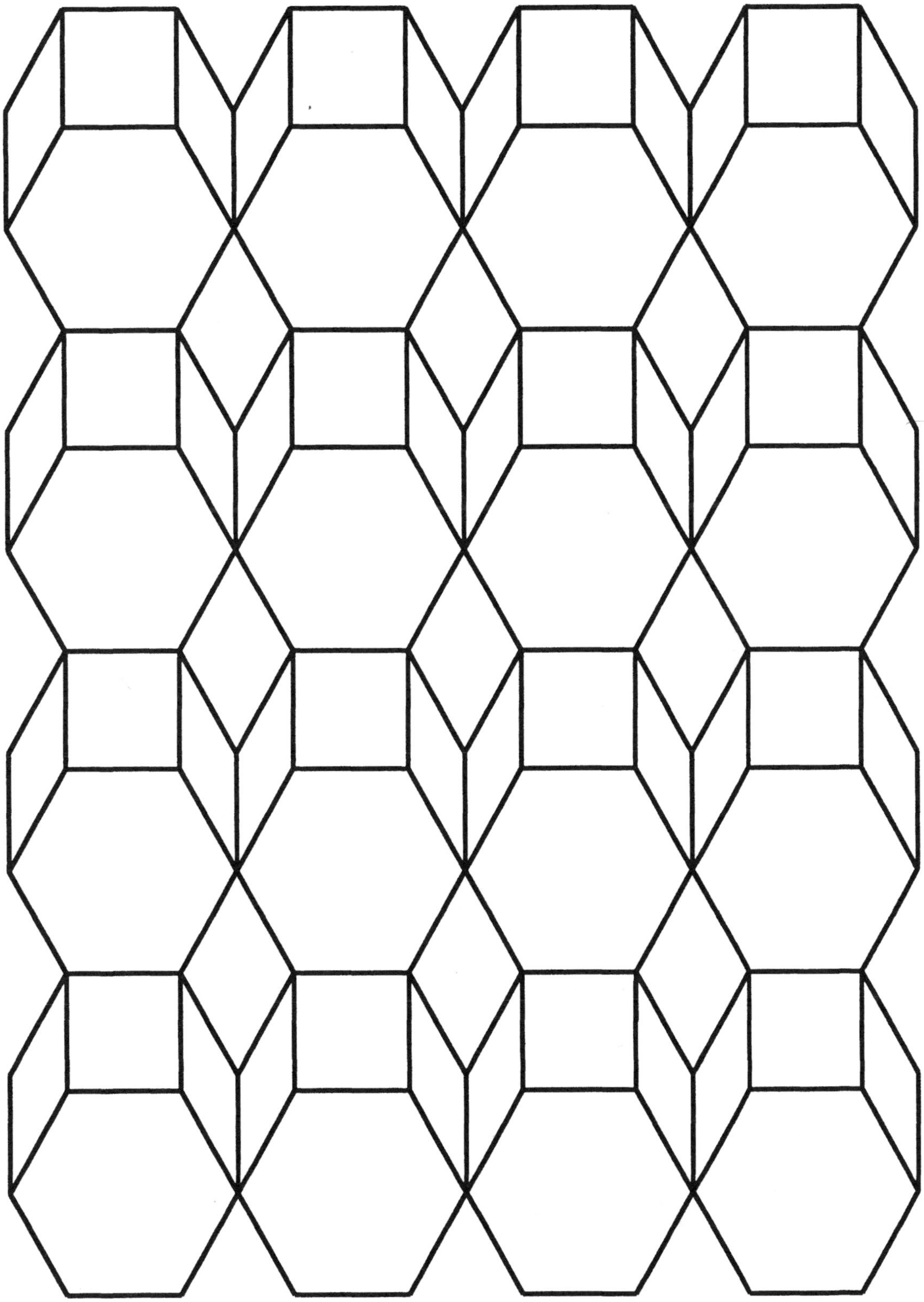

WHAT'S THE SAME?

1. Find two shapes that are the same. Draw a ring around the letters.

A B C D

2. Find two shapes that are the same. Draw a ring around the letters.

A B C D E

3. Which design is just like A? Draw a ring around the letter.

A B C D E

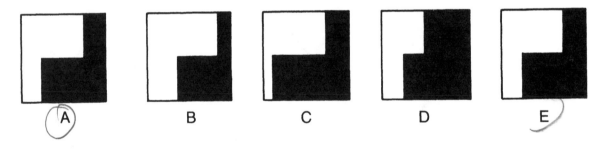

4. Find this shape. Color it.

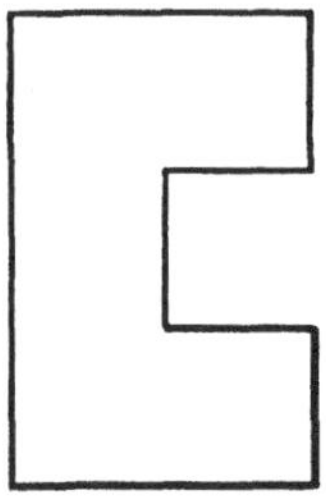

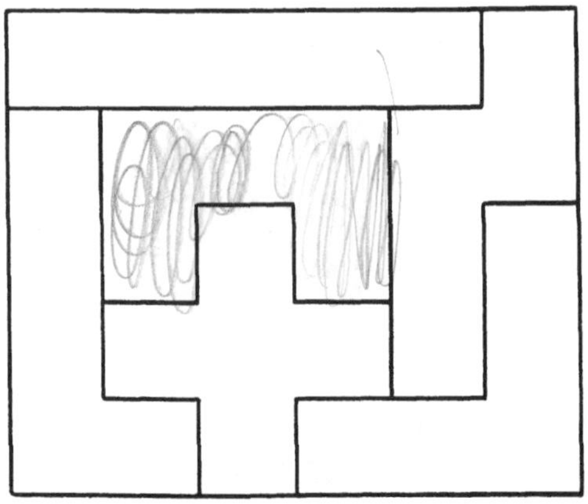

PUZZLE GIRL

Cut out the puzzle pieces. Fit the pieces together to make this picture.

CIRCLE MATCH

Draw a line between each of the circles that match.

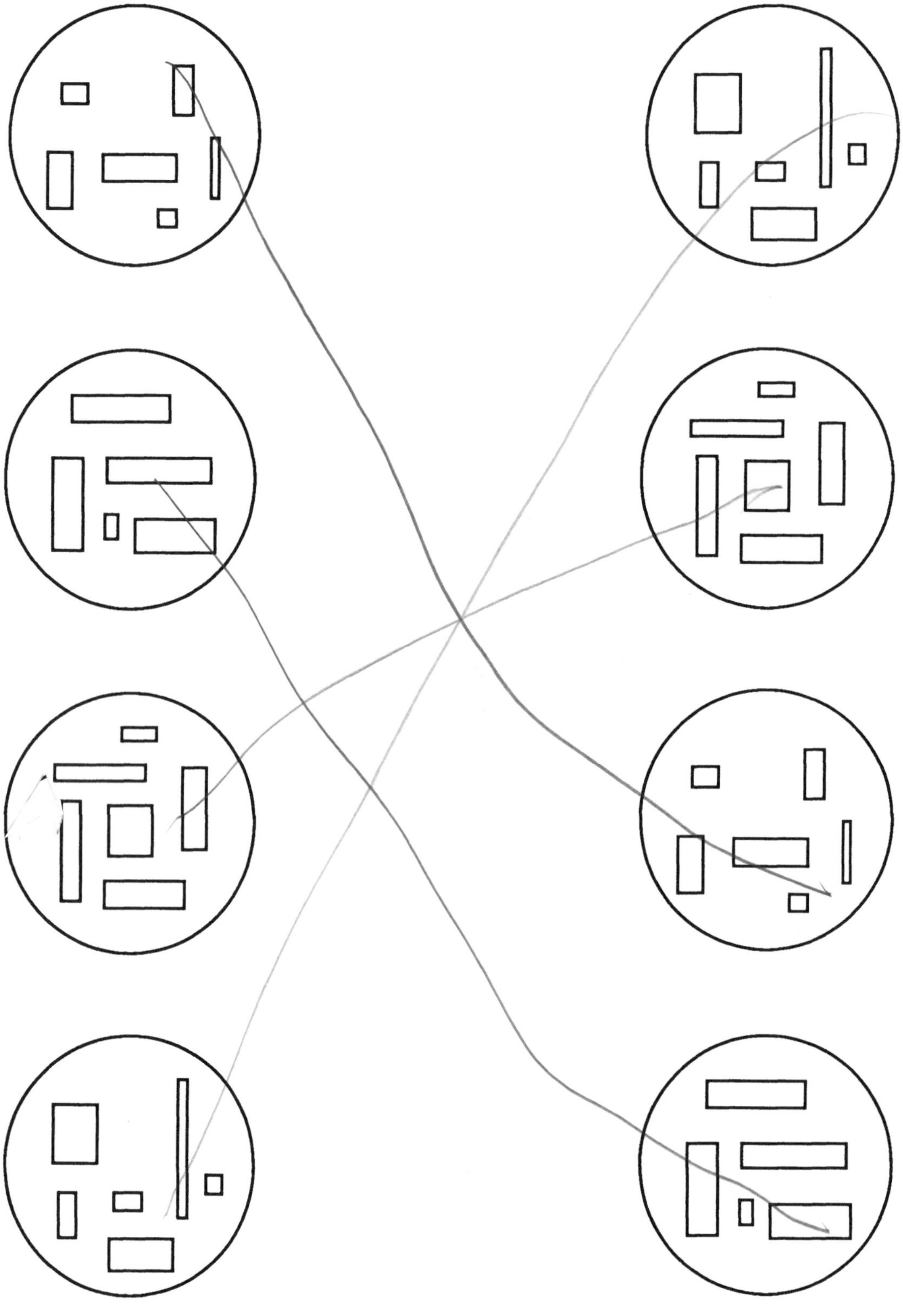

DOT DESIGN (II)

Copy each design.

1.

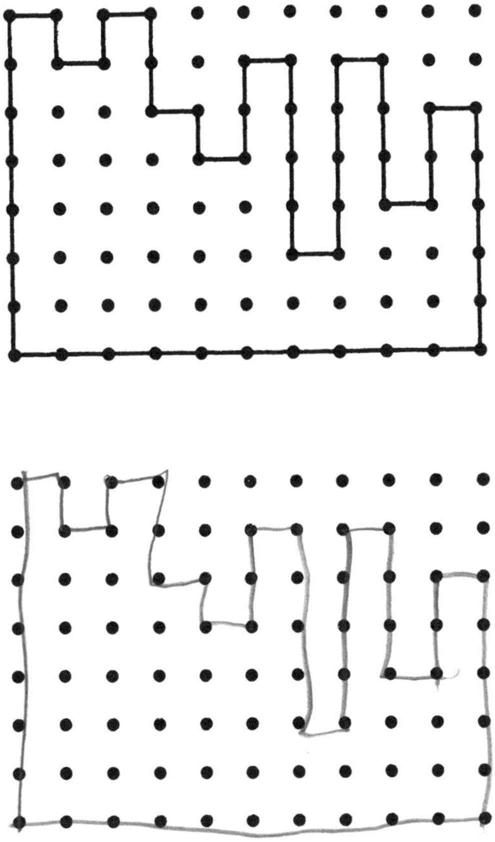

2.

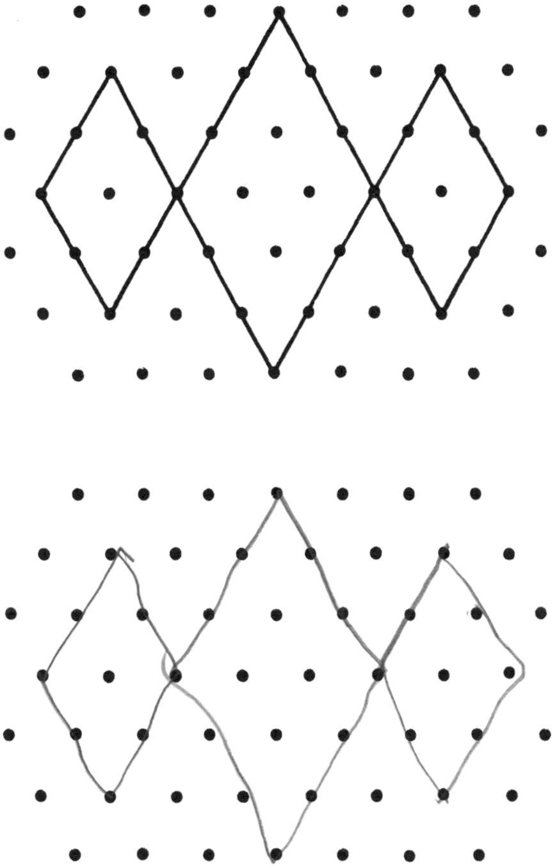

3.

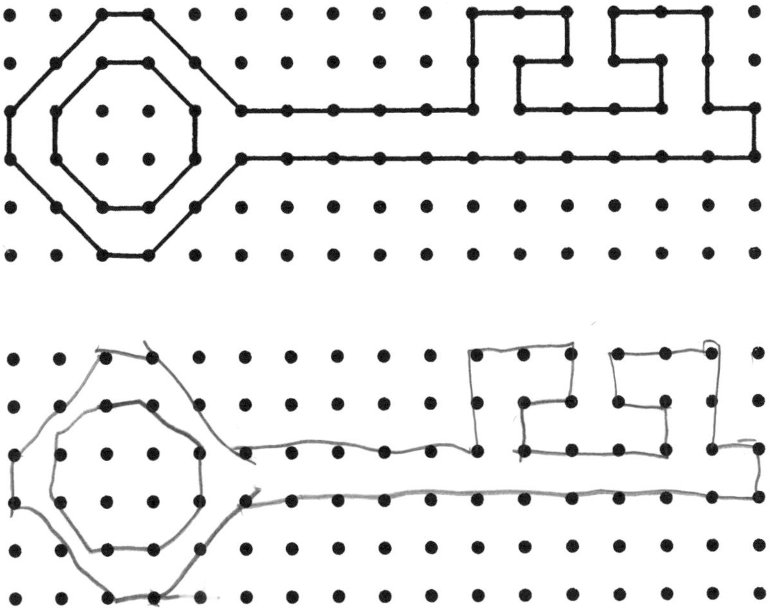

COLOR EACH SHAPE

1. Color each  .

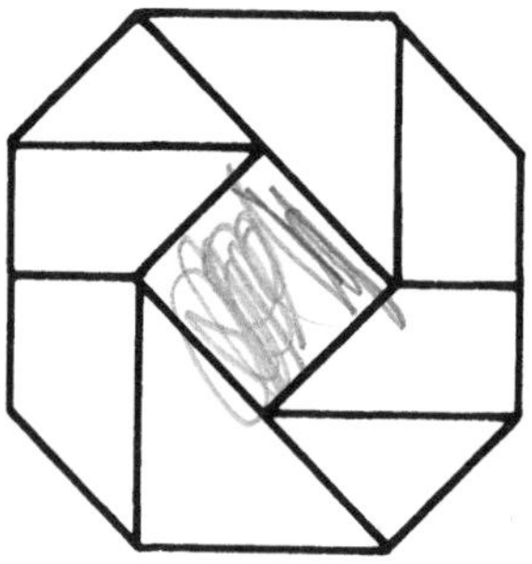

2. Color each 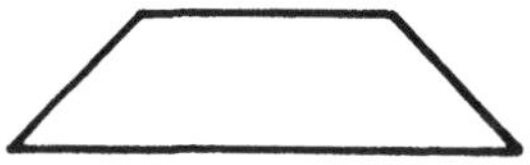 .

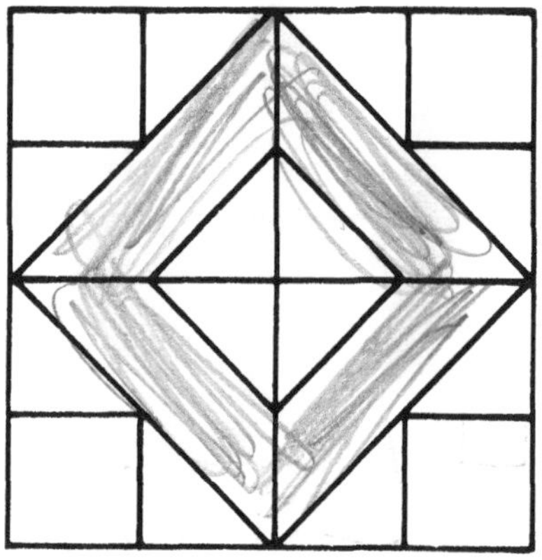

3. Color each  .

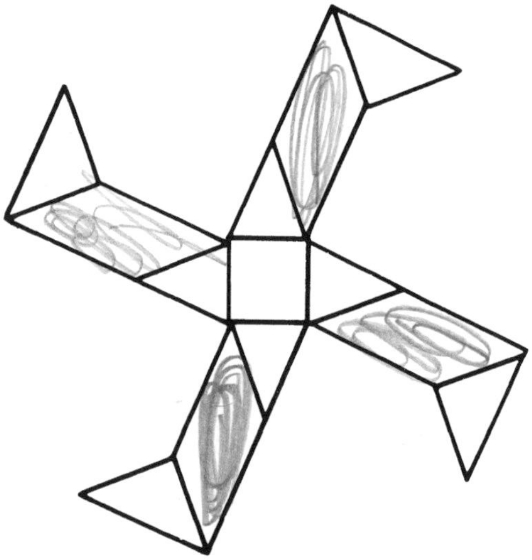

4. Color each 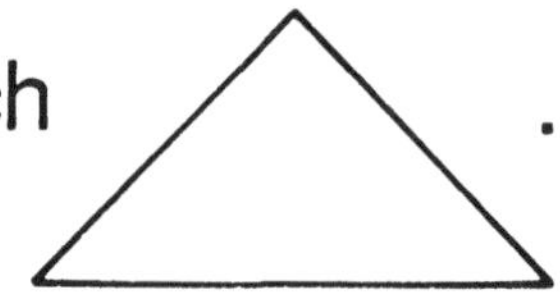 .

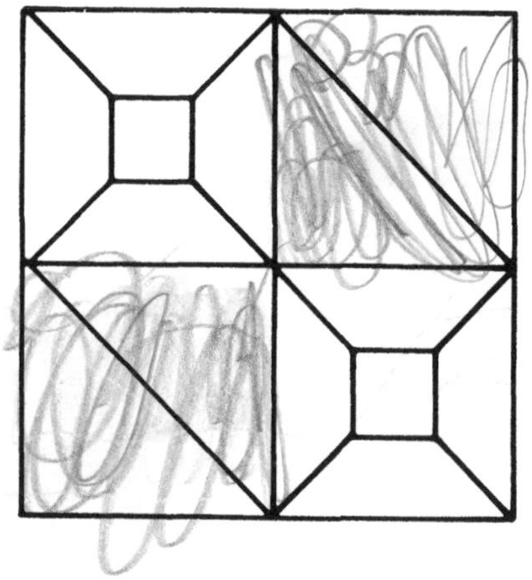

MISSING PIECE (I)

Write the letter of the missing piece in each of the six problems.

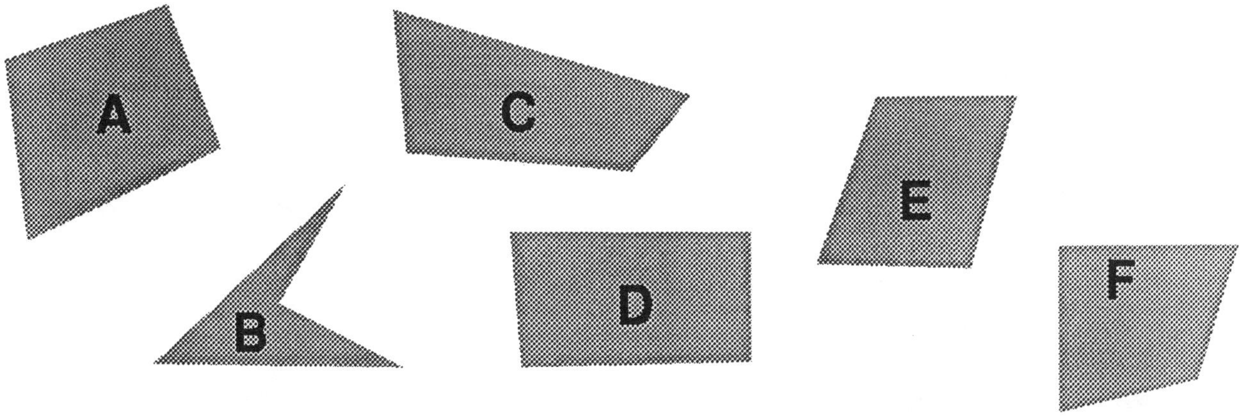
A
C
E
B
D
F

1.
D

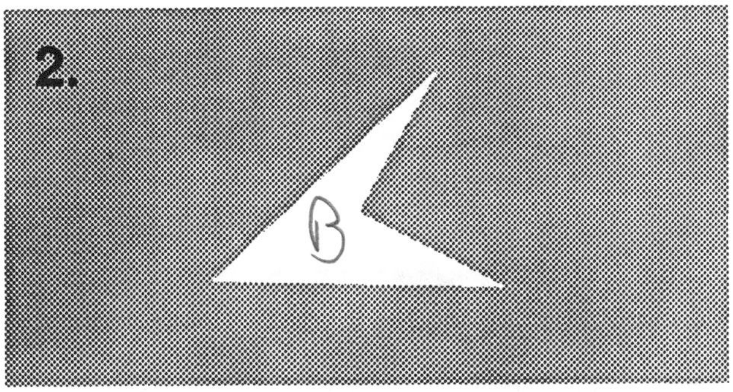
2.
B

3.
F

4.
E

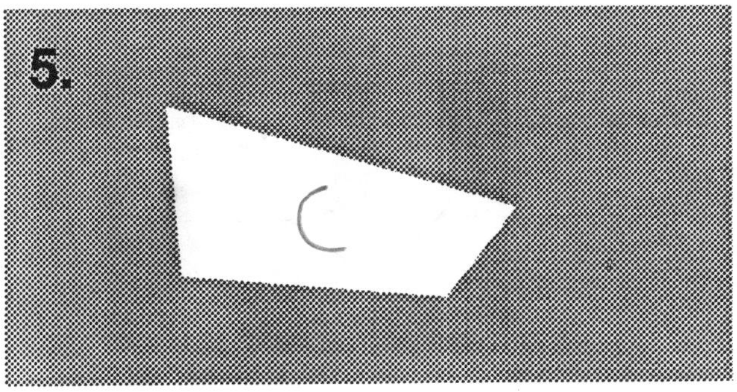
5.
C

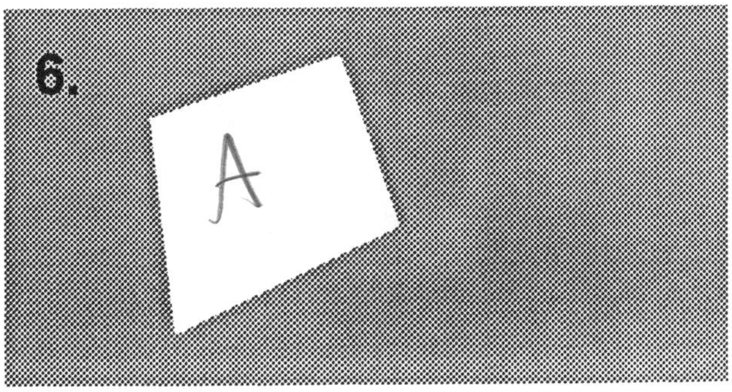
6.
A

RECTANGLE MATCH

Draw a line between each of the rectangles that match.

COLOR THE SHAPES (II)

Color the same shapes with the same color.

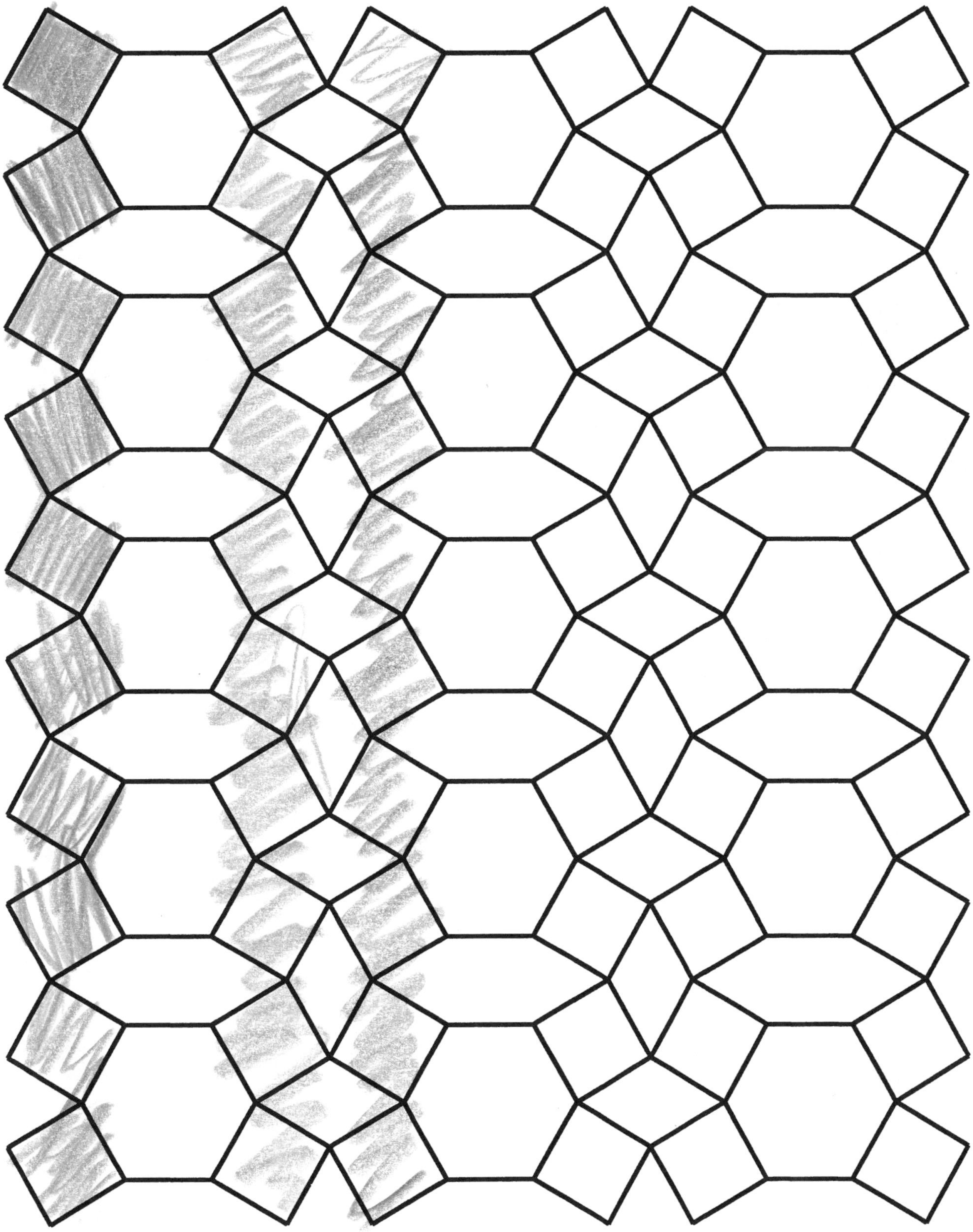

WHAT'S DIFFERENT?

Draw a ring around the shape in each row that is different.

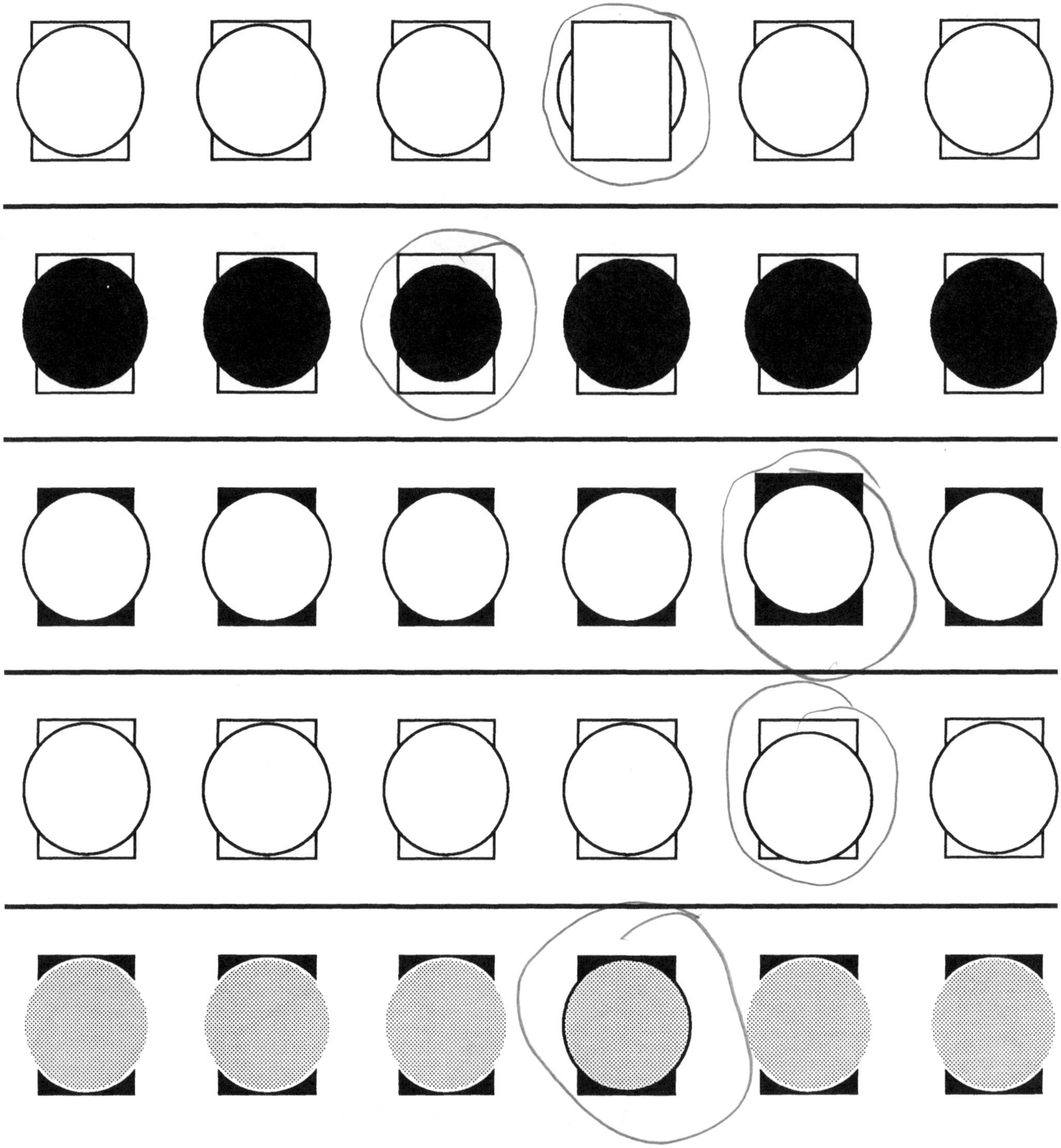

SURPRISE PACKAGES

▼▼

Write the letters of each matching pair of packages.

A and F　　C and G

H and B　　E and D

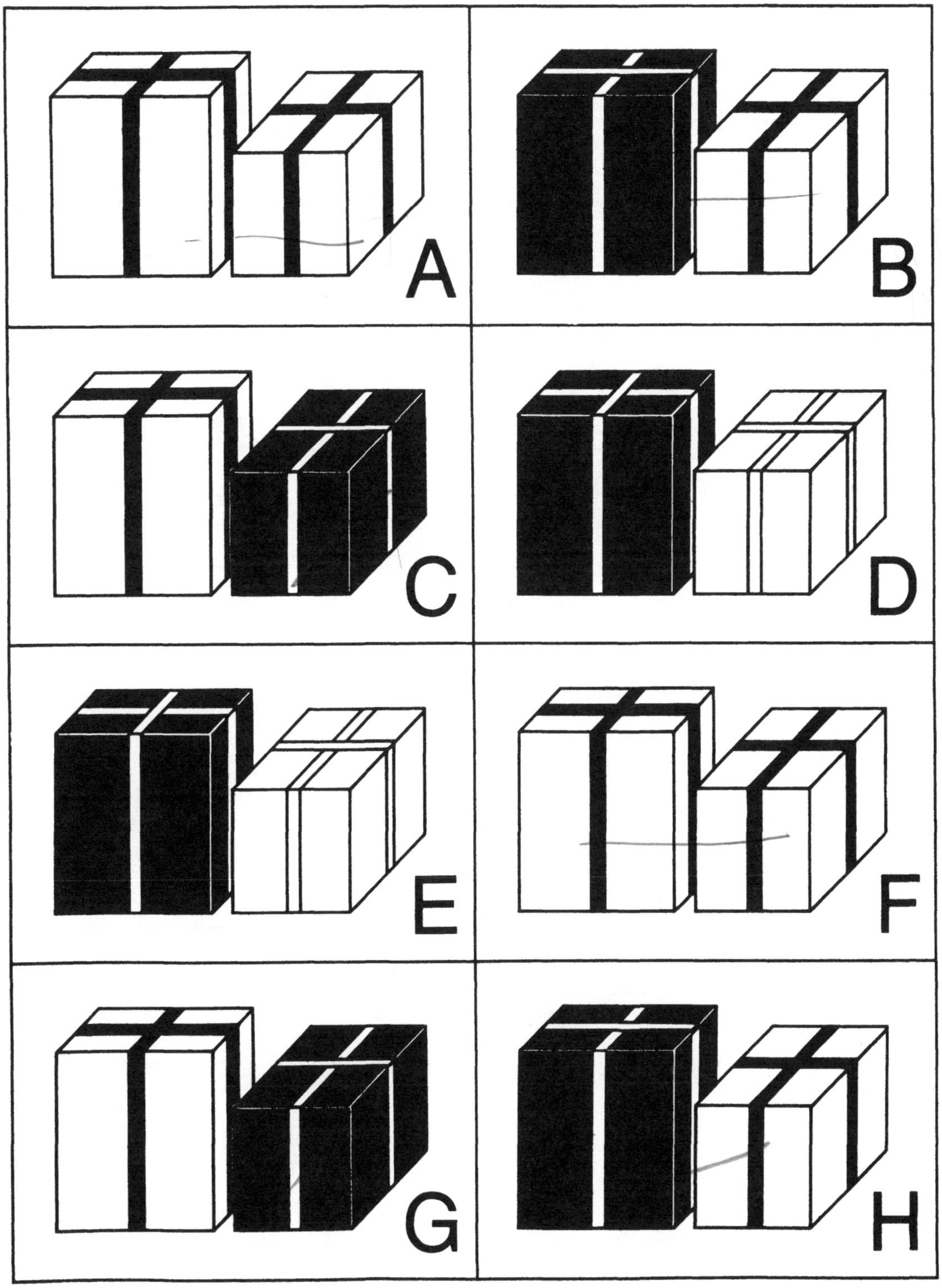
A
B
C
D
E
F
G
H

CARTOON PAIRS

Tell how the cartoons in each pair are different.

1. 1 is big one is small

TUNA
TUNA

2. 1 has frams & 1 doesen't

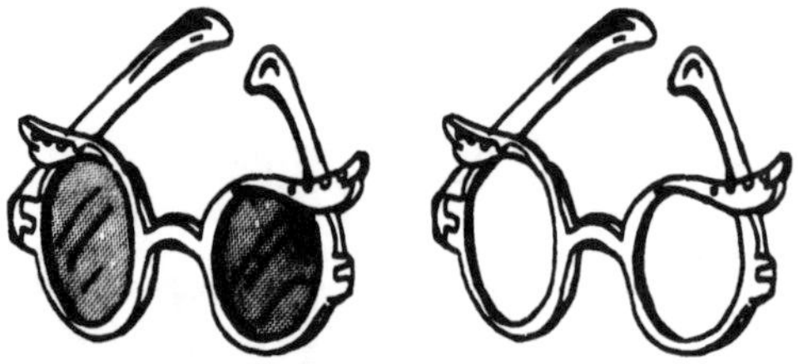

3. One has a sandcastle 1 doesent

4. They [illegible] differ times

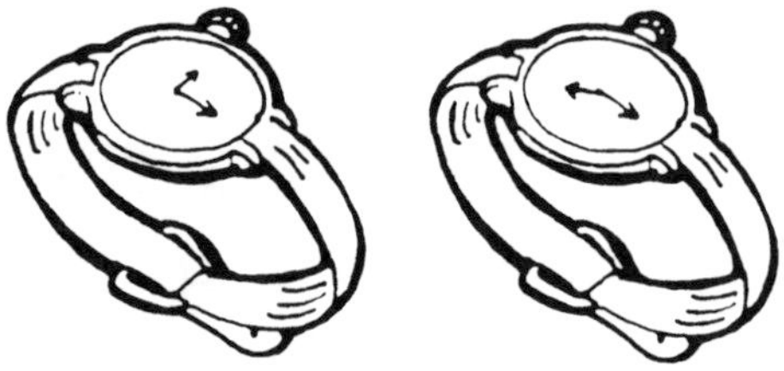

5.

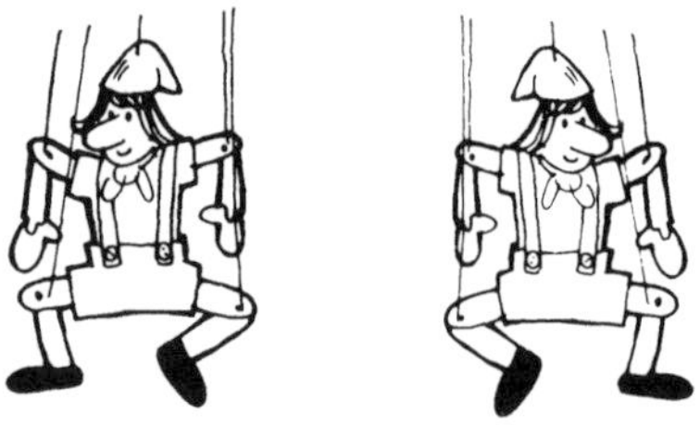

6.

7.

8.

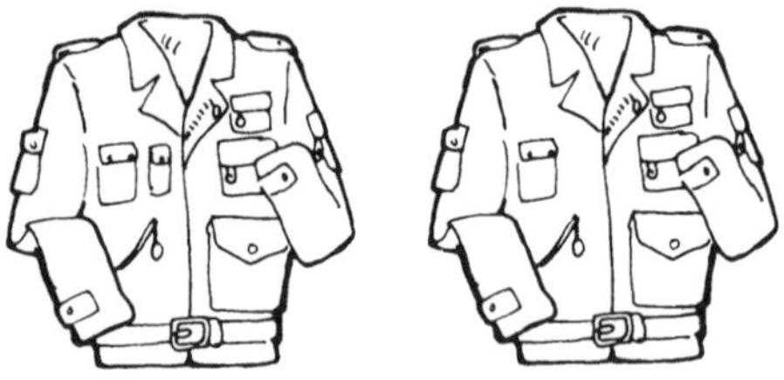

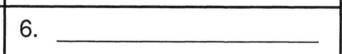

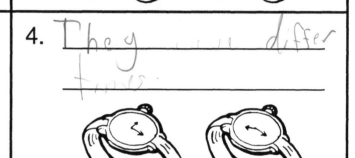

MORE DOT DESIGNS (I)

Copy each picture. Start at the lines given.

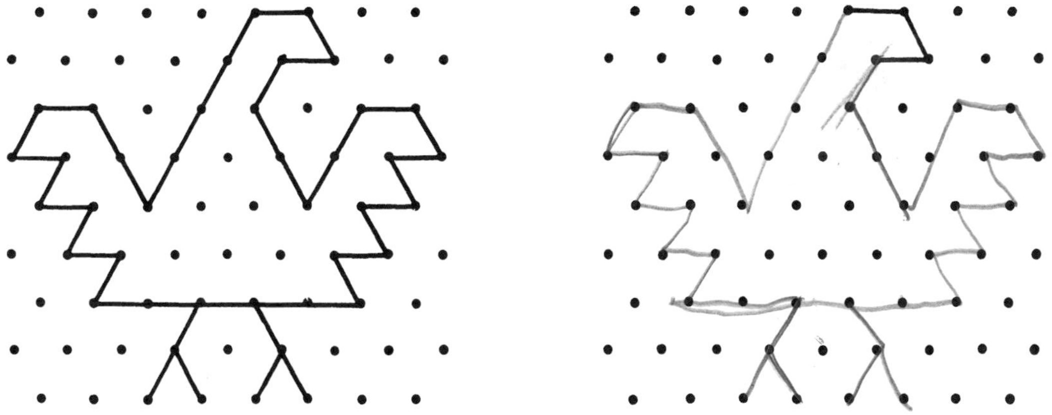

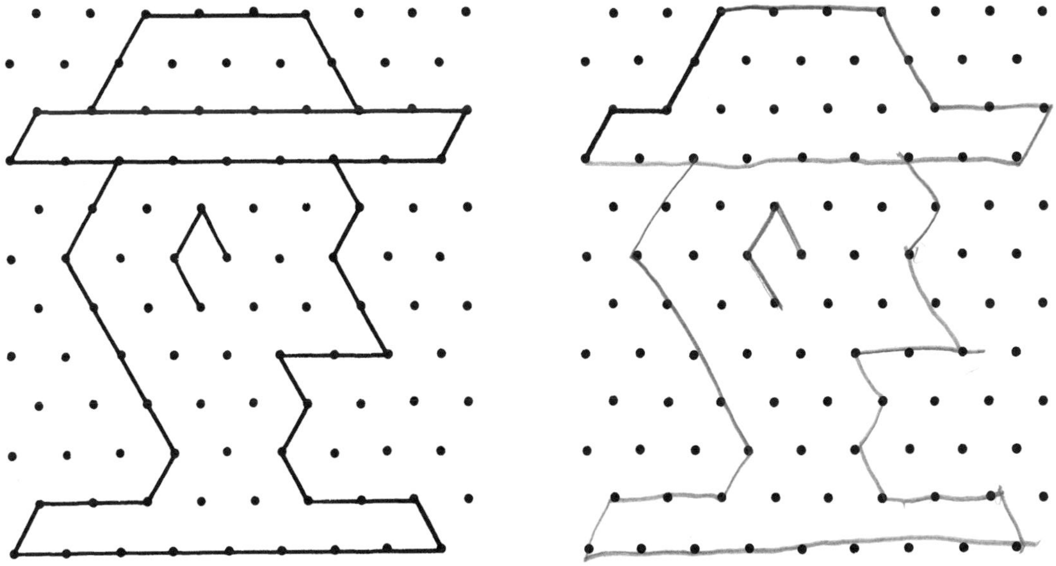

MATCH THE SHAPES

1. Find two shapes that are the same. Draw a ring around the letters.

A B C D

2. Find two shapes that are the same. Draw a ring around the letters.

A B C D E

3. Which design is just like A? Draw a ring around the letter.

A B C D E

4. Which pieces are the same? Write each letter in the shape that is the same.

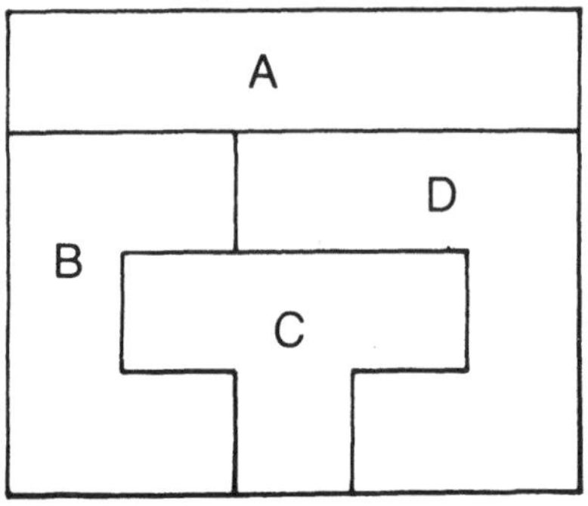
A
D
B
C

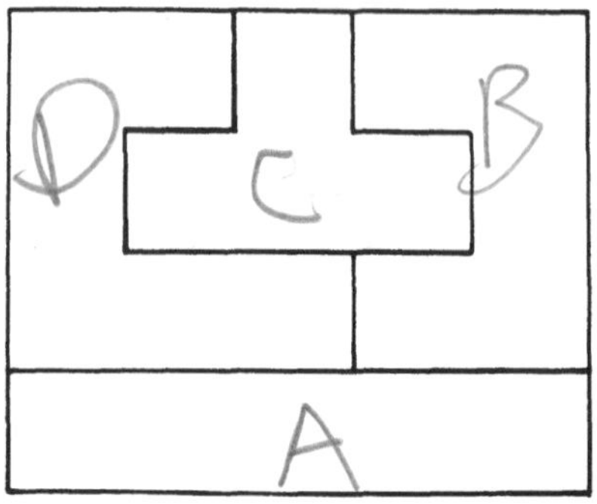

FIND THE SHAPE

Find the shape at the left in each box in the row.
Color it.

1.

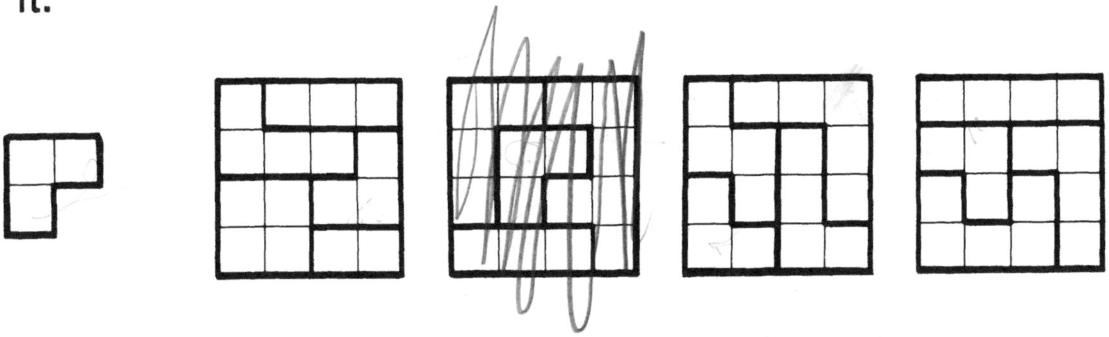

2.

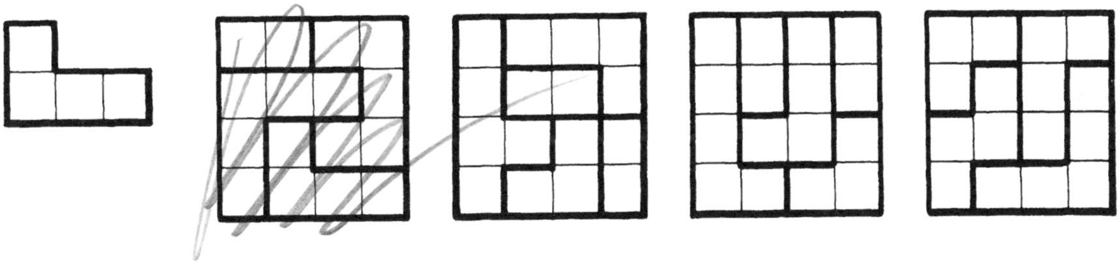

3.

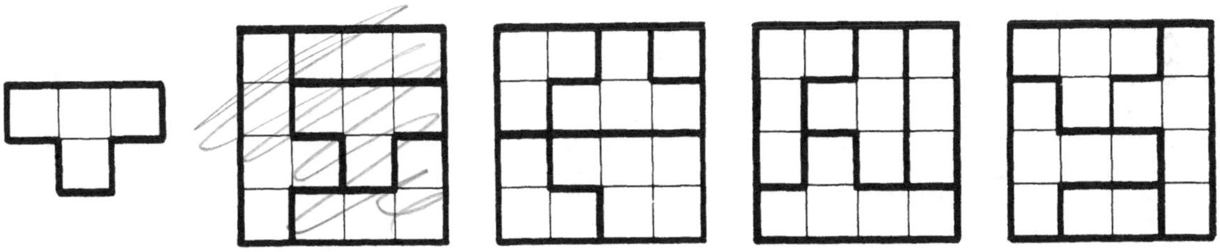

4.

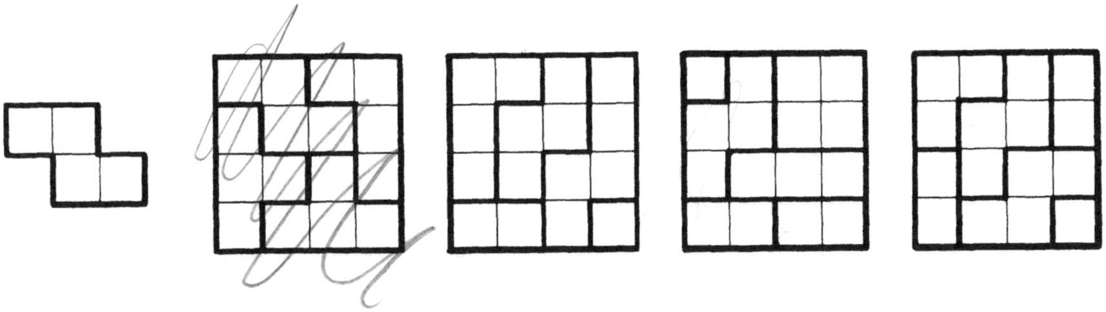

CALENDAR PUZZLE

▼▼

Cut out the puzzle pieces. Put them in order to make this calendar.

S	M	T	W	T	F	S
				1	2	3
4	5	6	7	8	9	10
11	12	13	14	15	16	17
18	19	20	21	22	23	24
25	26	27	28	29	30	31

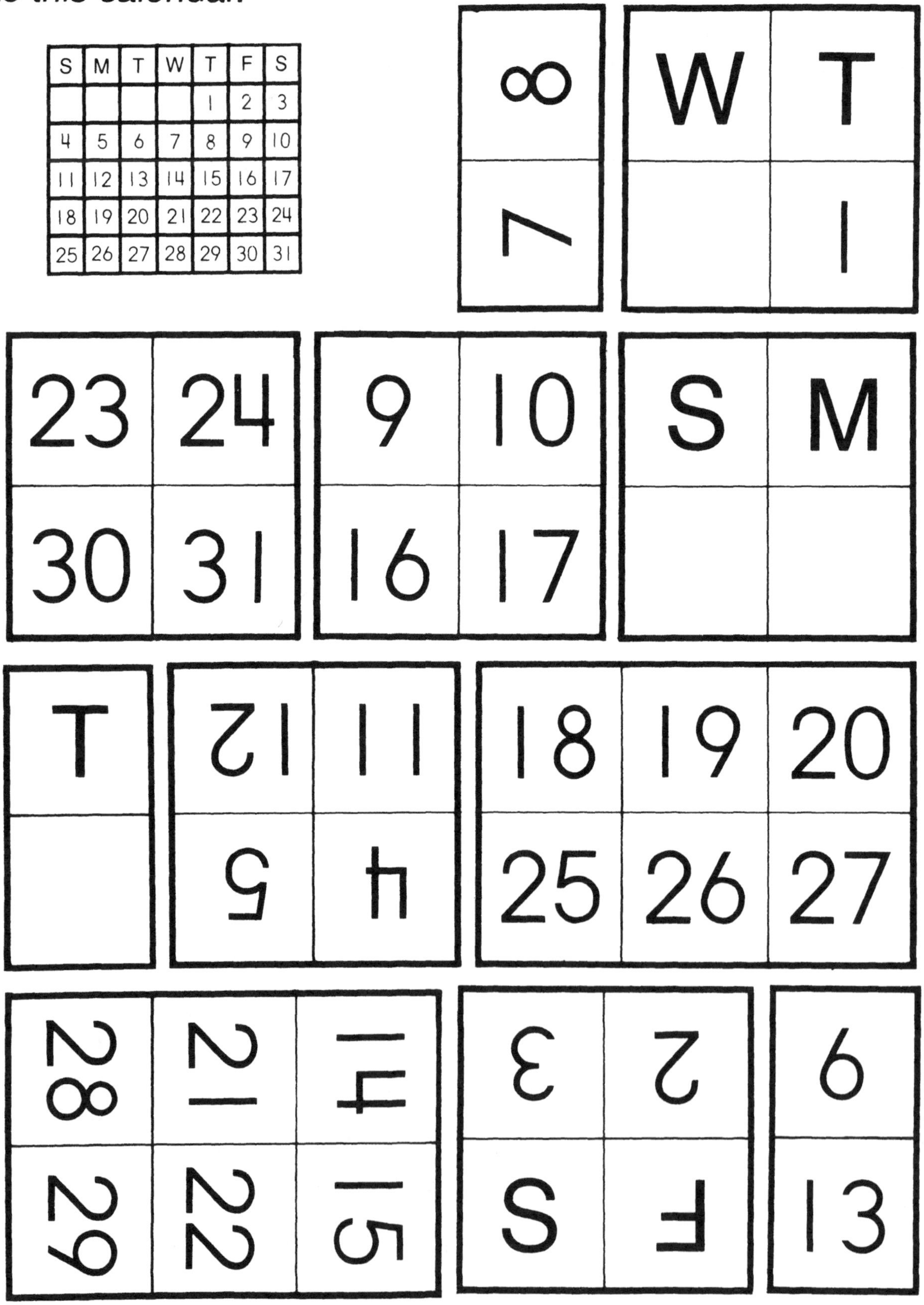

WHAT DO I SEE?

Teacher Sheet

A Group Visual Thinking Game

▼▼

Purpose

Students practice identifying shapes or colors and asking discriminating questions in a group activity.

Number of Students

A leader and one to thirty players.

How to Play

1. The leader locates an object in the room that everyone can see.
2. The leader states a clue (for example, "I see something brown" or "I see a circle.")
3. Players take turns asking questions that can be answered by "yes" or "no." If the leader answers "yes" to one of a player's questions, that player gets to ask another question.

Who Wins

The first player who guesses the object wins. This player then becomes the leader for the next round.

Sample Play

Leader: I see a circle.

Player 1: Is it on the floor?

Leader: No.

Player 2: Is it on the wall?

Leader: Yes.

Player 2: Is it the clock on the wall?

Leader: Yes!

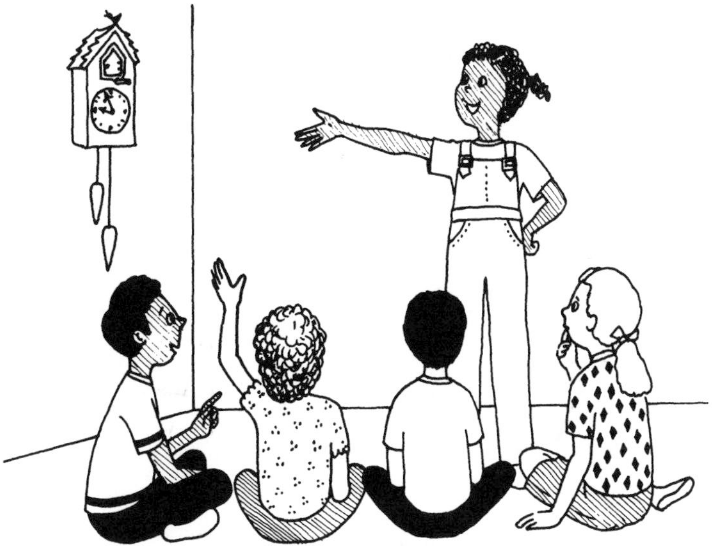

Variation

Limit the number of questions asked. For example, allow players only ten questions.

TURNED SHAPES (I) ▼▼

Each shape with a letter has been turned. Write the letter of the matching shape in each shape without a letter.

A
B
C
D
E
F
G

TURNED SHAPES (II)

▼▼

Each shape with a letter has been turned. Write the letter of the matching shape in each shape without a letter.

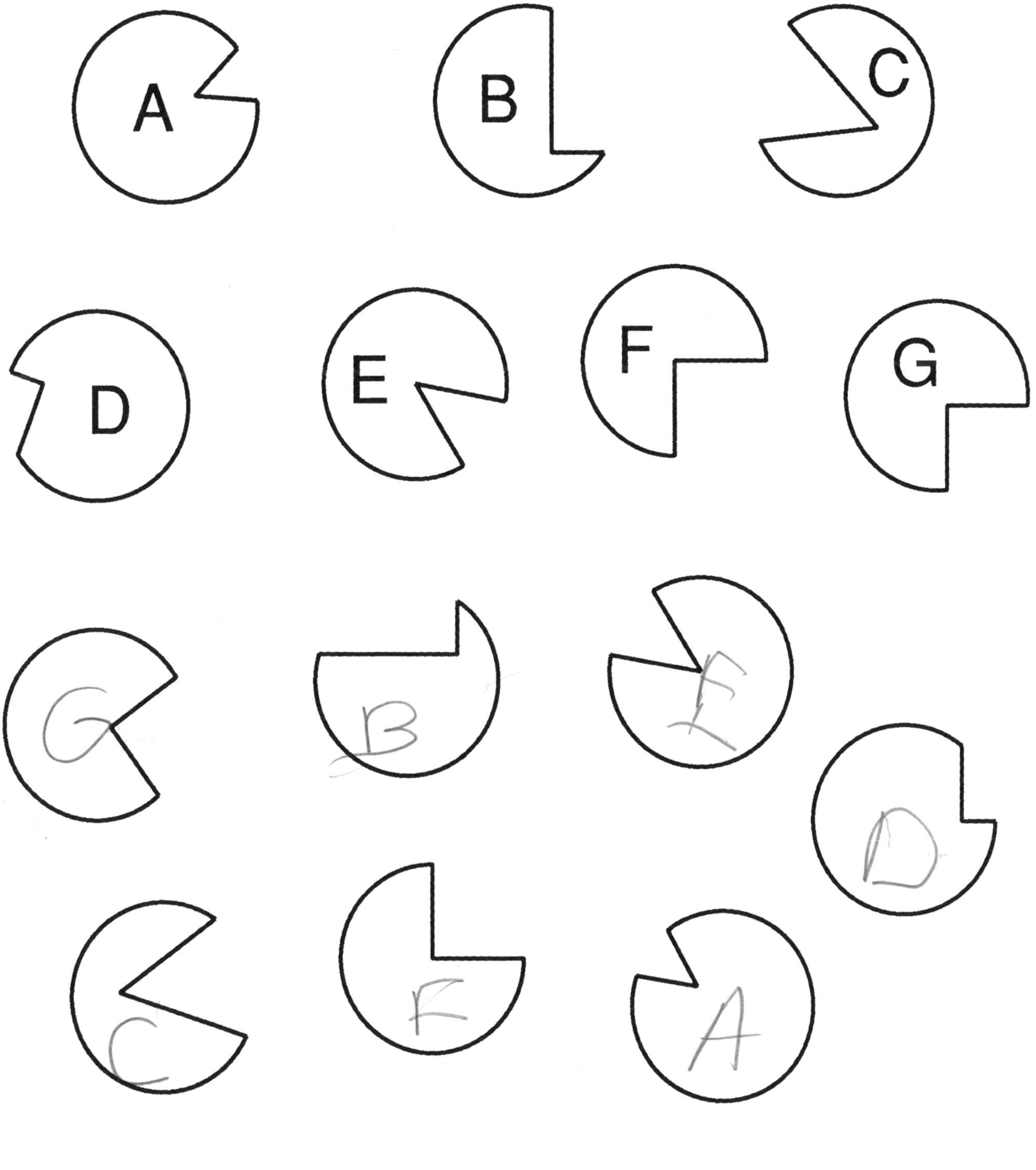
A
B
C
D
E
F
G
G
B
E
D
C
F
A

WHAT'S MY DESIGN? ▼▼

1. Which letters are the same above the line as below? Draw a ring around each one.

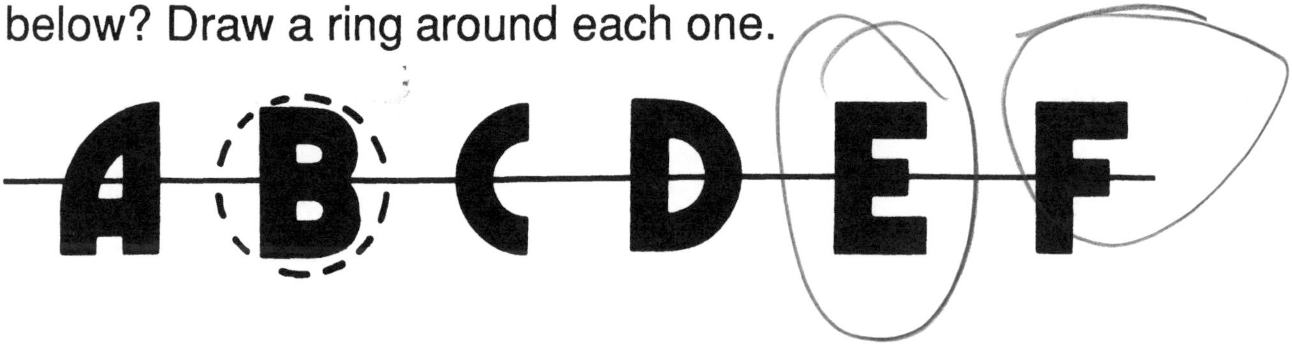
A B C D E F

2. Use a crayon or colored pencil. Copy the X on the lines.

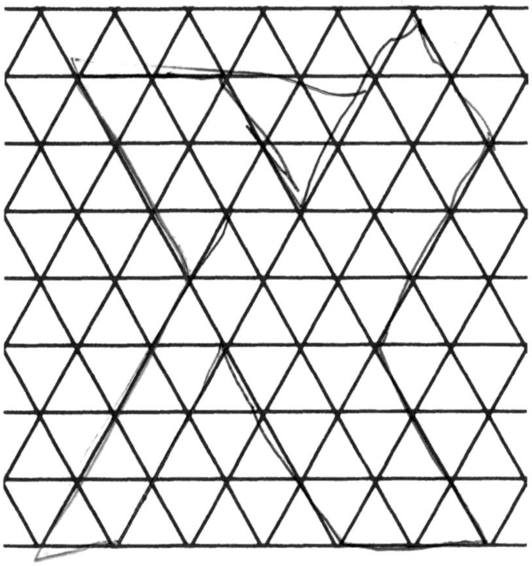

3. Use a crayon or colored pencil. Copy the design on the lines.

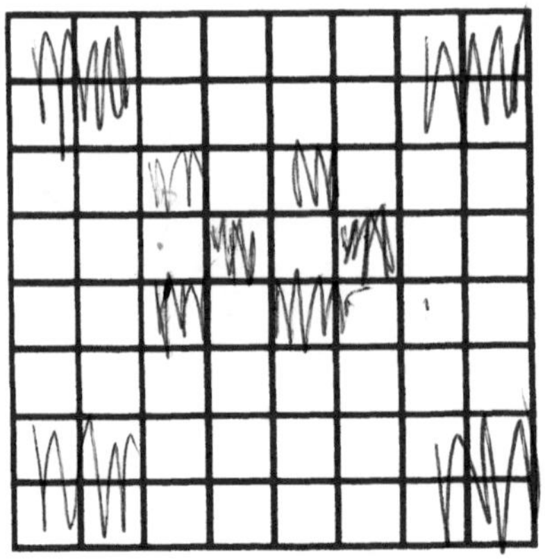

CONNECT THE DOTS

Follow these directions to make a puzzle. Draw each line as straight as you can. Do not lift your pencil.

Draw a line from 1 to 2.
Draw a line from 2 to 3.
Draw a line from 3 to 4.
Draw a line from 4 to 1.
Draw a line from 1 to 5.
Draw a line from 5 to 6.
Draw a line from 6 to 7.
Draw a line from 7 to 8.
Draw a line from 8 to 9.
Draw a line from 9 to 7.
Draw a line from 7 to 1.

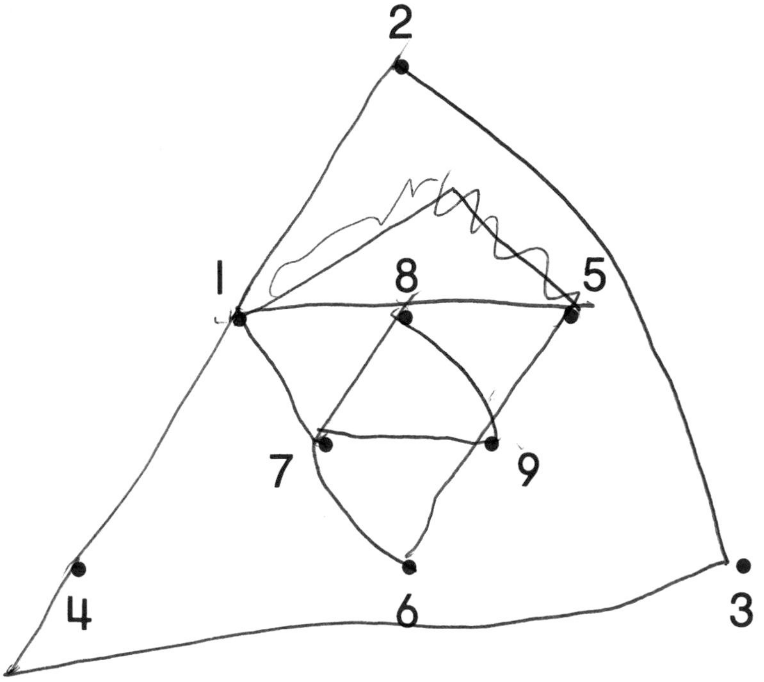
2
1
8
5
7
9
4
6
3

How many different triangles do you see?

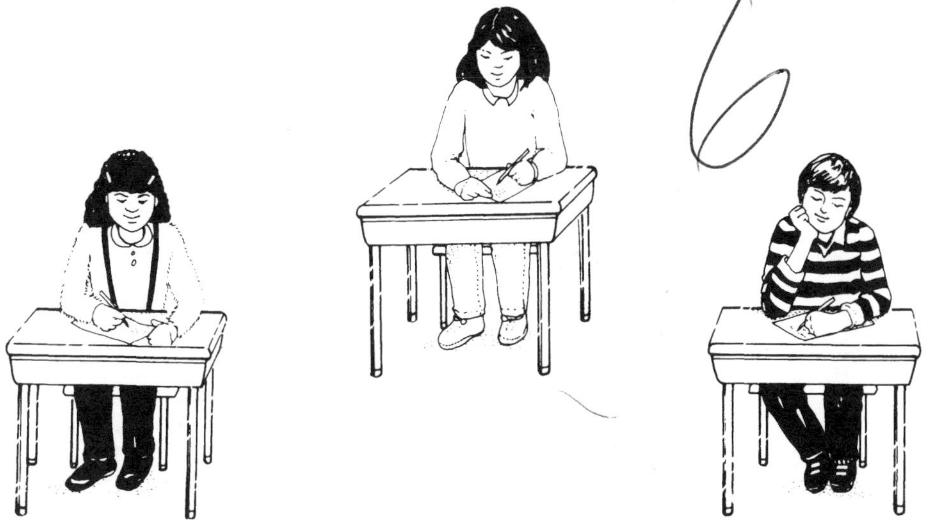

DIFFERENT STROKES

Draw a ring around the shape in each row that is different.

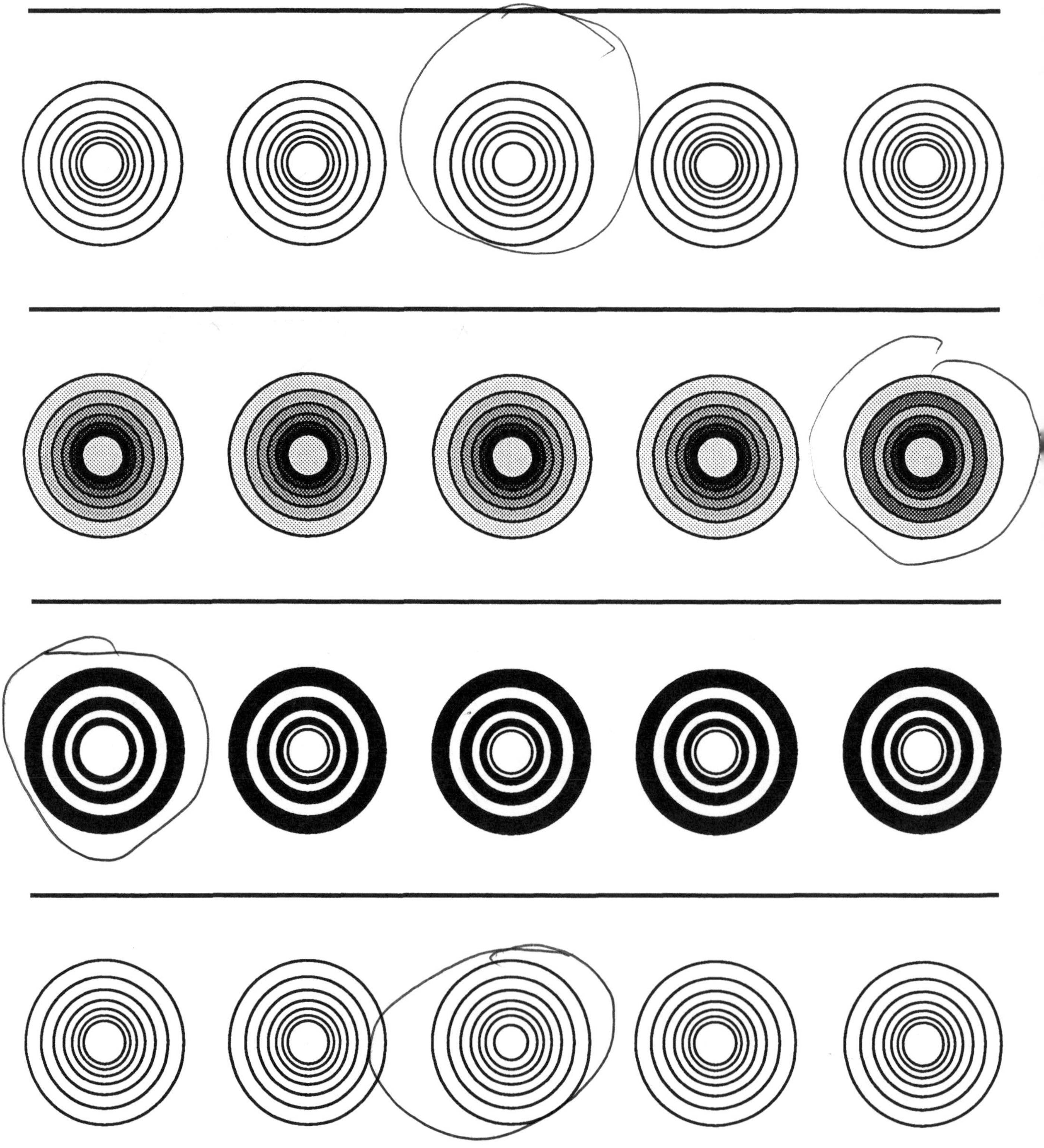

MISSING PIECE (II)

Write the letter of the missing pieces in each of the six problems.

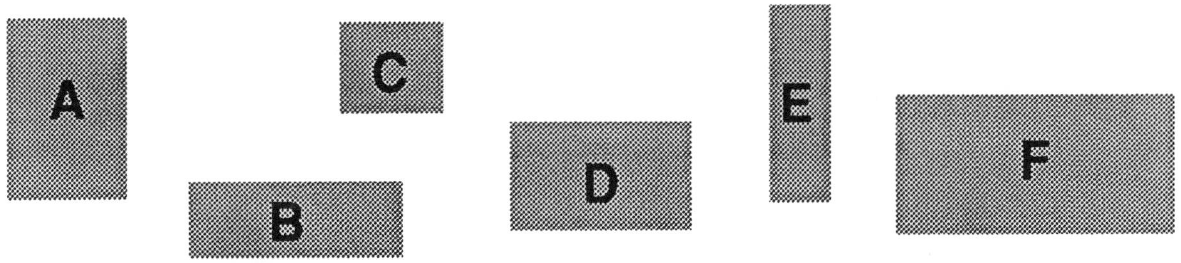
A
B
C
D
E
F

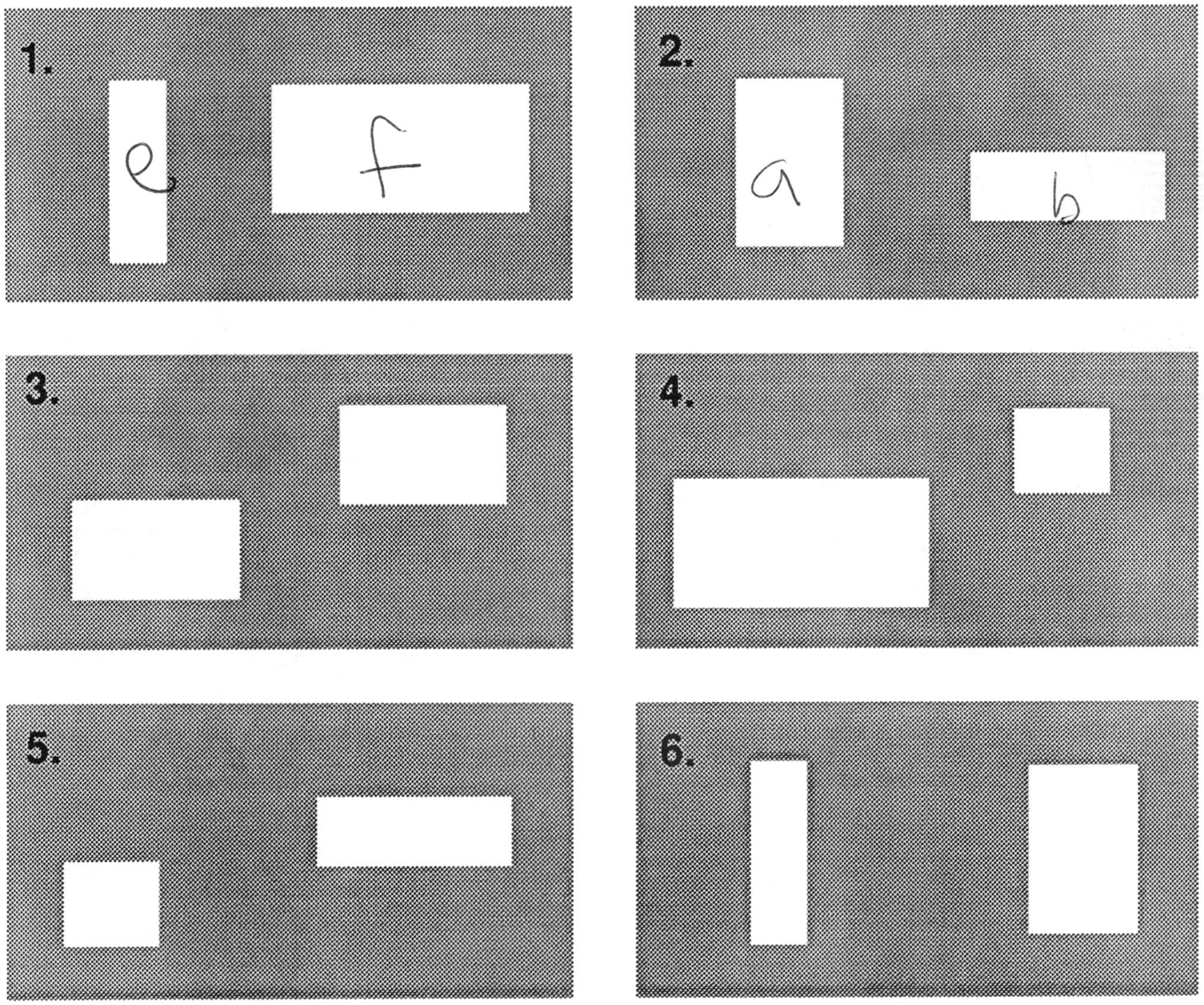
1.
e
f
2.
a
b
3.
4.
5.
6.

TRIANGLE MATCH

▼▼

Draw a line between each of the triangles that match.

CALCULATOR NUMBERS

▼▼

Connect the dots to draw each calculator number.

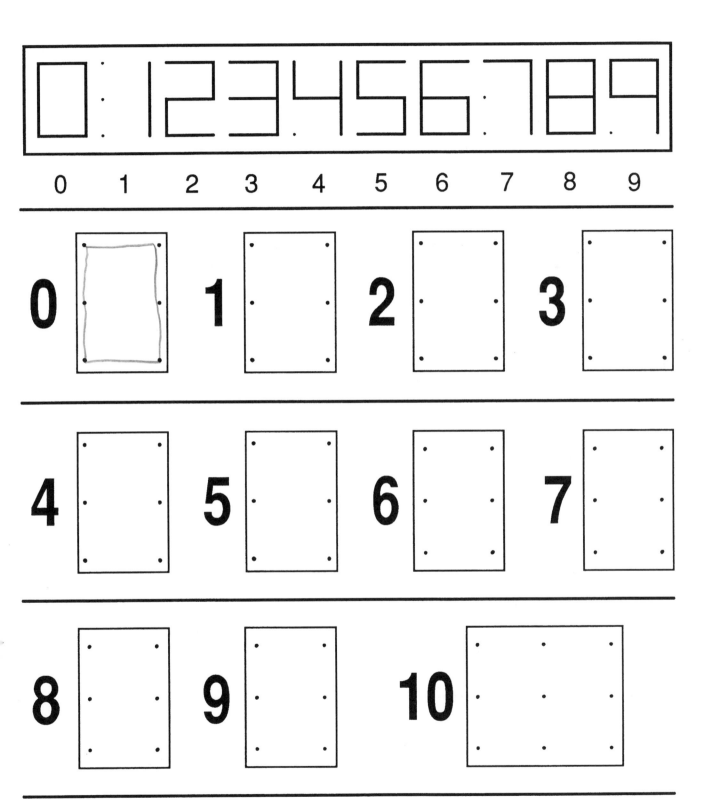

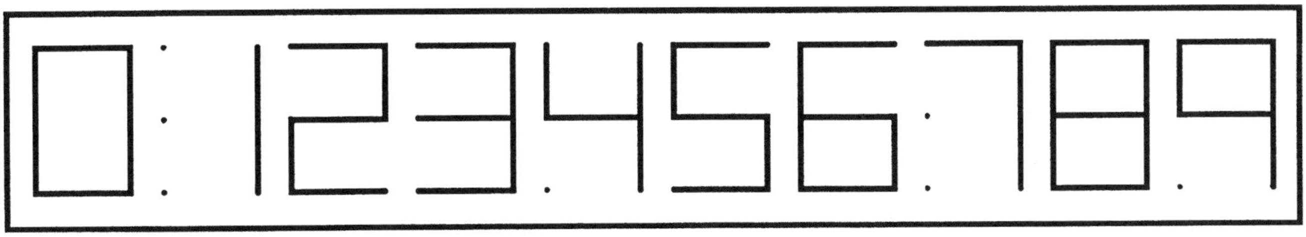

0 1 2 3 4 5 6 7 8 9

0 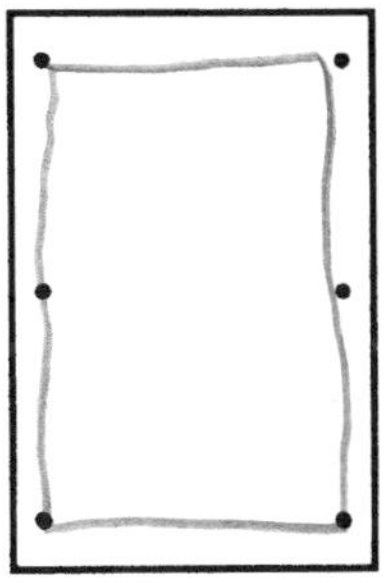 **1** 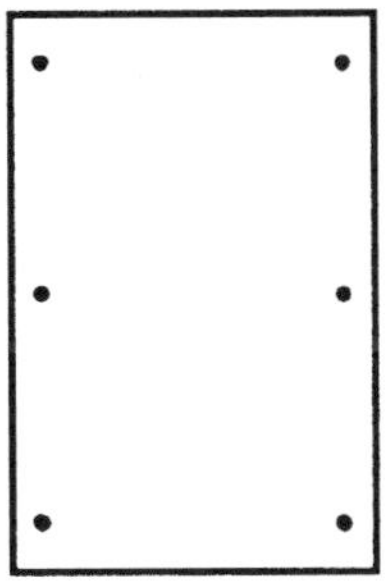 **2** 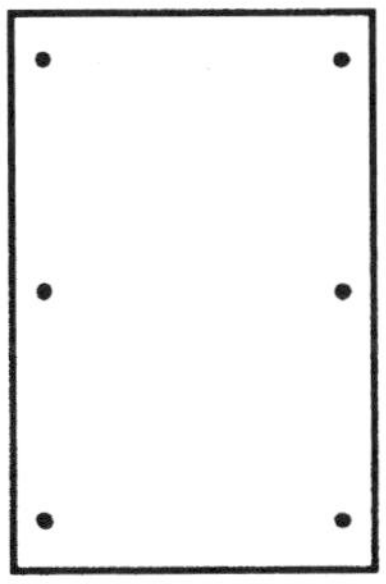 **3** 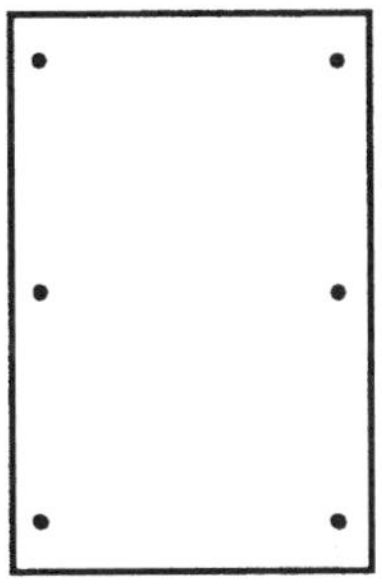

4 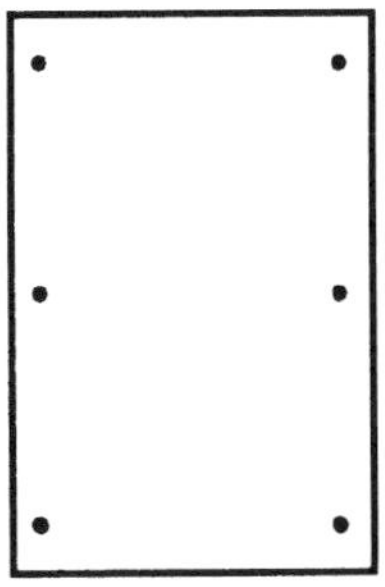 **5** 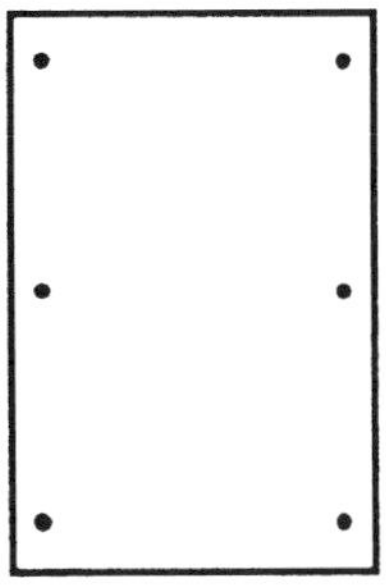 **6** 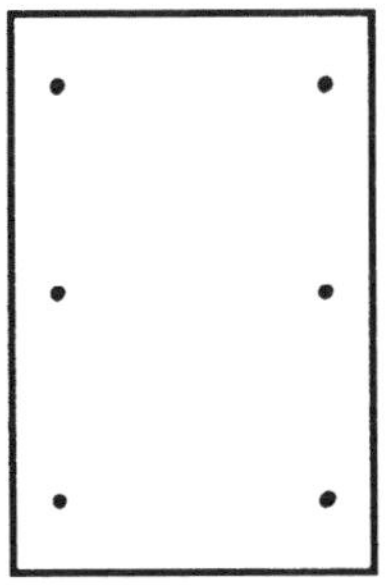 **7** 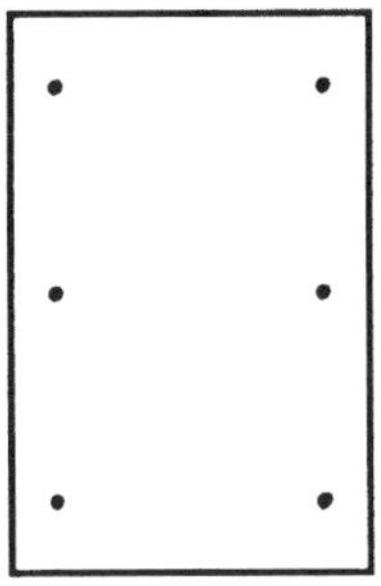

8 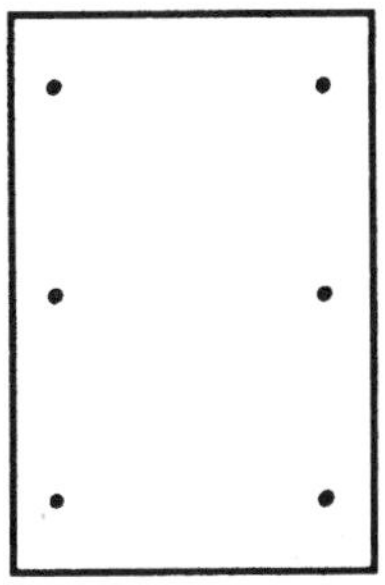 **9** 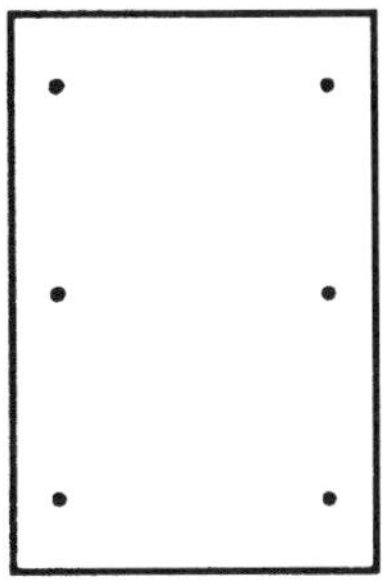 **10** 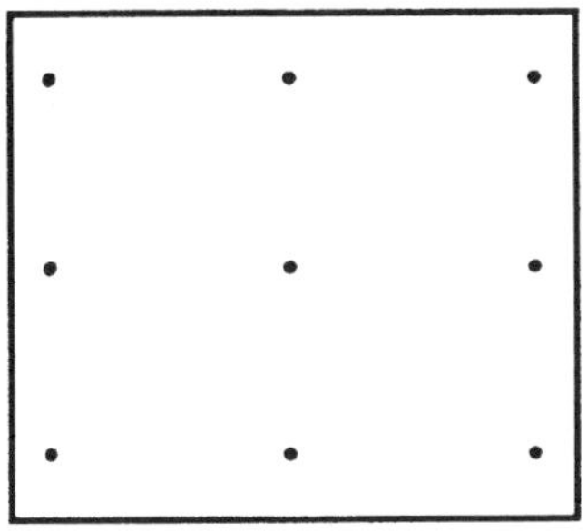

MAP PATHS (I)

Study the map. In each box, draw a ring around the one path that does *not* work.

MAP

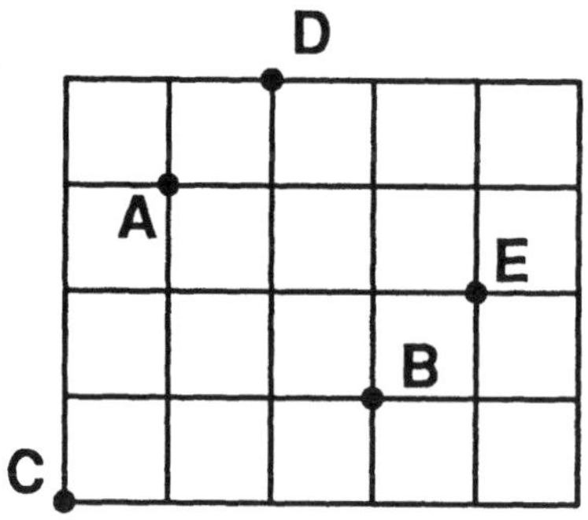
D
A
E
B
C

HITHER
TO THERE
YON
NOWHERE IN PARTICULAR

A to B

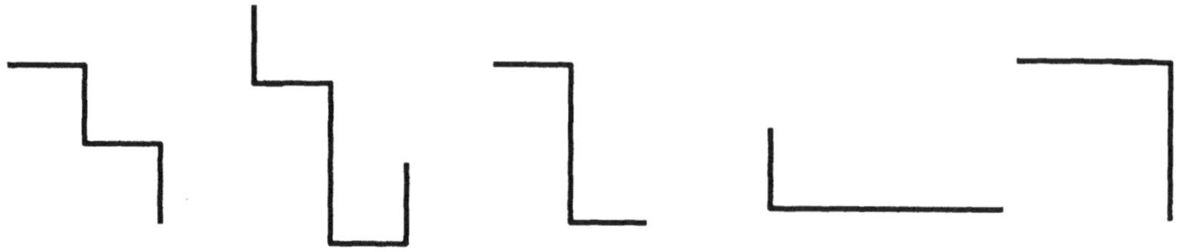

D to B

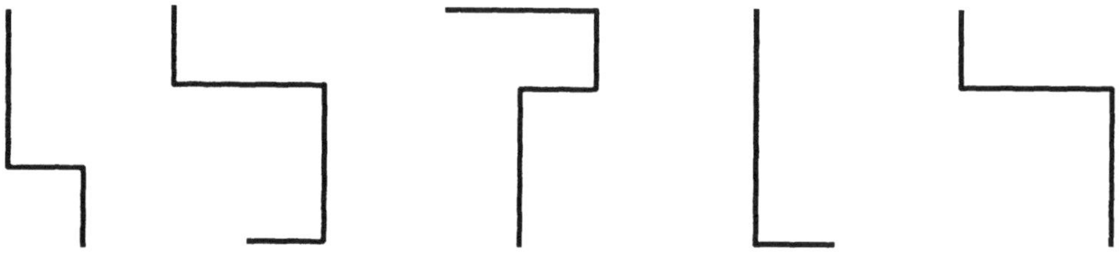

C to E

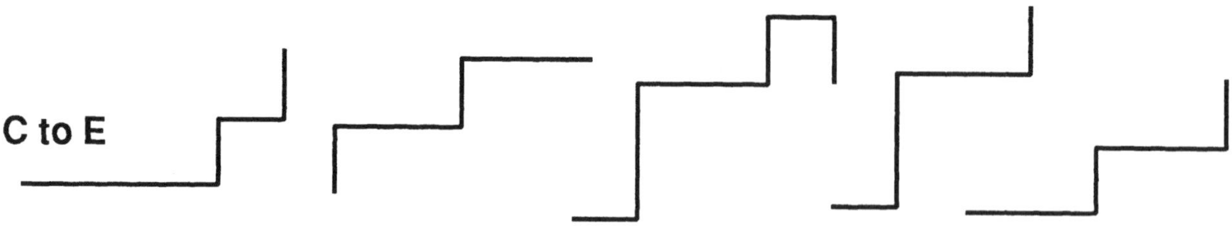

D to E

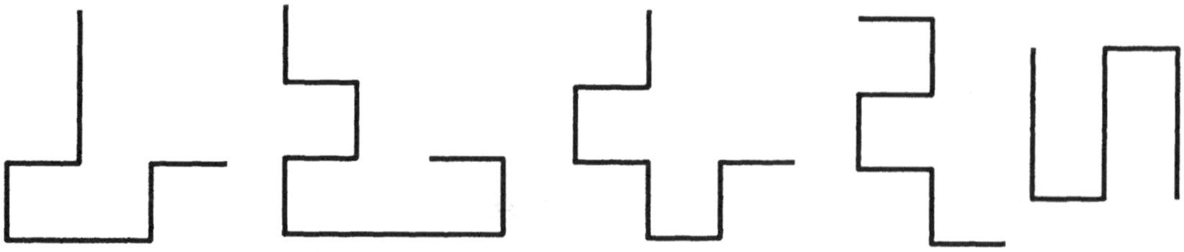

LETTER SHAPES

Choose a letter. Collect samples of this letter from newspapers, magazines, and other places.

Paste the letters in the space below. For example:

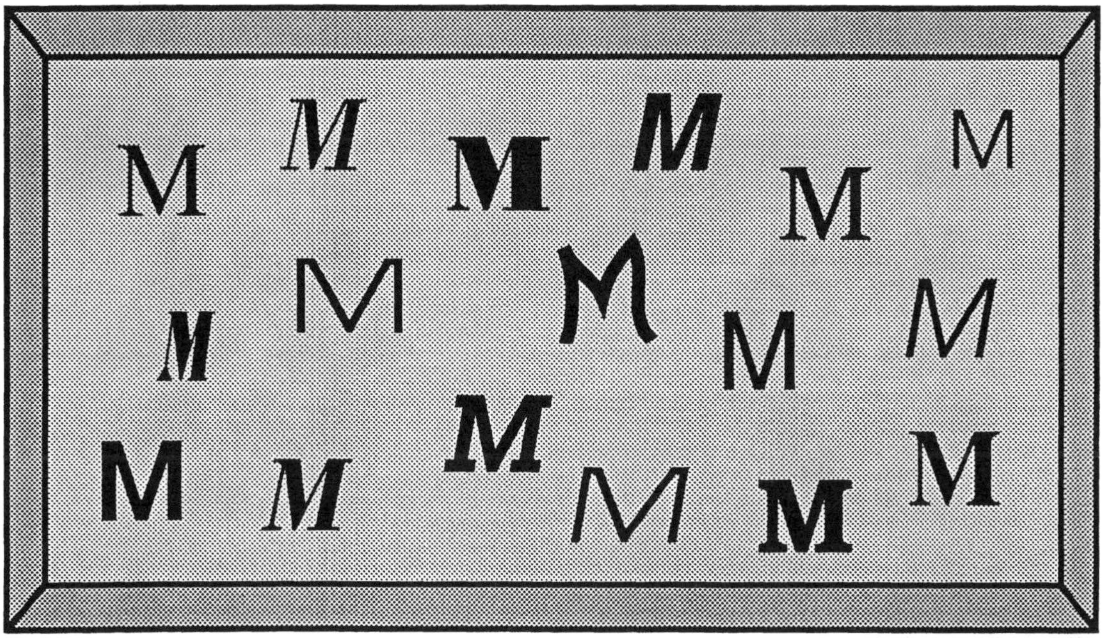

With the Whole Class: Decide on a letter. Then bring in BIG examples of this letter and put them on a bulletin board.

HEXAGON MATCH

Draw a line between each of the hexagons that match.

DIFFERENT DESIGNS

Draw a ring around the circle design in each row that is different.

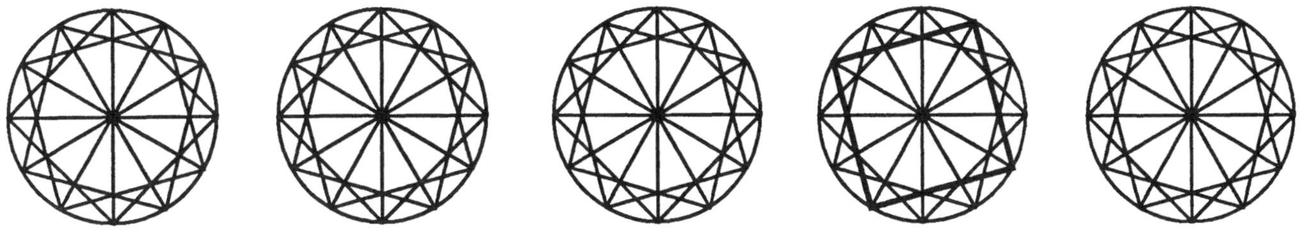

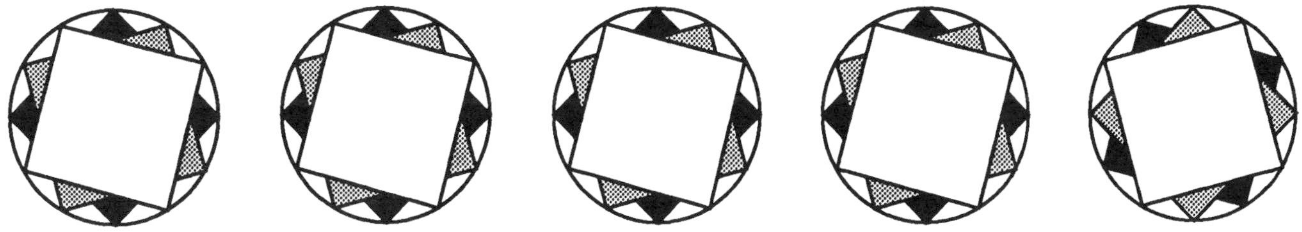

MORE DOT DESIGNS (II)

Copy each design. Start at the line given.

1.

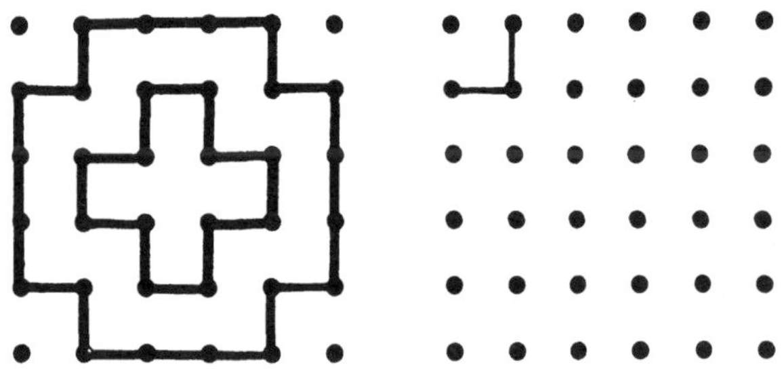

2.

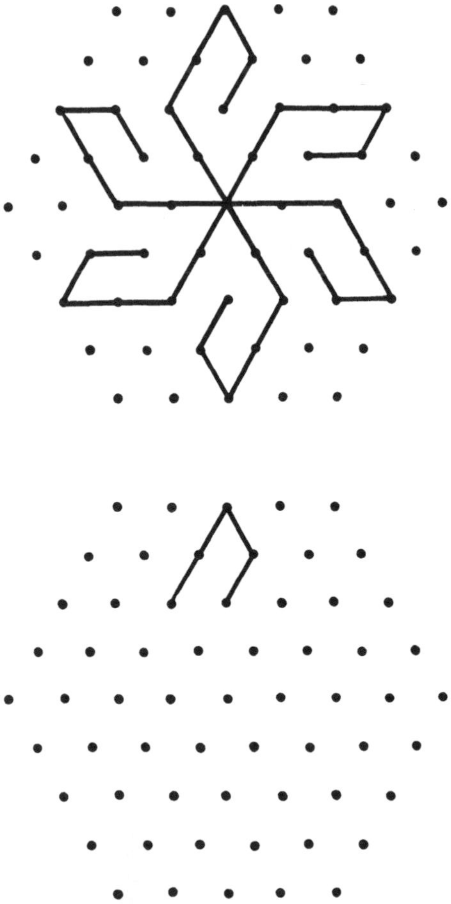

3.

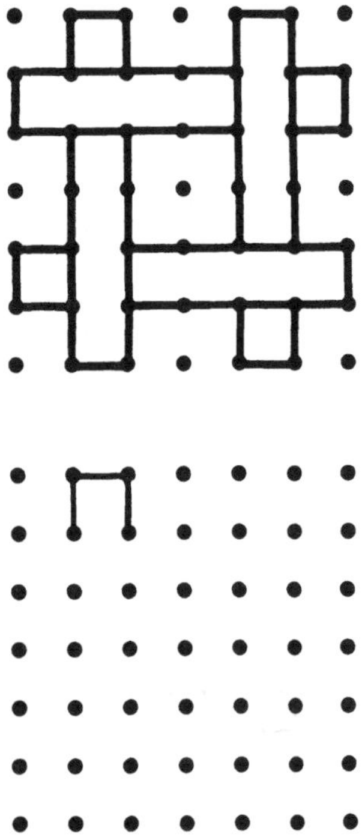

4.

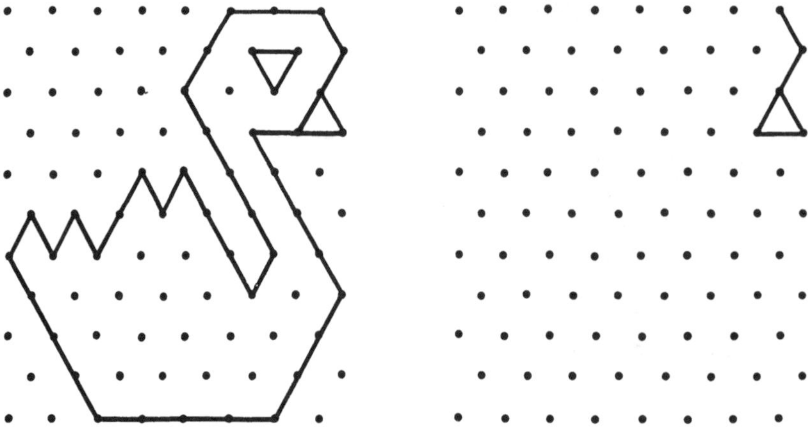

COLOR THE DESIGN

Copy each design with a colored pencil or crayon.

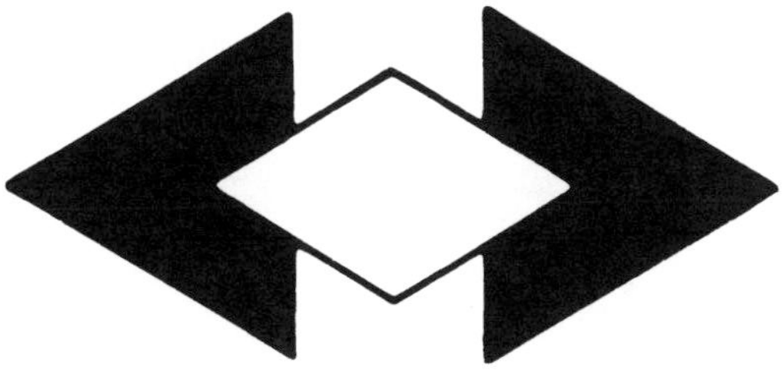

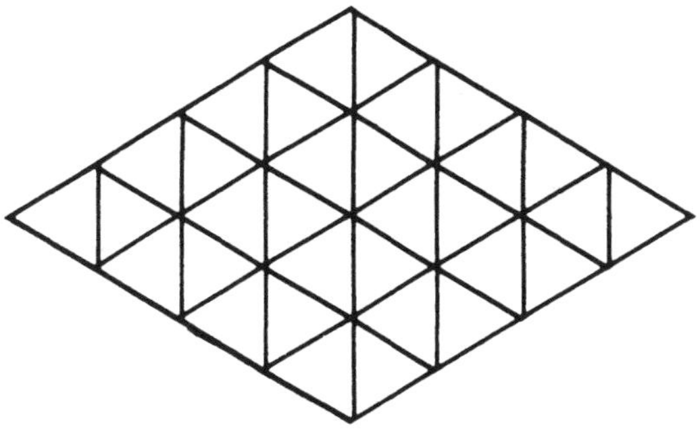

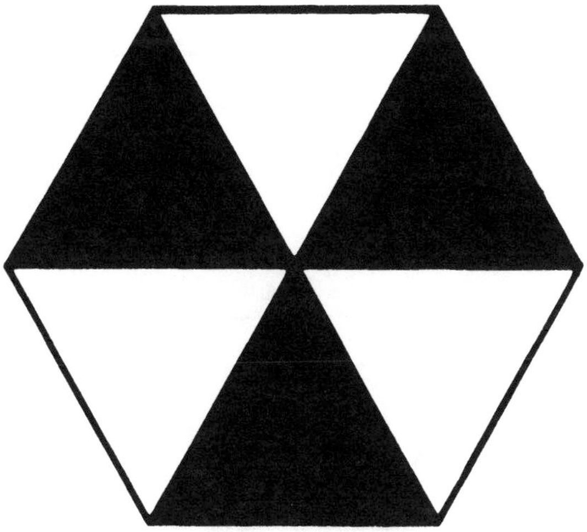

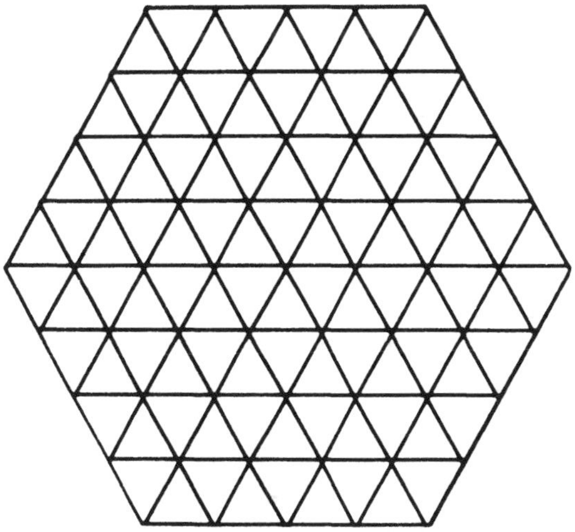

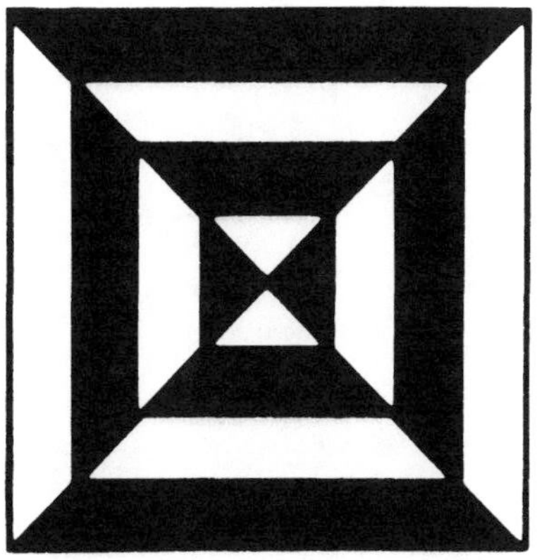

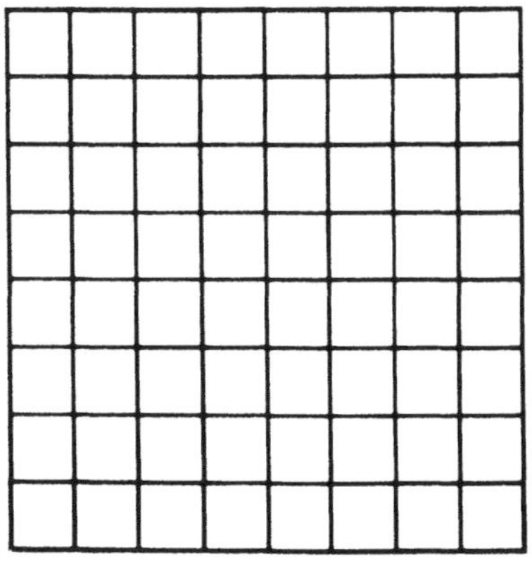

SHAPE MATCH

▼▼▼

Find the shape that matches the black one. Draw a ring around the letter.

1.

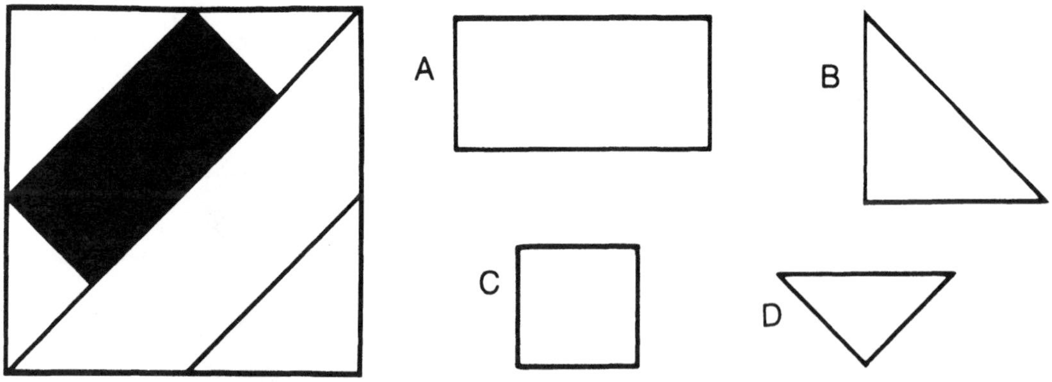
A
B
C
D

2.

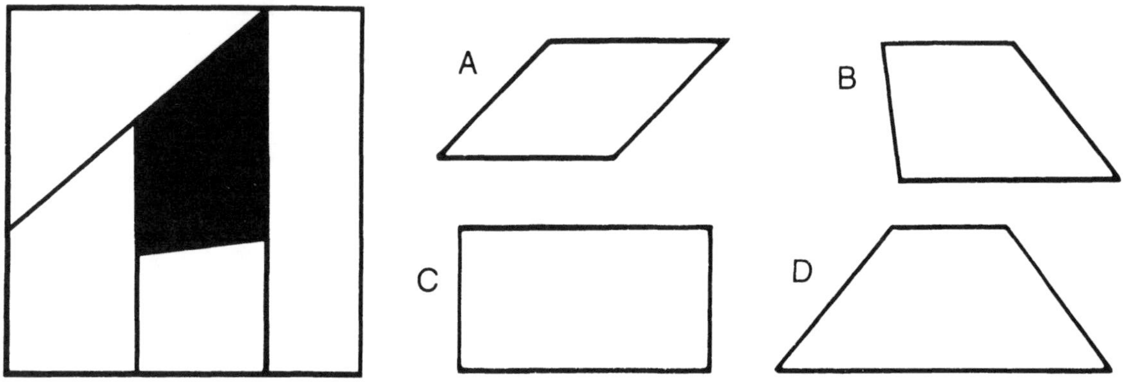
A
B
C
D

3.

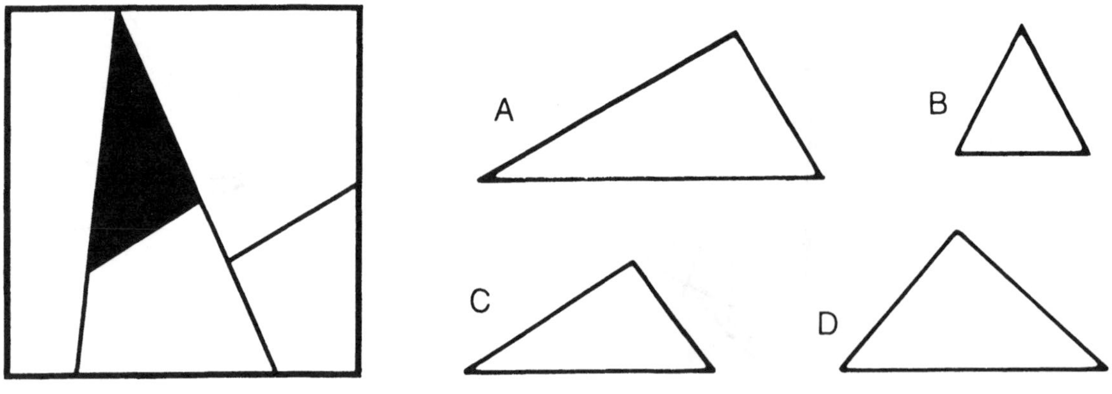
A
B
C
D

4.

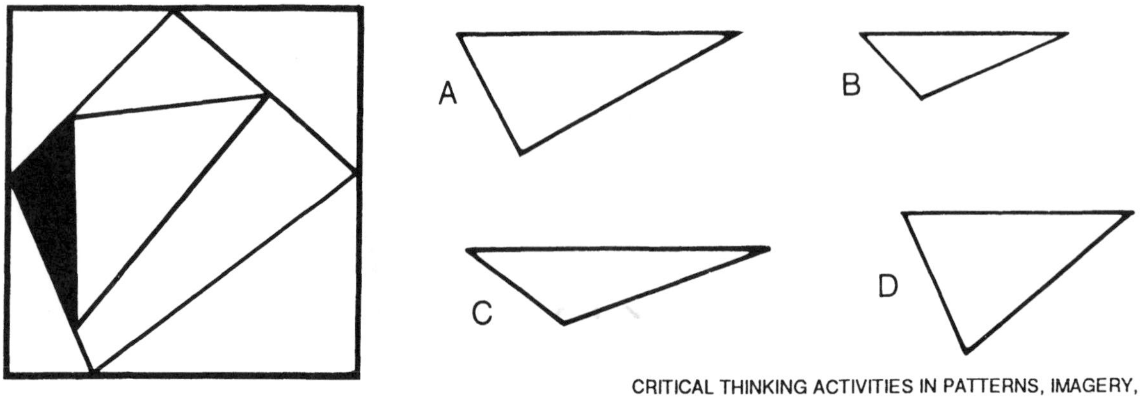
A
B
C
D

BALLOON PUZZLE

▼▼▼

Cut out the puzzle pieces. Fit the pieces together to make the balloon picture.

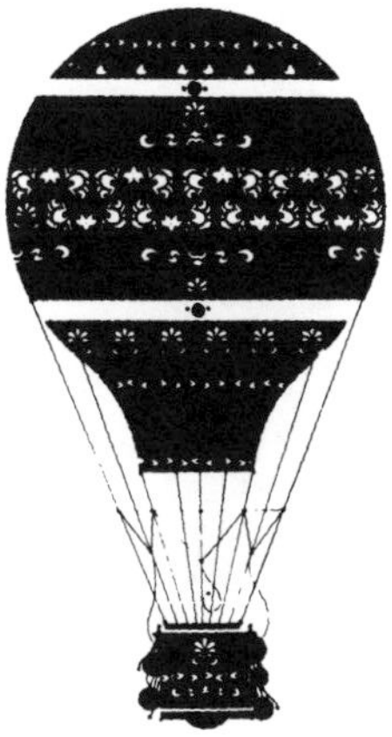

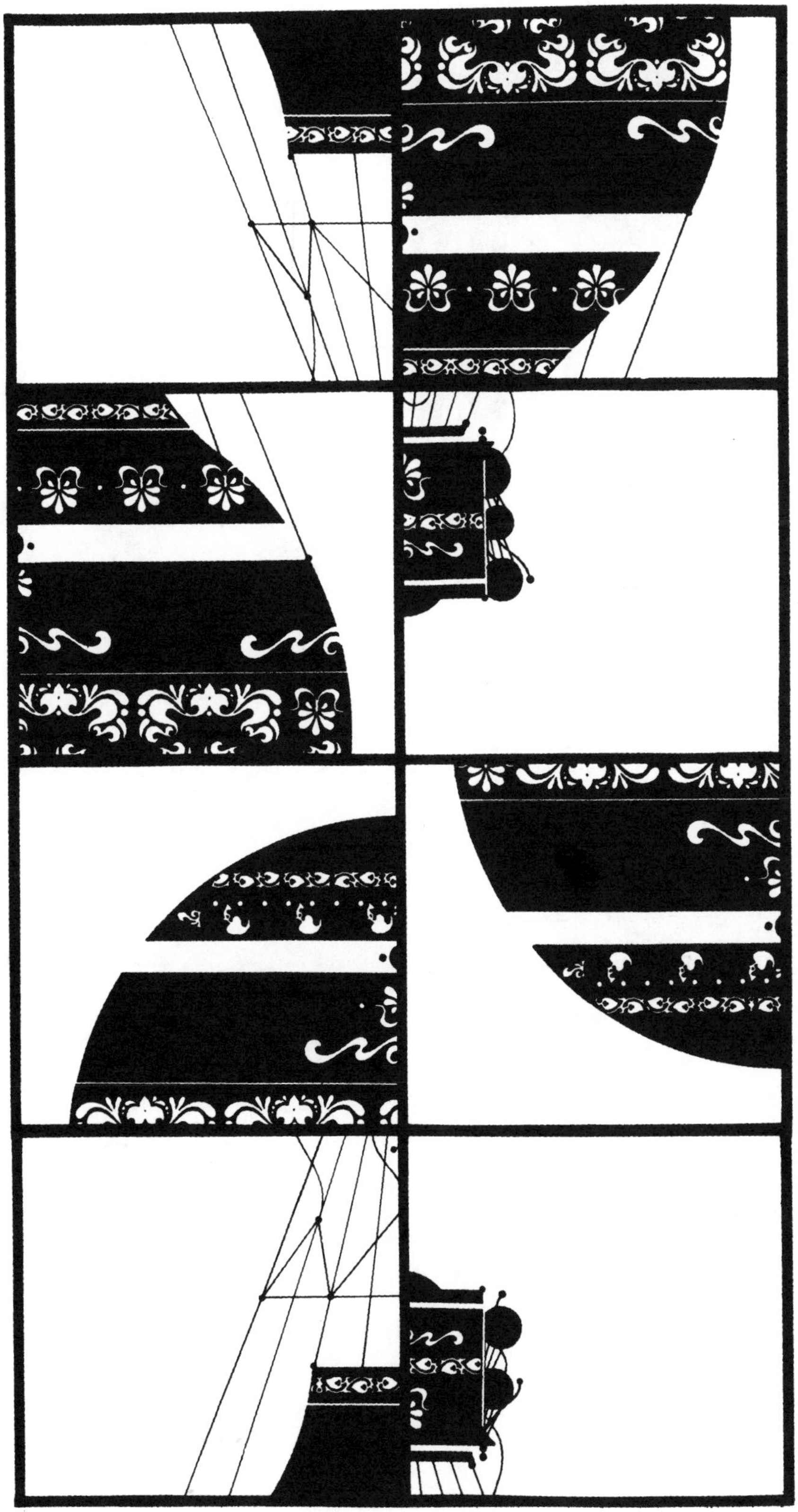

DIVIDED SHAPES

▼▼▼

1. Draw a ring around each letter that is the same on both sides of the line.

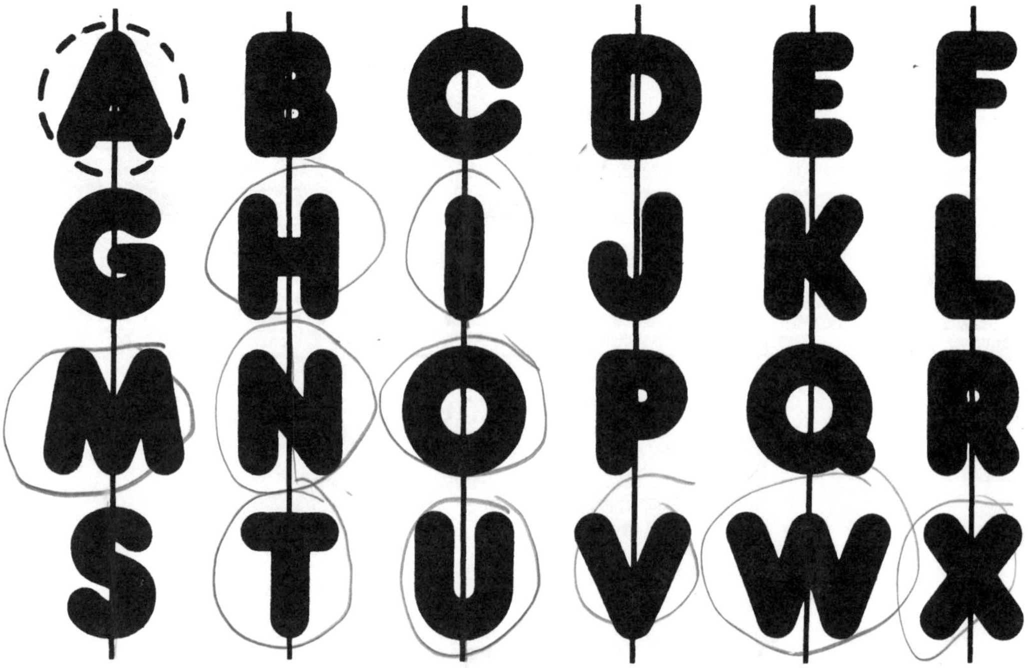
A B C D E F
G H I J K L
M N O P Q R
S T U V W X

2. Complete each picture. Make the right side the same as the left side.

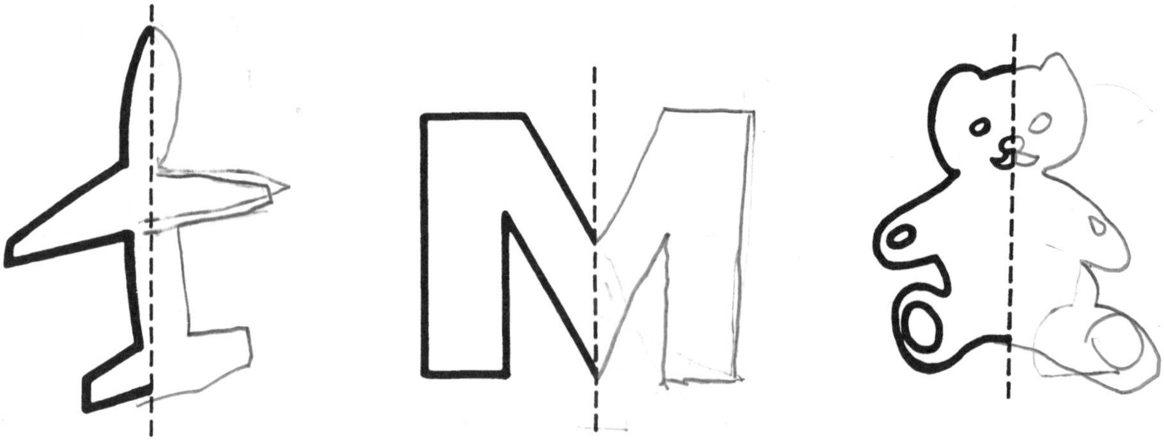

3. Divide each shape into two shapes that are the same. Try different ways of dividing the shapes. The first one is done for you.

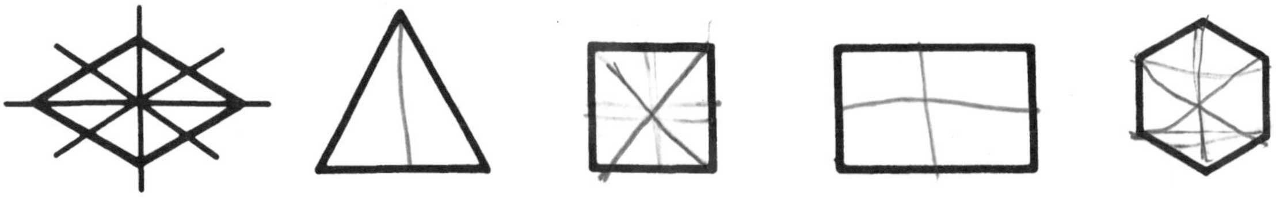

THE SAME DESIGN

1. Which design is exactly like A? Draw a ring around the correct letter.

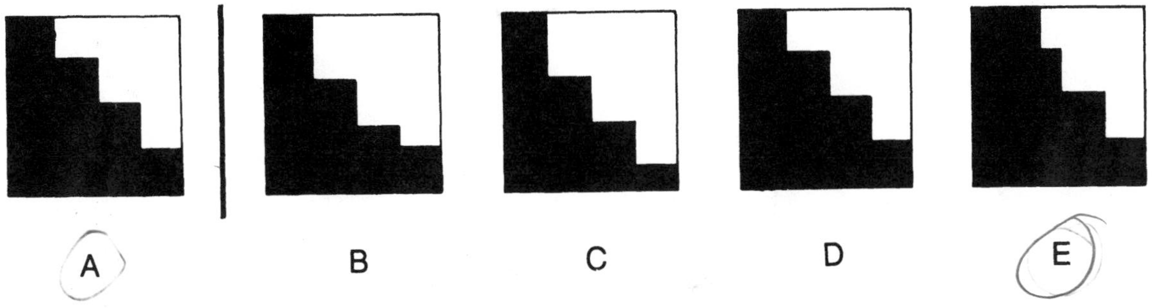
A
B
C
D
E

2. Find two designs that are the same. Draw a ring around the letters.

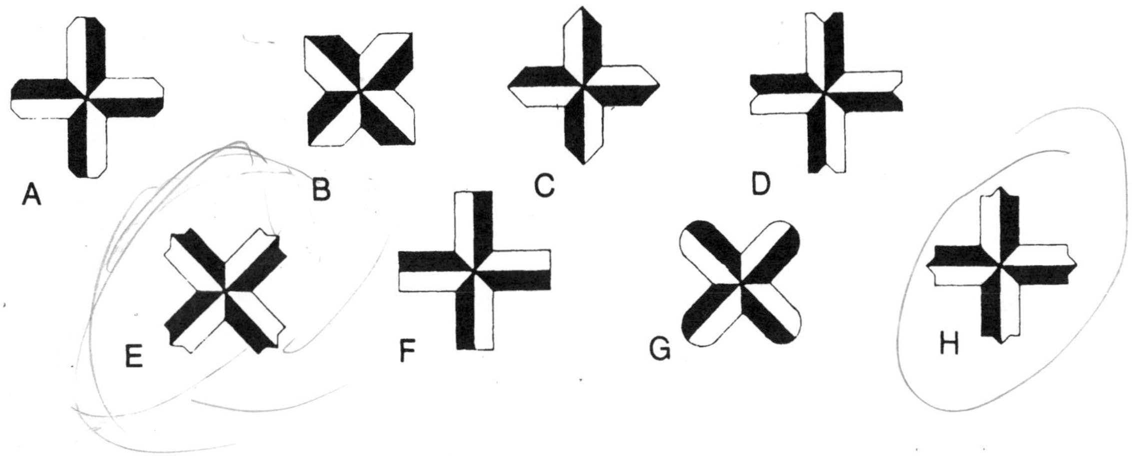
A
B
C
D
E
F
G
H

3. Which pieces are the same? Write the letter in the shape that is the same.

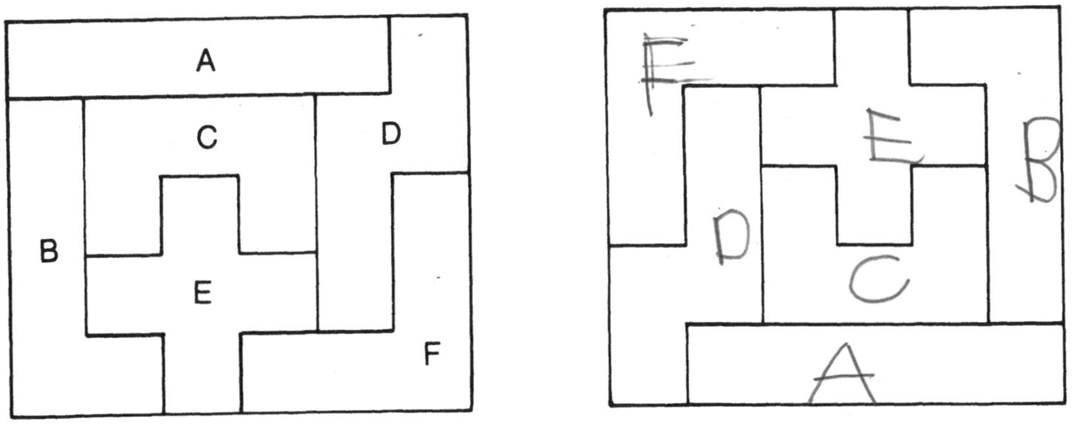
A
C
D
B
E
F

MISSING PIECE (III)

Write the letter of the missing pieces in each of the six problems.

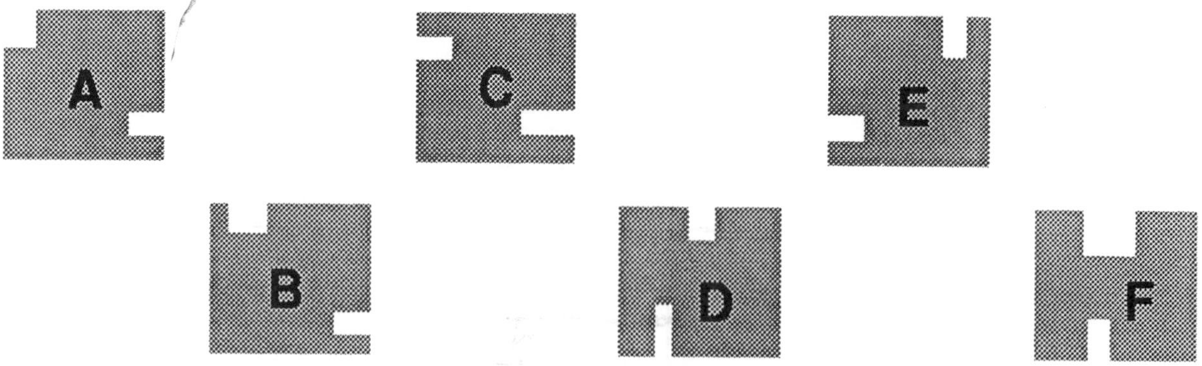
A
C
E
B
D
F

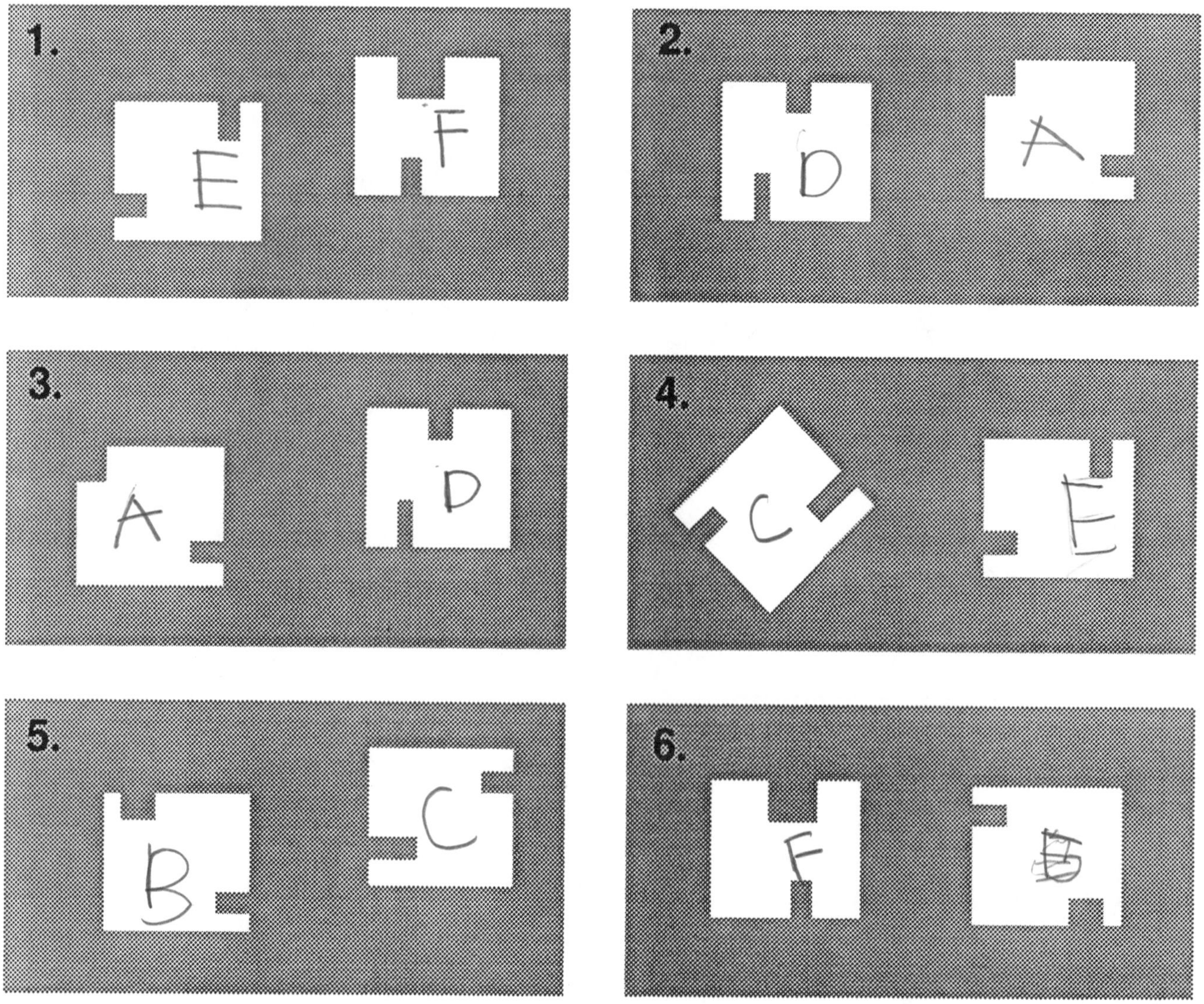
1.
E
F
2.
D
A
3.
A
D
4.
C
E
5.
B
C
6.
F

HOW MANY SHAPES? ▼▼▼

Draw a ring around the number of small shapes that fit into the large shape.

Example:

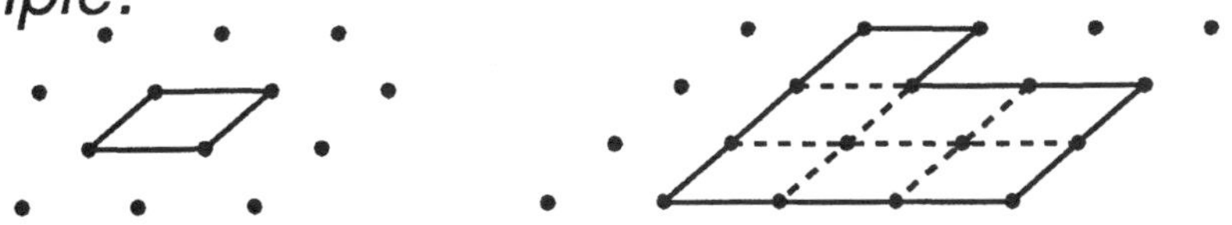

1 2 3 4
5 6 7 8
9 10 11 12

1. 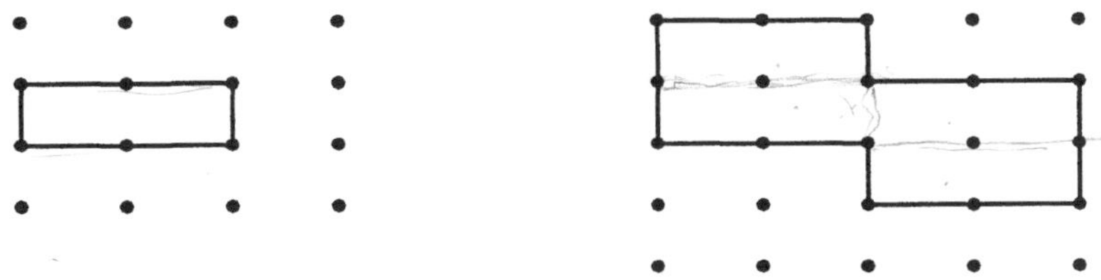

1 2 3 4
5 6 7 8
9 10 11 12

2. 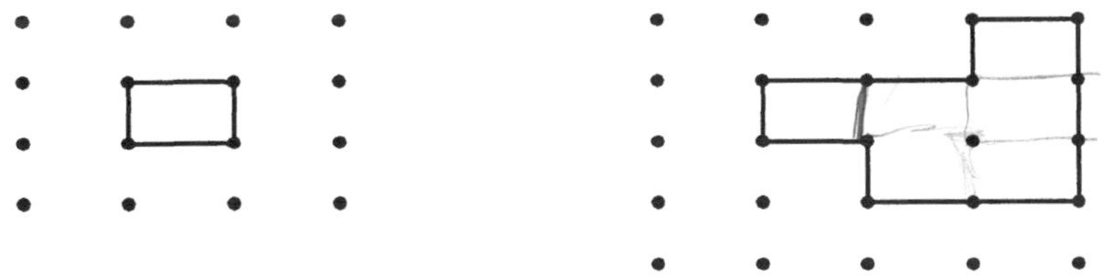

1 2 3 4
5 6 7 8
9 10 11 12

3. 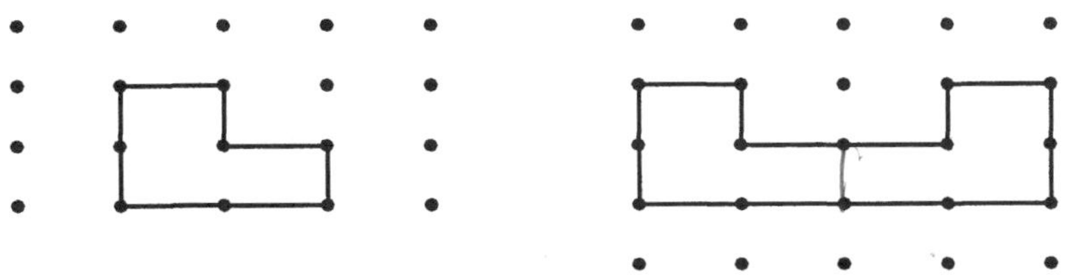

1 2 3 4
5 6 7 8
9 10 11 12

4. 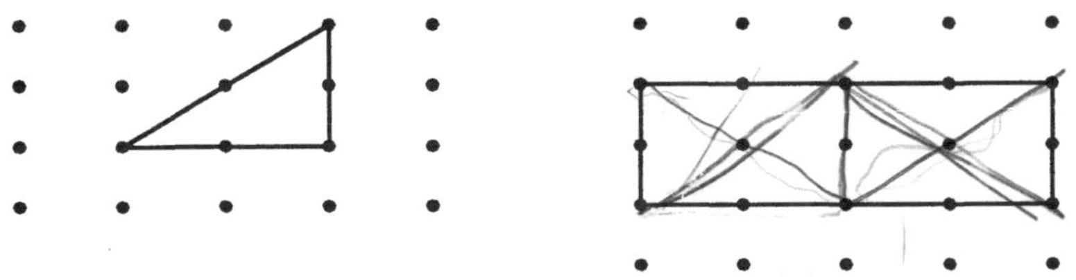

1 2 3 4
5 6 7 8
9 10 11 12

5. 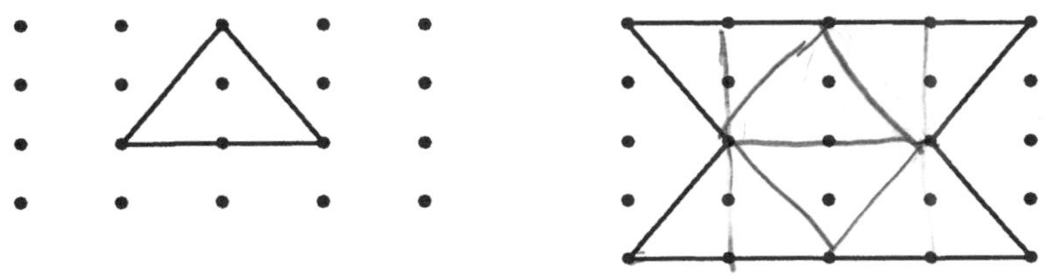

1 2 3 4
5 6 7 8
9 10 11 12

LETTER PERFECT

▼▼▼

Draw a ring around the two matching letters in each box.

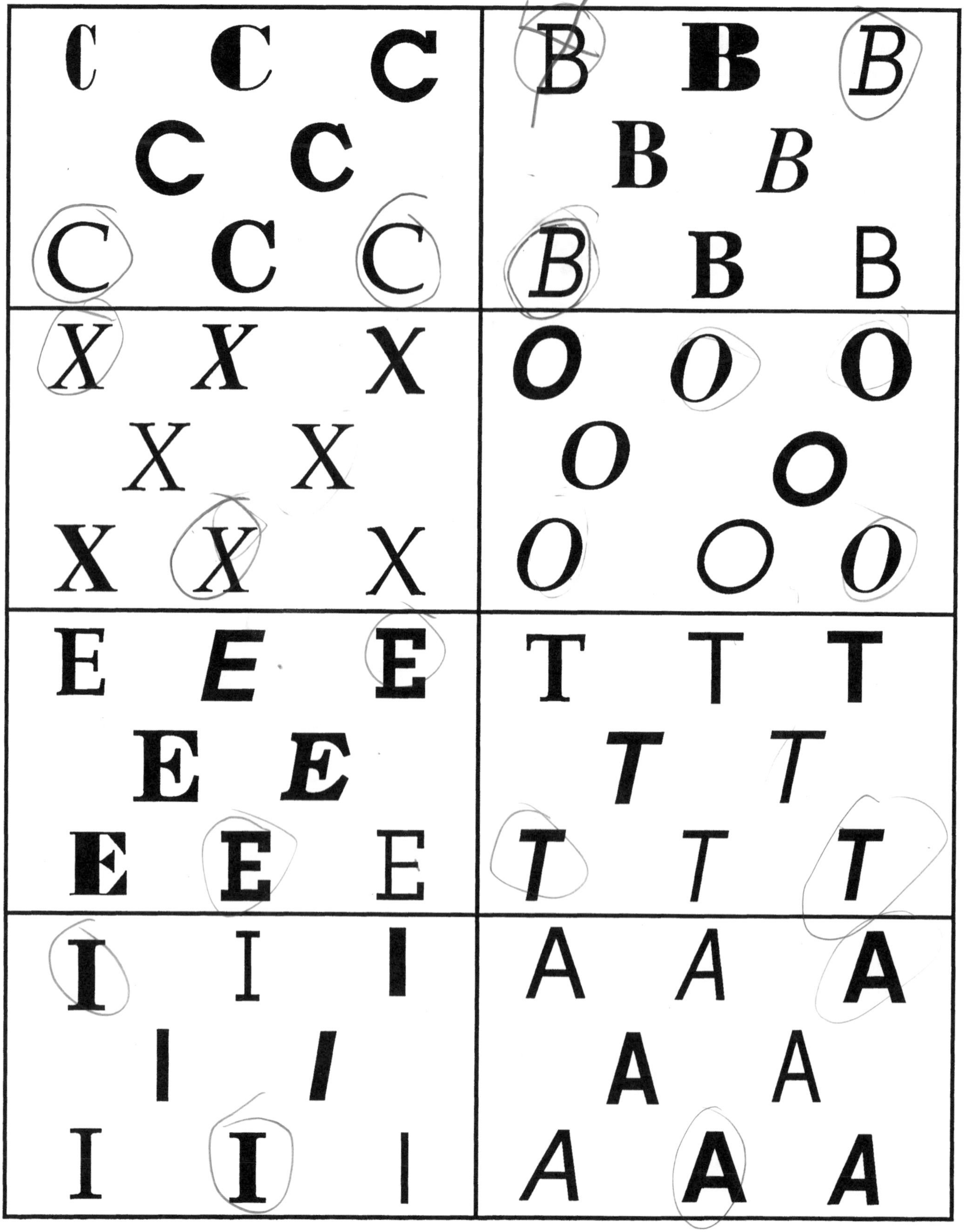

MATCH UP

▼▼▼

Draw a ring around the two matching shapes in each box.

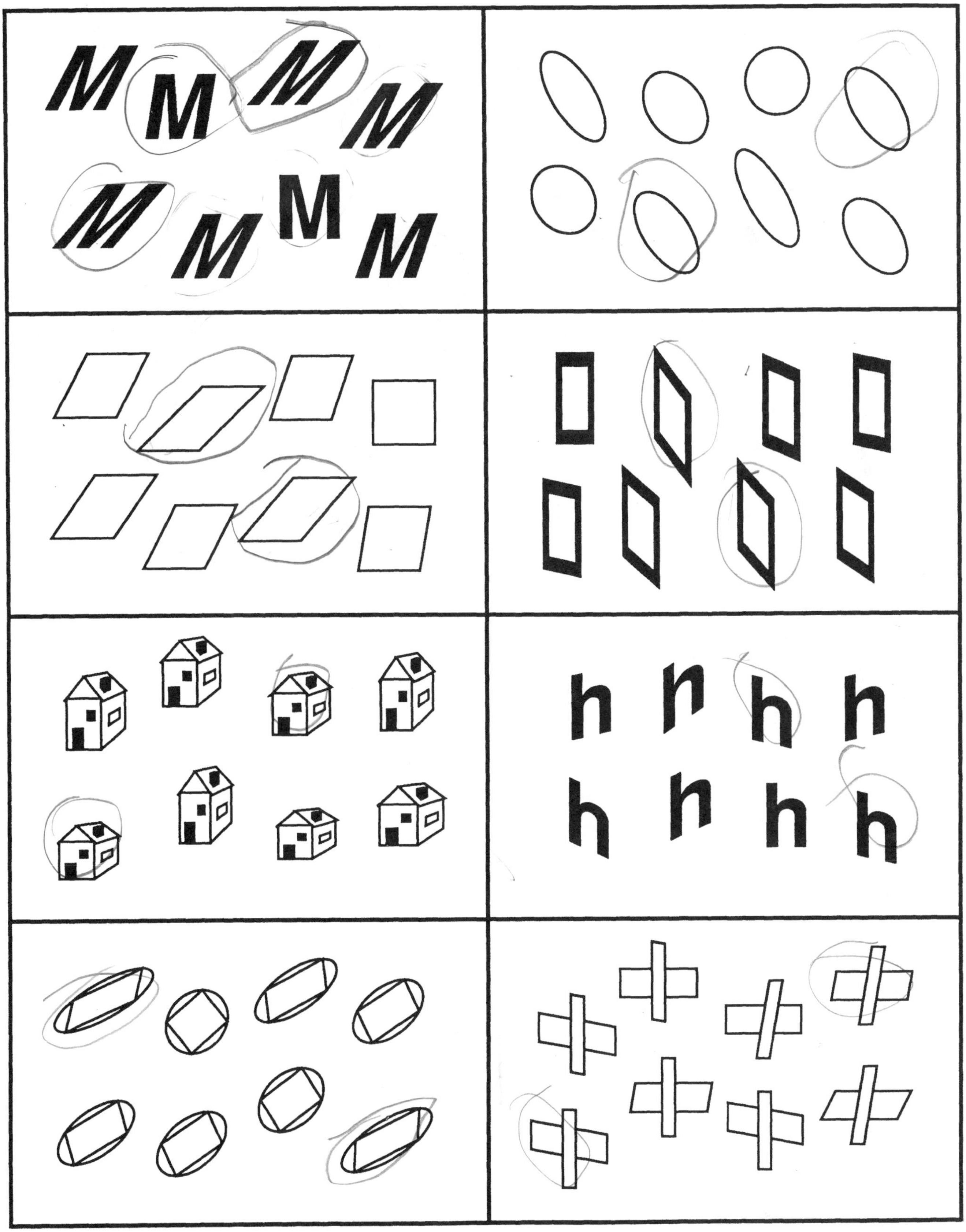

M M M M
M M M M
h h h h
h h h h

WHAT IS MY PAGE NUMBER?

Teacher Sheet

A Group Visual Thinking Game

▼▼▼

Purpose

Students practice visual estimation in a group activity.

Number of Students

A leader and one to thirty players.

How to Play

1. The leader selects a book and tells the players the total number of pages in the book.
2. The leader holds the book flat and opens it to a random page.
3. The leader asks, "What is my page number?" Each player puts his or her guess on a sheet of paper, writing in large numbers so that the leader can see the guesses.
4. After all of the players have written their guesses, the leader asks them to hold up their sheets of paper.

Who Wins

The player with the closest guess wins. This player then becomes the leader for the next round.

Sample Play

Leader: This book has 250 pages. (The leader opens the book to page 124, holding the book flat.)

Leader: What is my page number? (Players write their guesses on sheets of paper.)

Leader: Show your guesses. (Players hold up the sheets of paper with their guesses.)

Leader: Congratulations, Jill! Your guess of page 119 is closest.

Variation

The leader does *not* tell players the total number of pages first.

SHORTEST BOOK

Color the shortest book on each shelf.

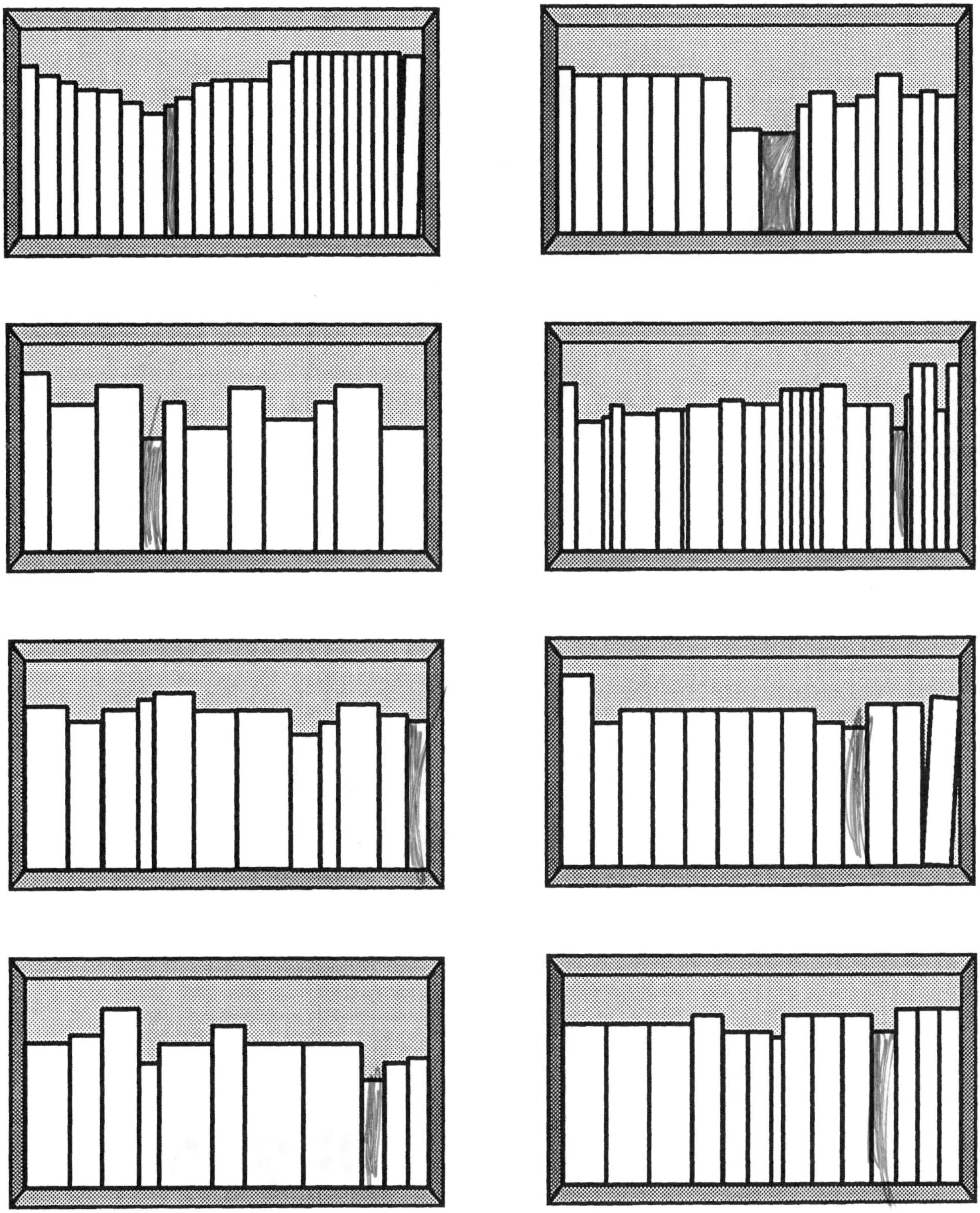

MAP ROUTES

Study the map. Draw a ring around the correct route in each problem.

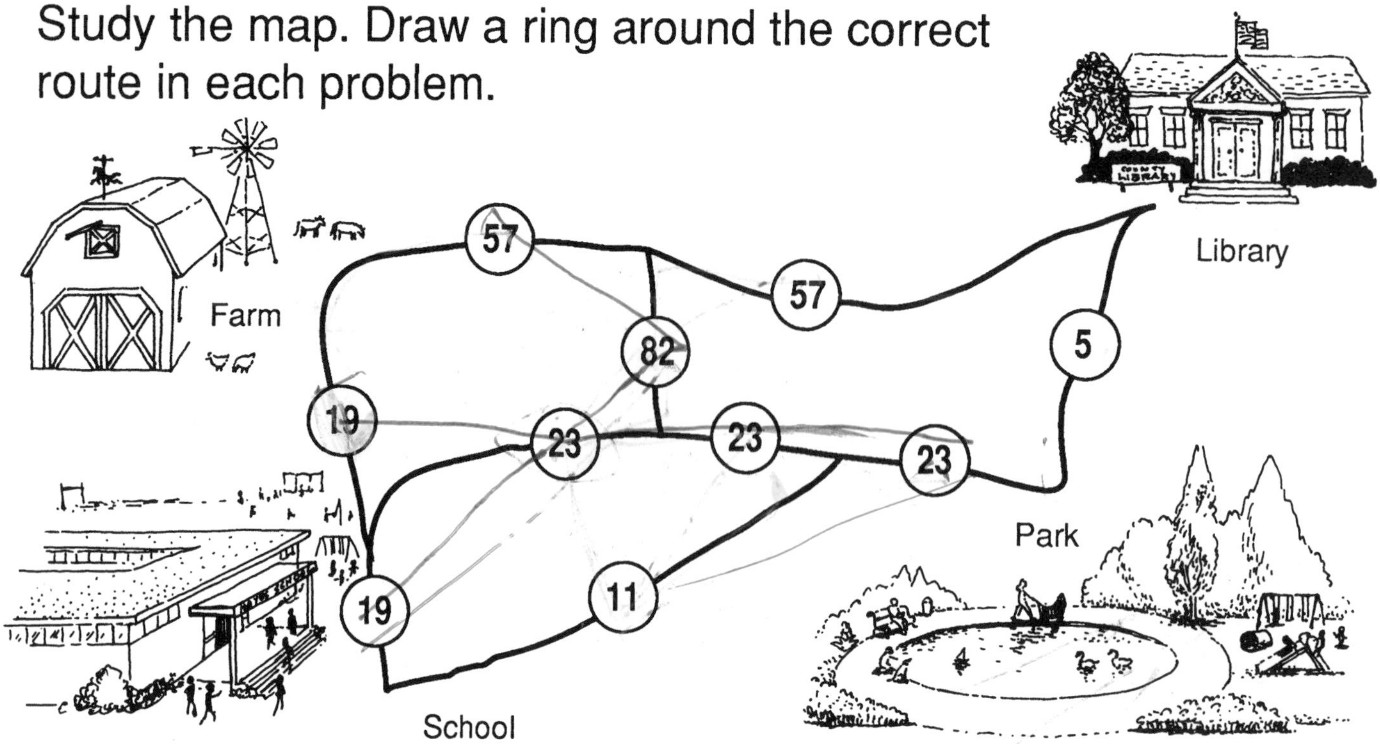

Farm
Library
57
57
82
5
19
23
23
23
Park
19
11
School

1.	School to Park	11 → 23 → 82 → 57	19 → 57
		11 → 23	19 → 23 → 82
2.	School to Library	11 → 23 → 19	19 → 23 → 82
		19 → 57	19
3.	Farm to Park	19 → 11	19 → 23
		57 → 82	57
4.	Farm to School	57 → 82 → 23	19
		57 → 5	19 → 23

MAP PATHS (II)

This is a map.

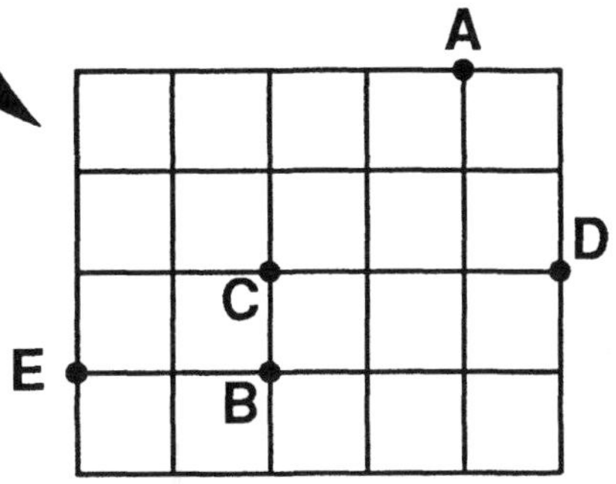
A
D
C
E
B

Study the map paths below. Draw a map on the grid that works for *all* of the map paths in each problem.

1.

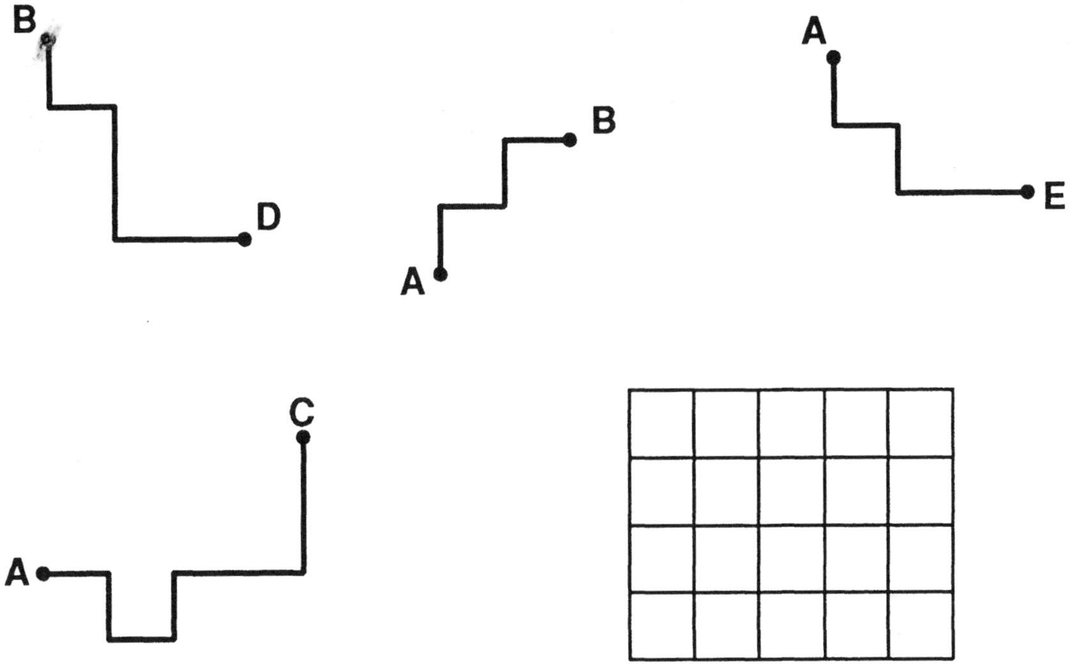
B
D
B
A
A
E
C
A

2.

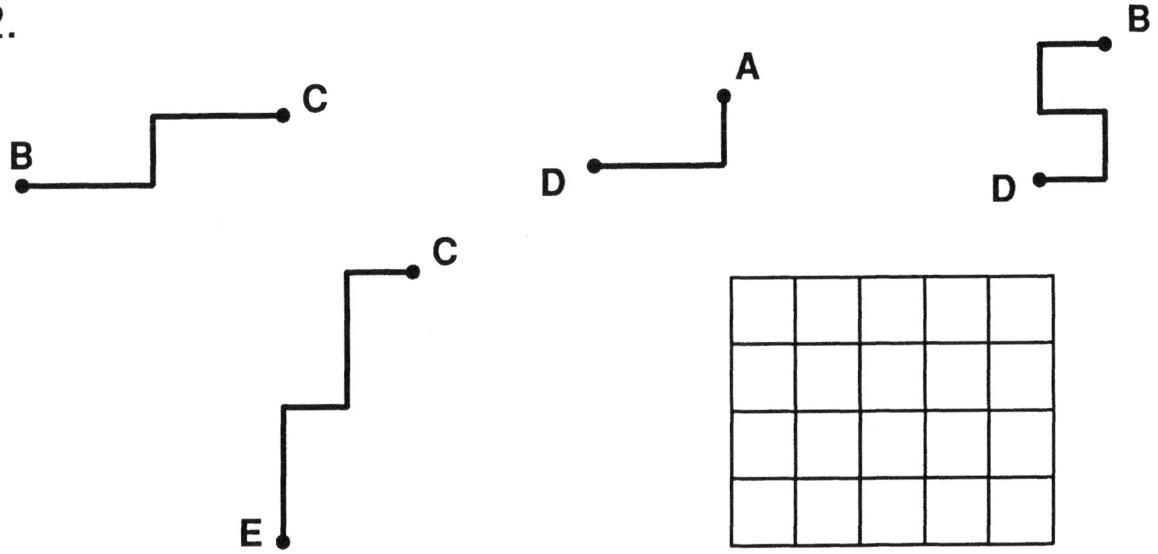
C
B
A
D
B
D
C
E

PART 3: LOGIC

DOG AND PUPPY

Draw a ring around each group that has the same relationship as dog has to puppy.

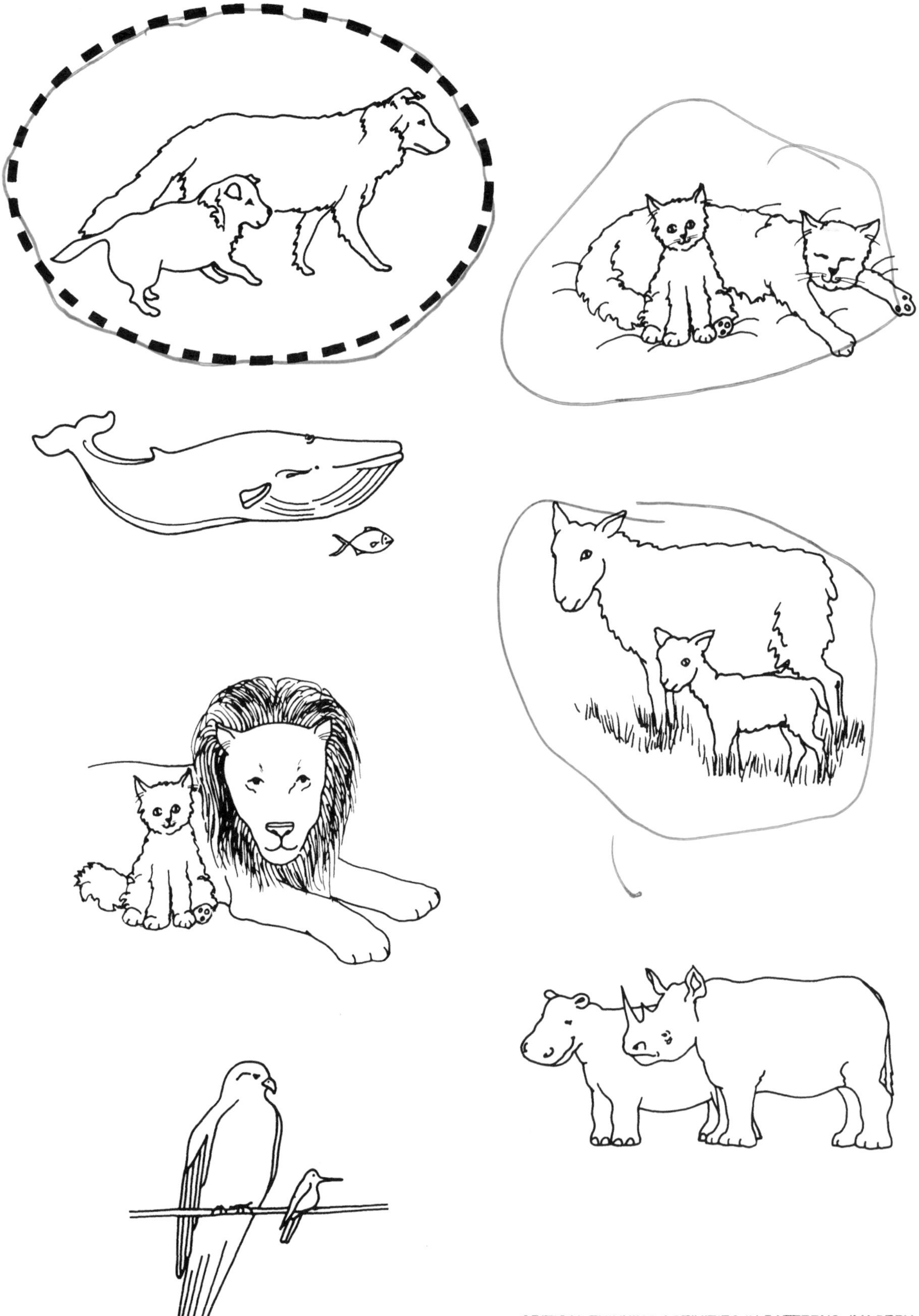

PICTURE LOGIC ▼

Look at the buses. The second one is a double-decker bus. Color the picture in each row that goes with the first picture in the same way the buses go together.

LIONS, HORSES, AND BEARS

Look at this picture.

A.		1	2	3	4	5
B.		1	2	3	4	5
C.		1	2	3	4	5
D.	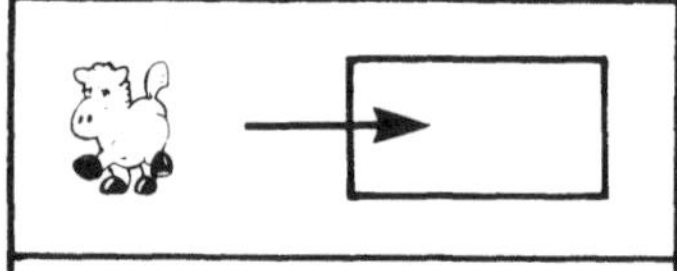	1	2	3	4	5
E.	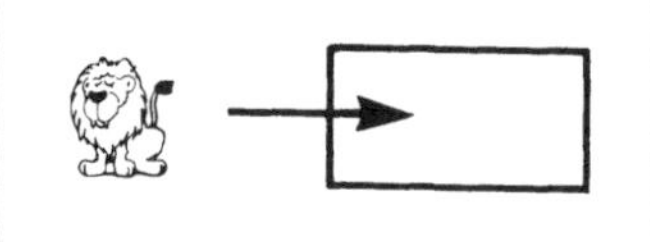	1	2	3	4	5

Row A—Draw a ring around the number of lions in the circle.

Row B—Draw a ring around the number of lions *not* in the circle.

Row C—Draw a ring around the number of animals in the circle.

Row D—Draw a ring around the number of horses in the rectangle.

Row E—Draw a ring around the number of lions in the rectangle.

A DOG'S LOGIC

Look at this picture.

A.		1 2 3 4 5 6 7 8
B.		1 2 3 4 5 6 7 8
C.		1 2 3 4 5 6 7 8
D.		1 2 3 4 5 6 7 8

Row A—Draw a ring around the number of dogs in the circle.

Row B—Draw a ring around the number of dogs in the square.

Row C—Draw a ring around the number of dogs *not* in a shape.

Row D—Draw a ring around the number of dogs in all.

LOGIC BUTTERFLIES

Look at this picture.

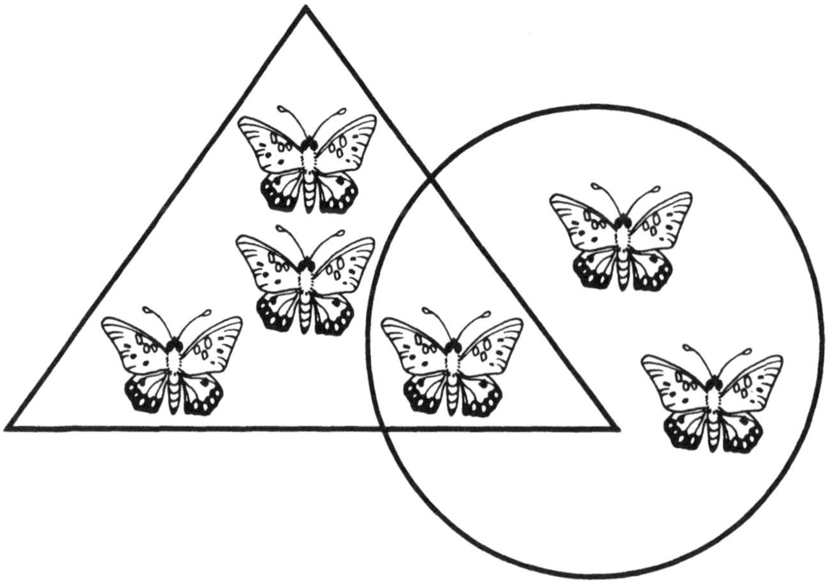

A.		1 2 3 4 5 6
B.		1 2 3 4 5 6
C.	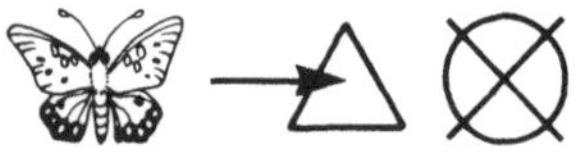	1 2 3 4 5 6
D.	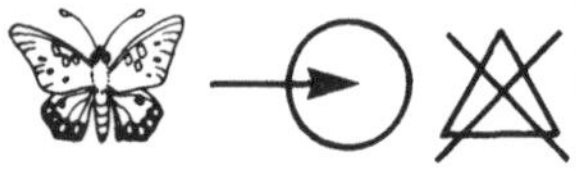	1 2 3 4 5 6
E.		1 2 3 4 5 6

Row A—Draw a ring around the number of butterflies in the triangle.

Row B—Draw a ring around the number of butterflies in the circle.

Row C—Draw a ring around the number of butterflies in the triangle only.

Row D—Draw a ring around the number of butterflies in the circle only.

Row E—Draw a ring around the number of butterflies in all.

FLOWERS AND SNOWFLAKES

Look at this picture.

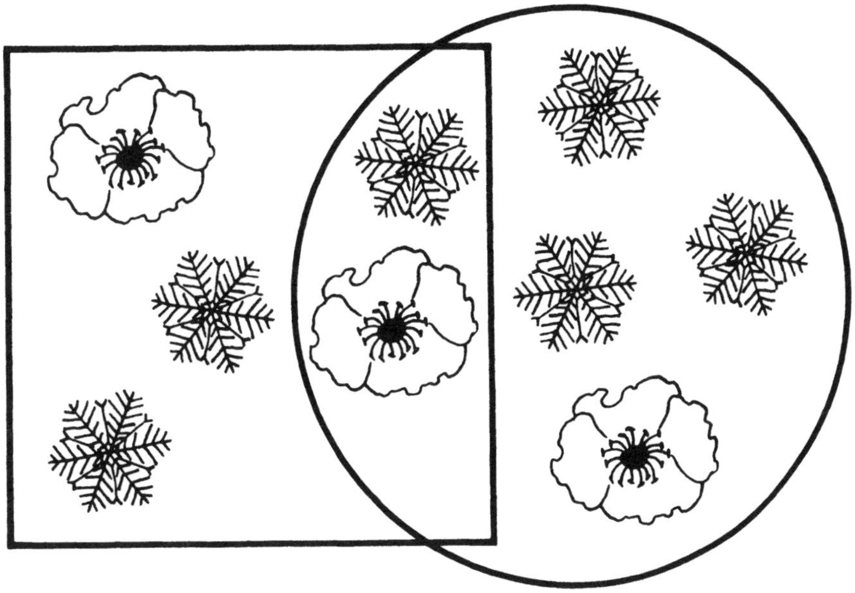

A.	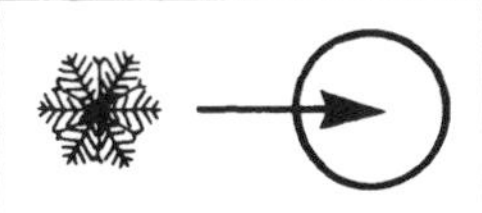	1	2	3	4	5	6	7	8	9
B.	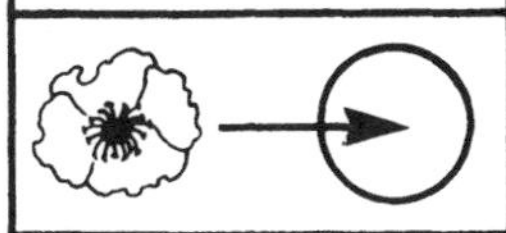	1	2	3	4	5	6	7	8	9
C.	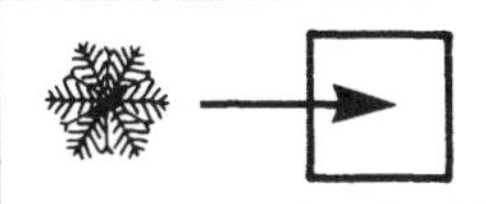	1	2	3	4	5	6	7	8	9
D.	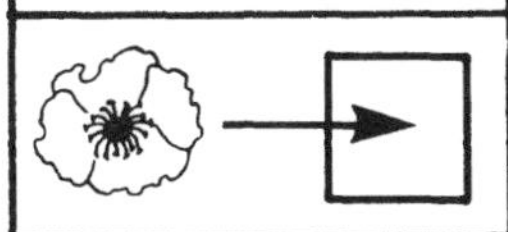	1	2	3	4	5	6	7	8	9
E.	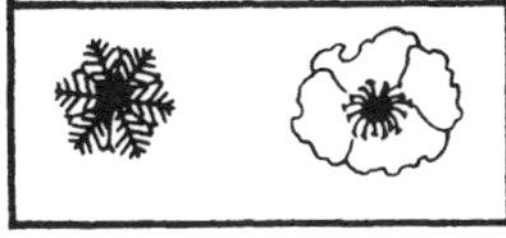	1	2	3	4	5	6	7	8	9

Row A—Draw a ring around the number of snowflakes in the circle.

Row B—Draw a ring around the number of flowers in the circle.

Row C—Draw a ring around the number of snowflakes in the square.

Row D—Draw a ring around the number of flowers in the square.

Row E—Draw a ring around the number of snowflakes and flowers in all.

TREE LOGIC CHART

Look at this picture. Fill in the chart.

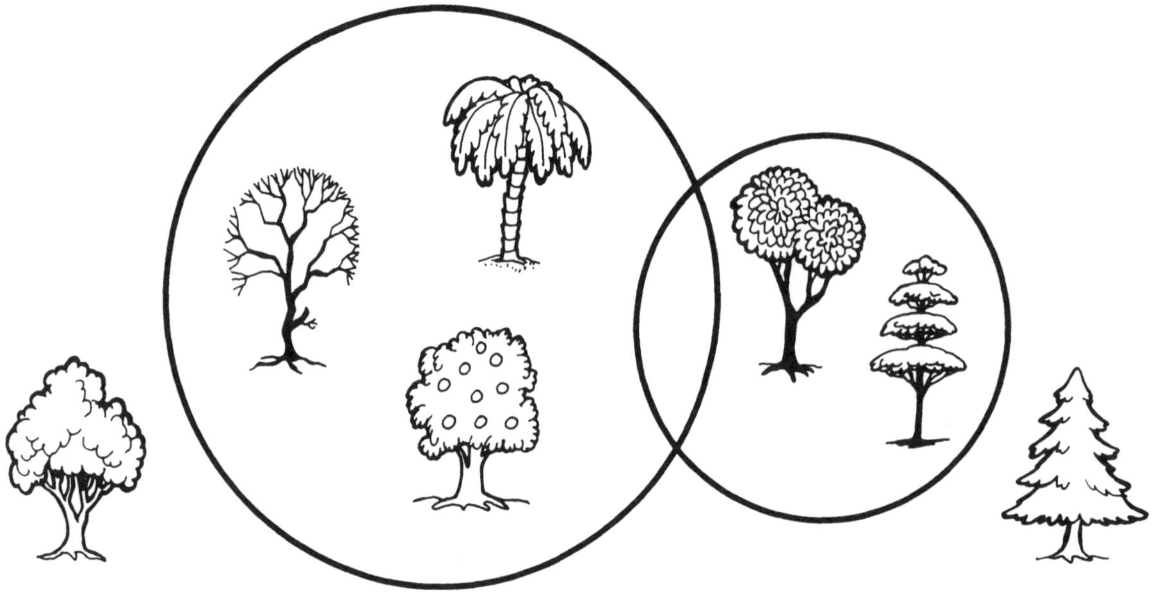

	Tally	Number
How many trees are in the small circle?	I I	2
How many trees are in the big circle?		
How many trees are *not* in a circle?		
How many trees are there in all?		

LEAF LOGIC CHART

Look at this picture. Fill in the chart.

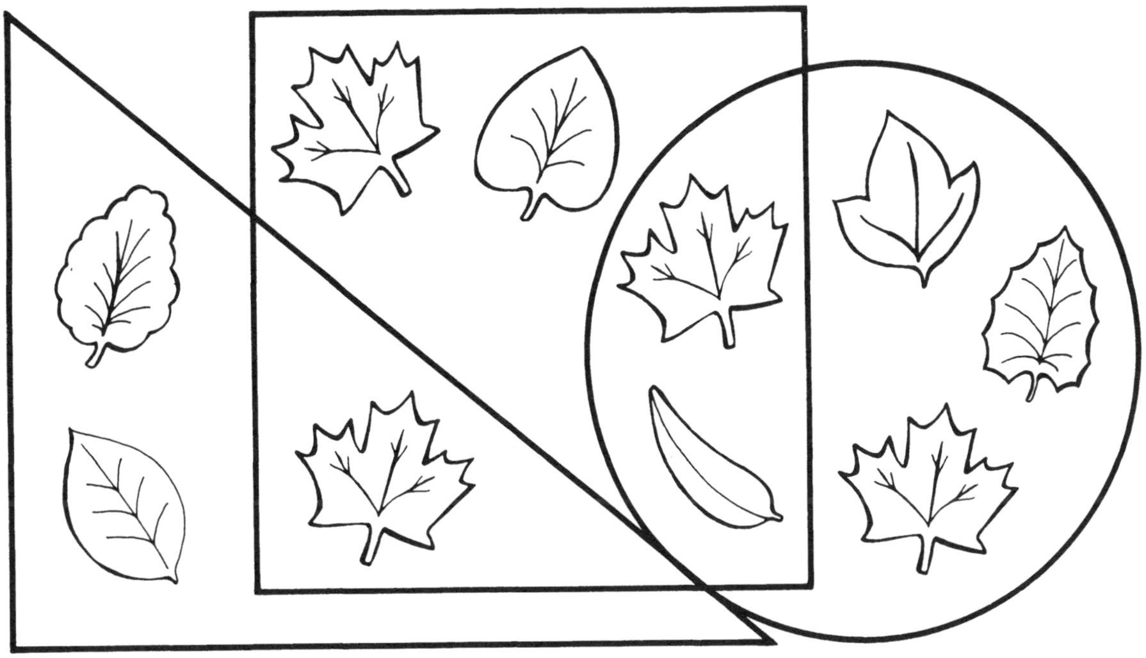

	Tally	Number
How many leaves are in the circle?	𝍸	5
How many leaves are in the triangle?		
How many leaves are there in all?		
How many leaves are in both the circle and the square?		
How many leaves are in both the square and the triangle?		

CATS AND DOGS

Look at this picture. Fill in the chart.

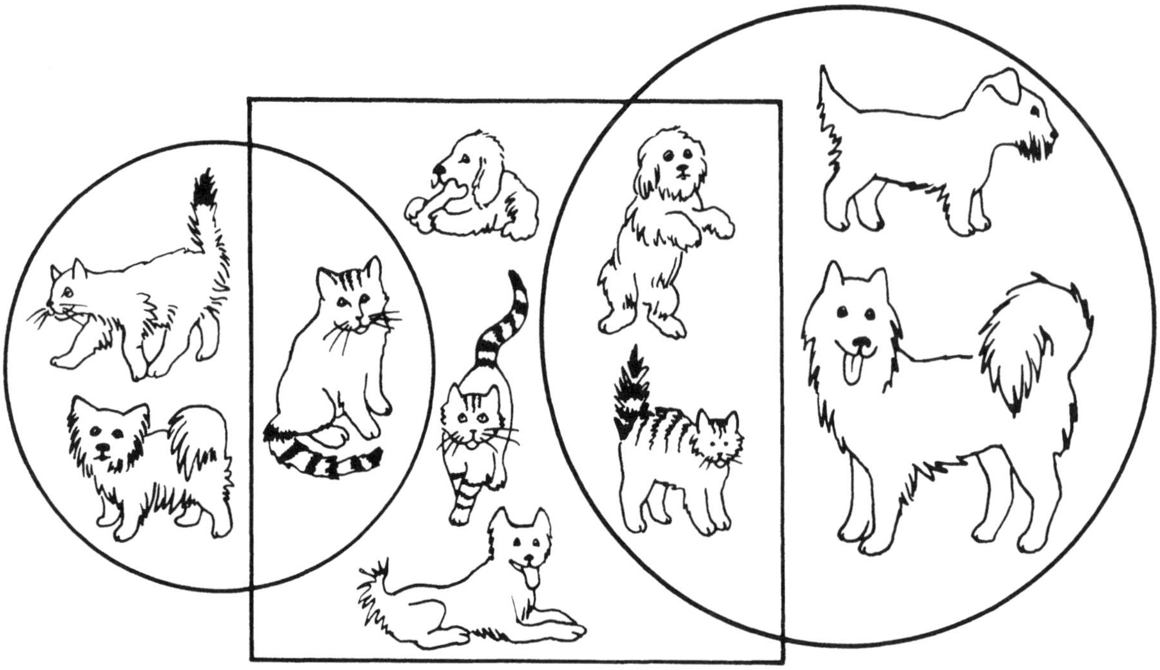

	Tally	Number
How many cats are in the big circle?		
How many dogs are in the square?		
How many cats are in the small circle?		
How many animals are in the square only?	I I I	3
How many animals are in the small circle only?		

BOYS AND GIRLS

Look at this picture. Fill in the chart.

	Tally	Number
How many children are inside the circle?		
How many children are outside the circle?		
How many boys are inside the circle?		
How many girls are outside the circle?		
How many children are there in all?		

SQUARE LOGIC

Look at this picture. Fill in the chart.

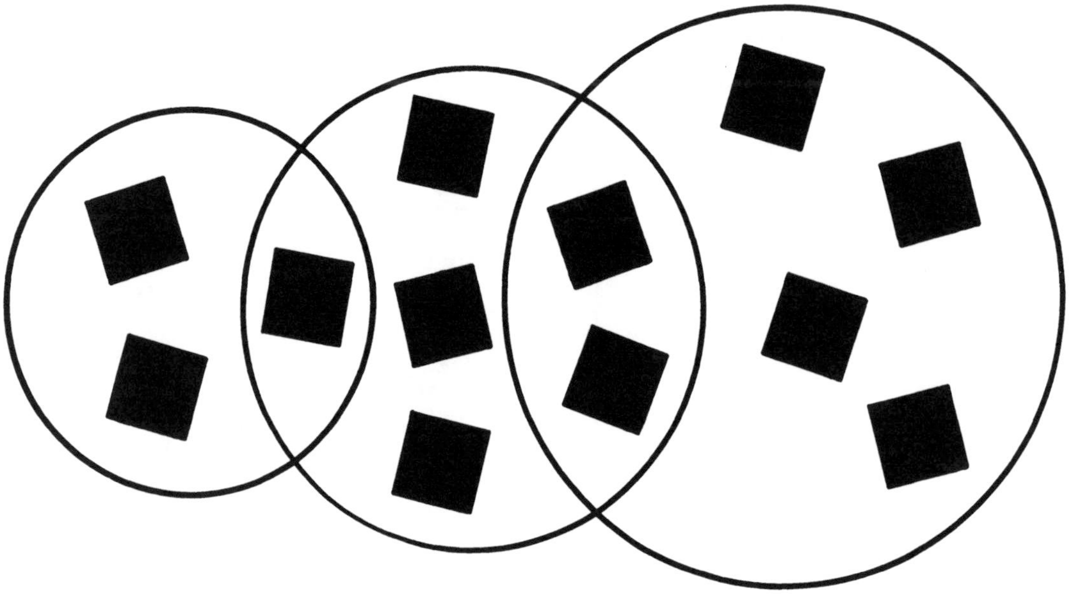

	Tally	Number
Squares in the big circle:		
Squares in the small circle:		
Squares in the middle circle:		
Squares in both big and middle circles:	I I	2
Squares in both small and middle circles:		

ANIMAL LOGIC

Look at this picture. Fill in the chart.

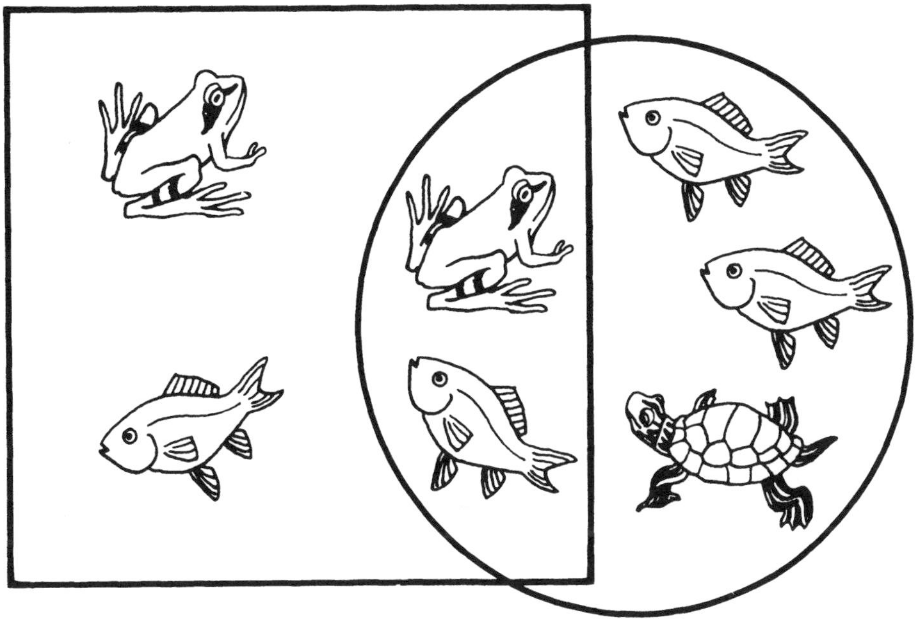

	Tally	Number
Frogs in the circle:		
Frogs in the square:		
Fish in the circle:		
Fish in the circle only:	I I	2
Frogs in the square only:		
Turtles in the square:		
Turtles in the circle:		

WHAT'S COMMON? (I)

Draw a ring around the things all the shapes in each box have in common.

Example:

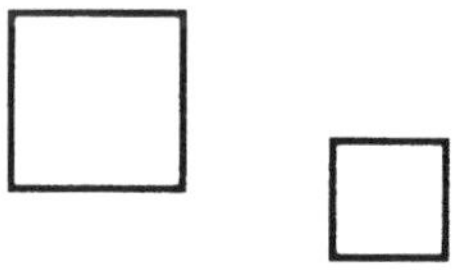

same shape (circled)
same size
same color (circled)

1.

same shape
same size
same color

2.

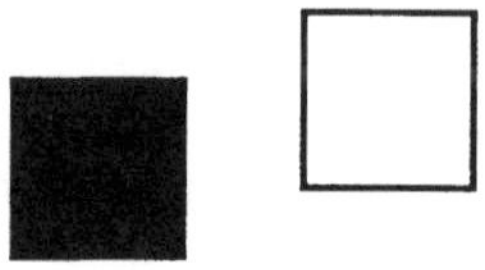

same shape
same size
same color

3.

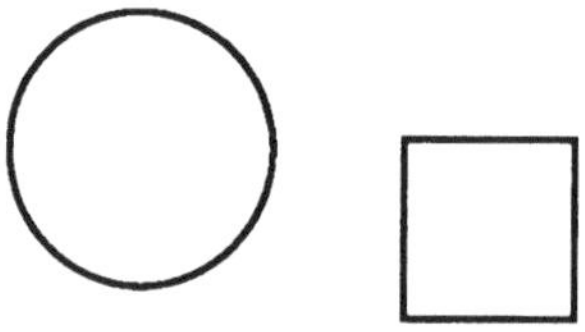

same shape
same size
same color

4.

same shape
same size
same color

5.

same shape
same size
same color

6.

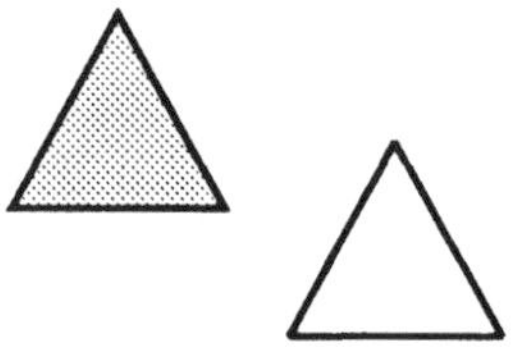

same shape
same size
same color

7.

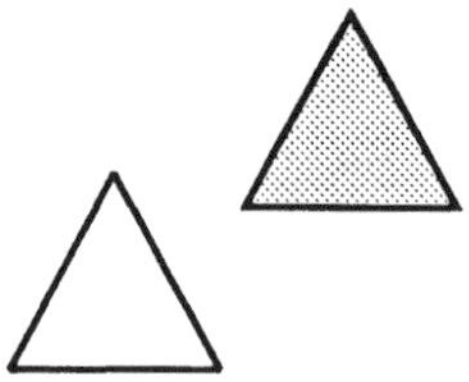

same shape
same size
same color

8.

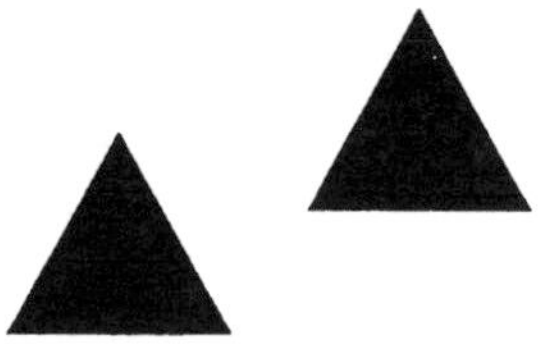

same shape
same size
same color

WHAT FIRST? (I)

Draw a ring around what you do first.

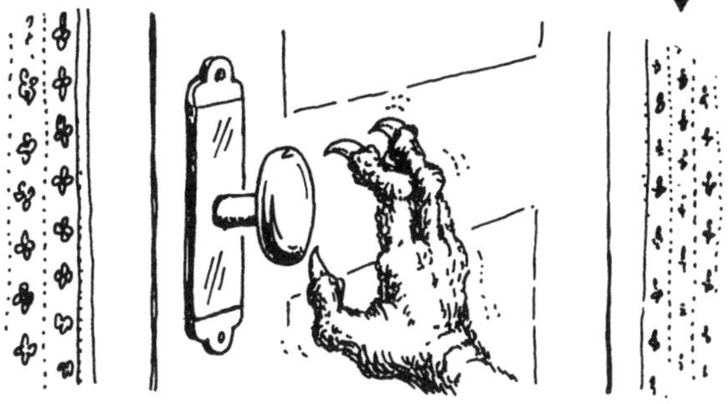

Example: A. Open the door.

(B.) Turn the door knob.

1. A. Put on your shoes. B. Tie the shoe laces.	**2.** A. Drink a glass of milk. B. Pour a glass of milk.
3. A. Go to sleep. B. Turn out the bedroom light.	**4.** A. Turn on the water. B. Take a shower.
5. A. Open a jar of peanut butter. B. Take peanut butter out of the refrigerator. C. Spread peanut butter on bread.	**6.** A. Get in the car. B. Drive away. C. Fasten your seat belt.
7. A. Read the book. B. Borrow the book from the library. C. Return the book to the library.	**8.** A. Put bread in the toaster. B. Eat toast. C. Plug in the toaster.

BIRD LOGIC

▼▼

Look at this picture. Fill in the chart.

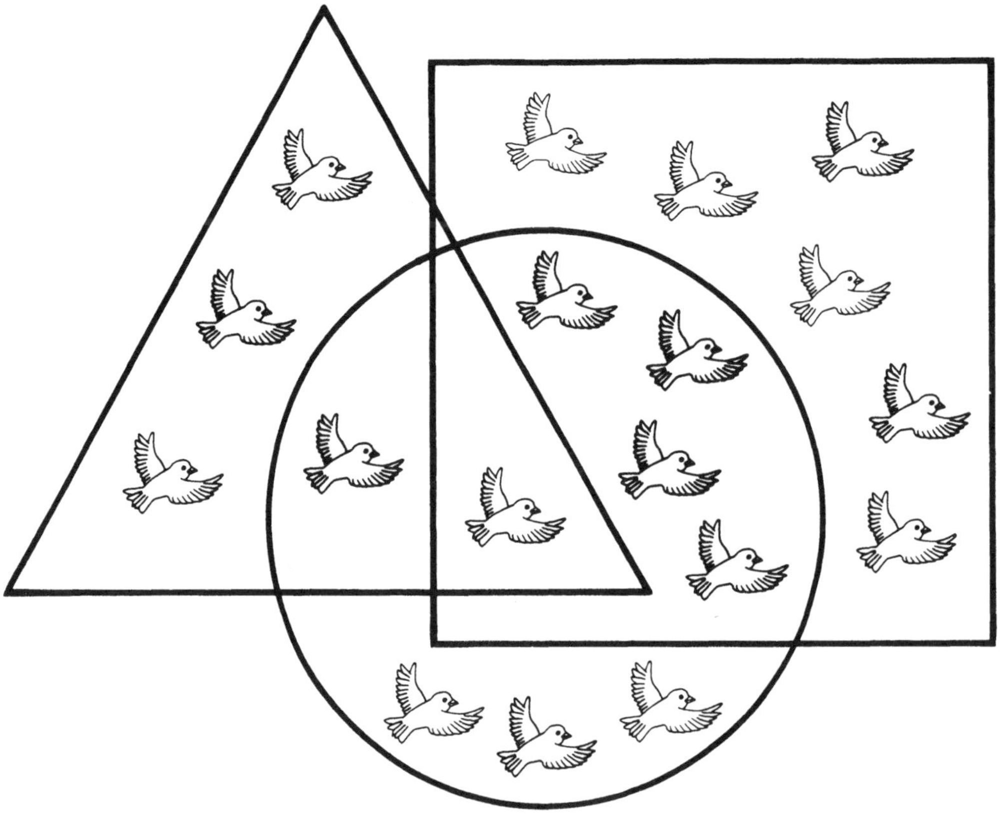

	Number
Birds in the square:	
Birds in the square only:	6
Birds in the circle:	
Birds in both the circle and the square:	5
Birds in both the circle and the triangle:	
Birds in the triangle only:	
Birds in the circle, the triangle, and the square:	

JET LOGIC

▼▼

Look at this picture. Fill in the chart.

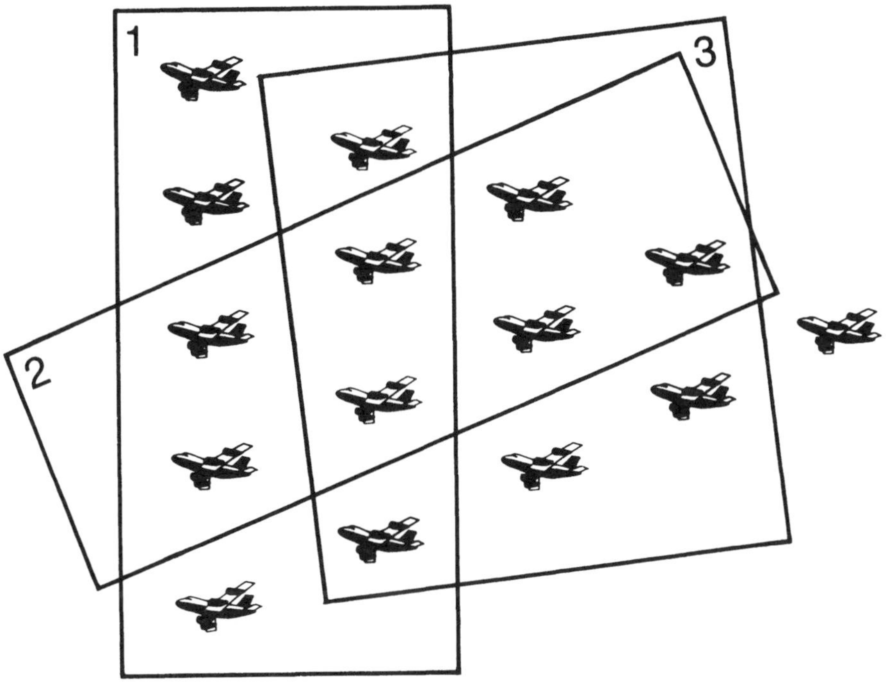

1
2
3

	Number
Jets *not* in a rectangle:	
Jets in all:	
Jets in rectangle 1:	
Jets in rectangle 2:	
Jets in rectangle 3:	
Jets in both rectangles 1 and 3:	4
Jets in both rectangles 2 and 3:	
Jets in all three rectangles:	

SHAPE LOGIC

Look at this picture. Fill in the chart.

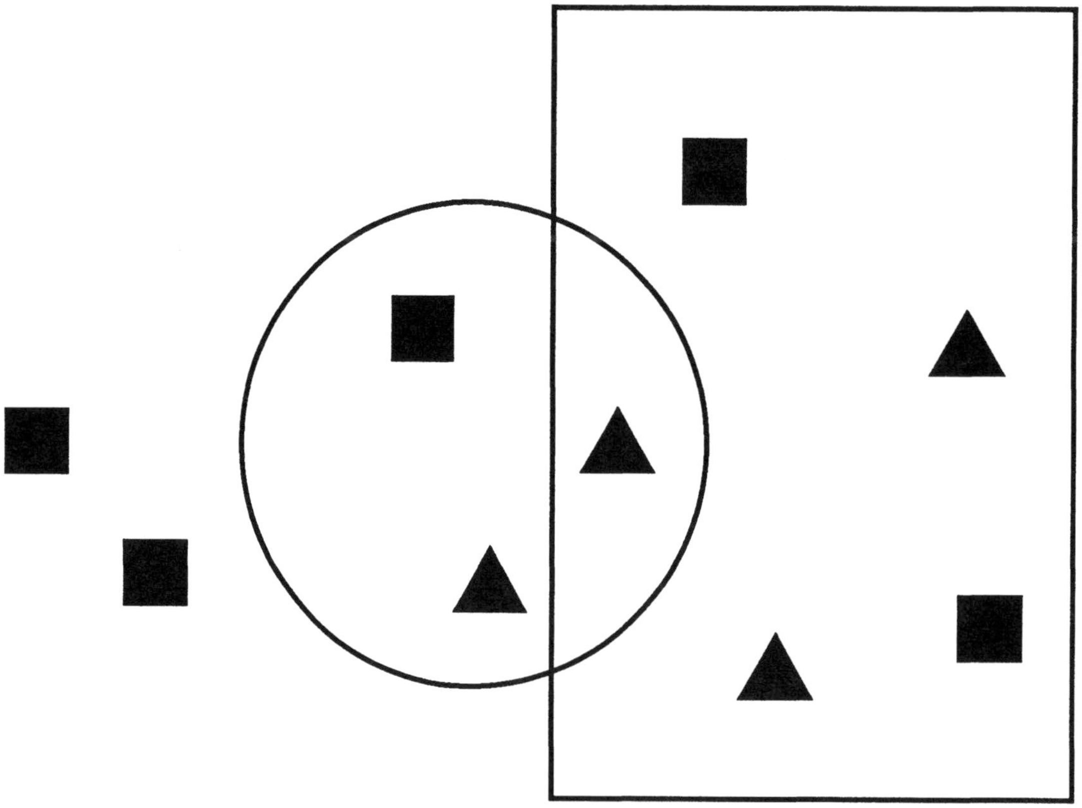

	Number
▲ in the rectangle:	
▲ in the circle:	
■ in the circle:	
■ in the rectangle:	
■ *not* in any shape:	
▲ in all:	
■ in all:	

COUNT THE CONES ▼▼

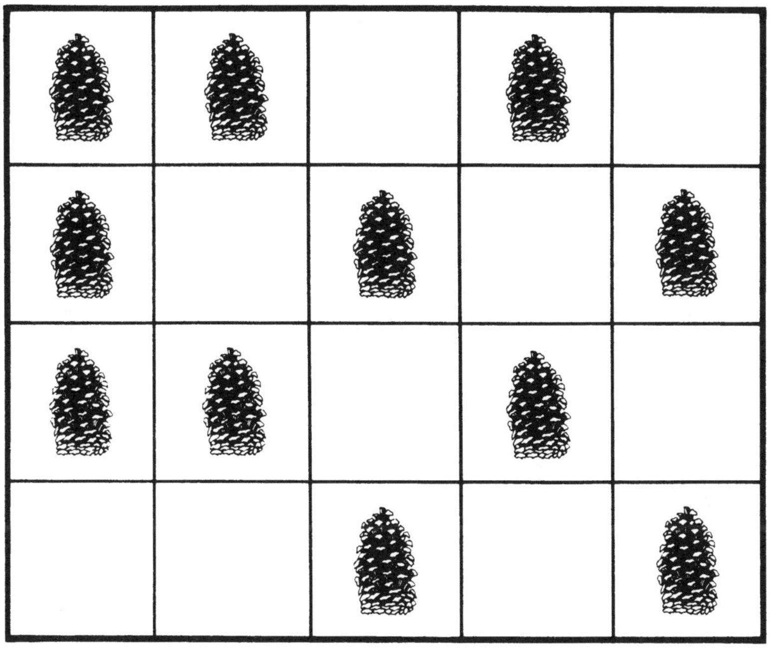

1. How many pine cones are *not* in the top row? _____
2. How many pine cones are *not* in the bottom row? _____
3. How many pine cones are *not* in the two middle rows? _____
4. How many pine cones are *not* in the top two rows? _____
5. How many pine cones are there in all? _____
6. How many blank spaces are there in all? _____

SQUARES AND CIRCLES

▼▼

Look at this picture. Fill in the chart.

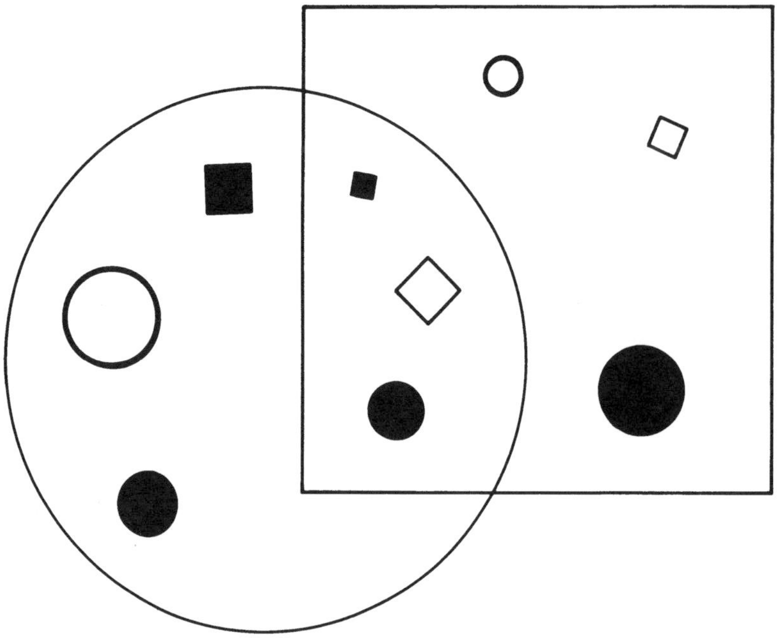

	Number
Circles in the big circle:	
Squares in the big square:	
Circles in the big circle only:	2
Squares in the big square only:	
Squares in both big shapes:	2
Circles in both big shapes:	
Circles in the big square only:	
Squares in the big circle only:	

LOGIC LEAVES

▼▼

Look at this picture. Fill in the chart.

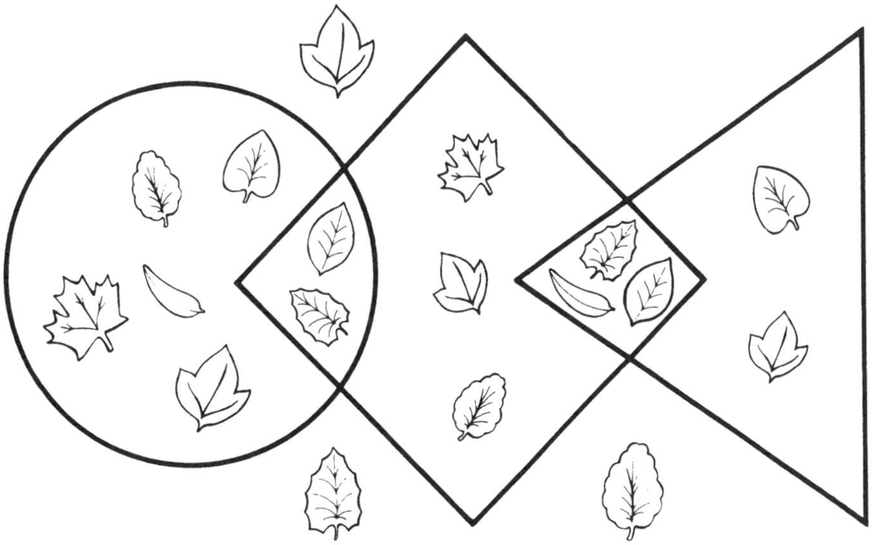

	Number
Leaves in the circle only:	
Leaves in the square only:	
Leaves in the triangle only:	
Leaves in both the circle and the square:	
Leaves in both the square and the triangle:	
Leaves in neither the circle nor the triangle:	
Leaves not in any shape:	
Leaves on the page:	

WHAT'S COMMON? (II)

Draw a ring around the things all the shapes in each box have in common.

Example:

same shape

same size

same color

1.

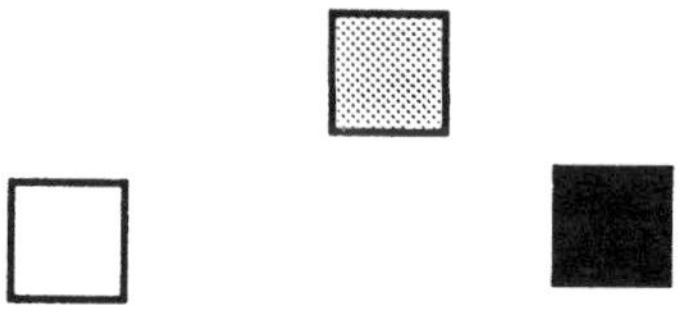

same shape

same size

same color

2.

same shape

same size

same color

3.

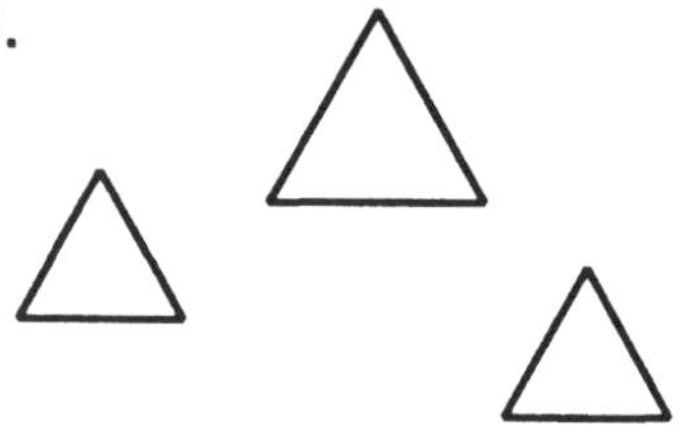

same shape

same size

same color

4.

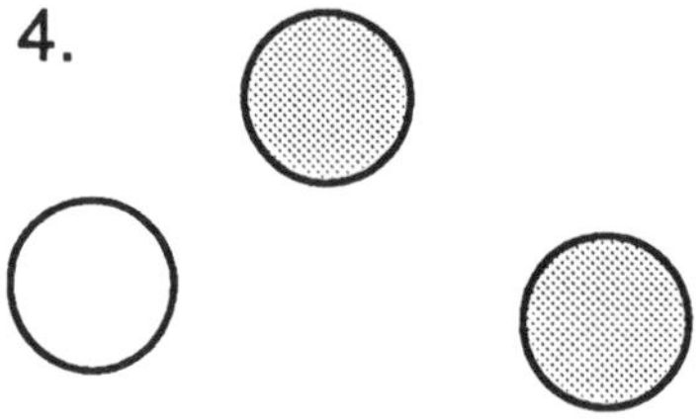

same shape

same size

same color

5.

same shape

same size

same color

6.

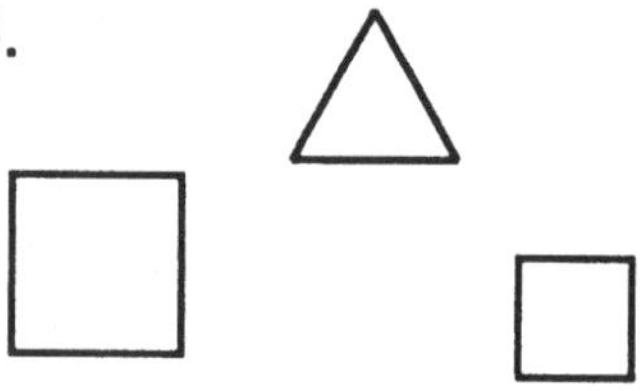

same shape

same size

same color

7.

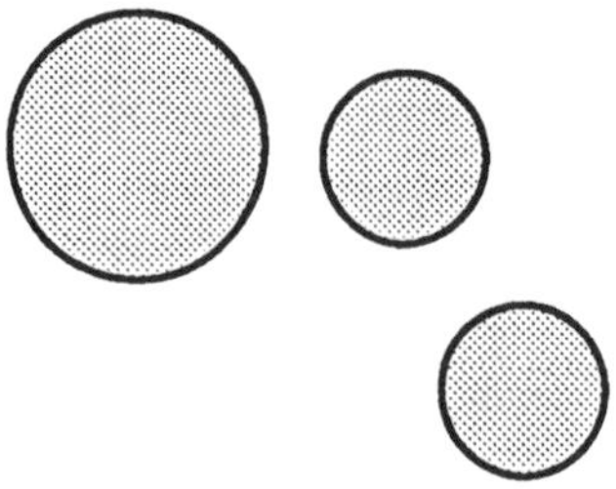

same shape

same size

same color

8.

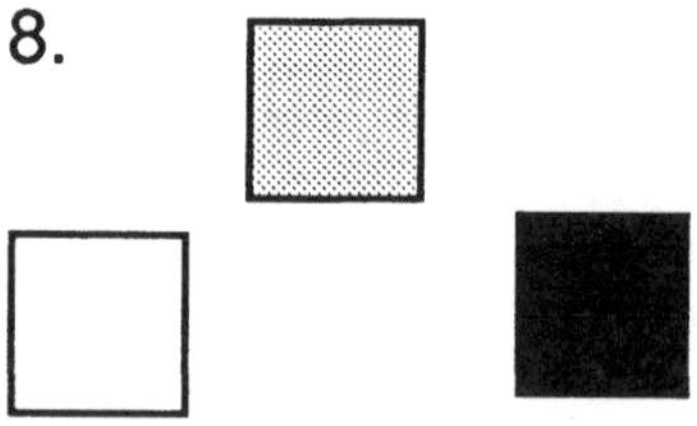

same shape

same size

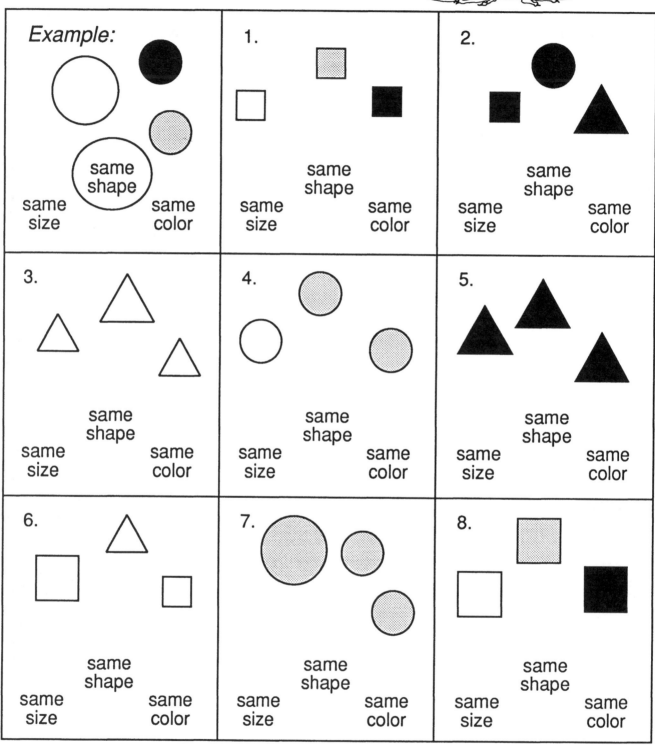

same color

MISSING WORDS

▼▼

Match the numbers with the right word names.
Write the missing word in the empty box.

Example:

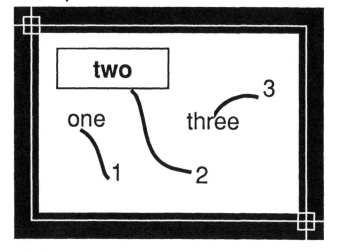

two

3

one three

1 2

1.

2 seven

4

7

two

2.

1 3

six one

6 three 8

3.

2 four 8

two

eight

5 4

4.

9 ten 3

7 seven

three 10

5.

nine 0

9

6 1

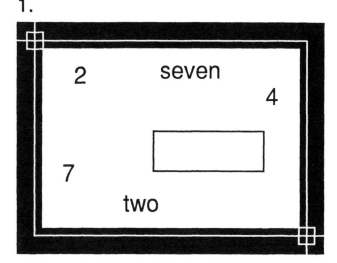

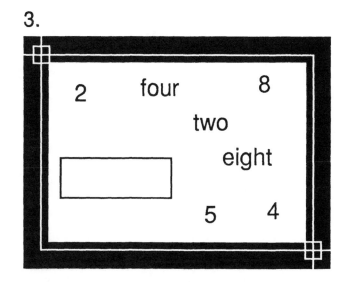

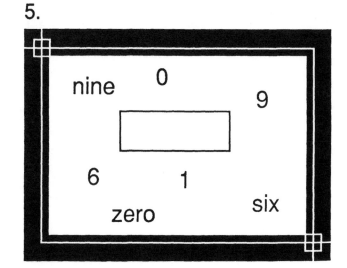

zero six

NUMBER NAMES

▼▼

The word names for the numbers are in the puzzle. Draw a ring around the words you find.

1. Find these numbers:

1
2
10

T	E	N
W	O	W
O	N	E

2. Find these numbers:

1
2
9
10

T	W	O	N
E	C	O	B
N	I	N	E
O	P	E	N

3. Find these numbers:

4
5
6
7

T	A	F	O	U	R
O	S	I	X	B	O
L	I	V	E	C	A
M	S	E	V	E	N

RELATIONSHIPS

▼▼

Choose the best answer to complete these sentences. Draw a ring around the right word.

1. Cat is to kitten as dog is to	dish bark puppy tail
2. Car is to road as boat is to	motor fish sail lake
3. Hat is to head as mitten is to	snow hand cold winter
4. Finger is to hand as toe is to	foot pull missle leg
5. Cow is to milk as chicken is to	feathers rooster egg hen

Fill in the blanks:

6. Fish is to water as bird is to ________________.

7. Black is to white as stop is to ________________.

8. Saw is to carpenter as brush is to ________________.

9. Cocker Spaniel is to dog as ___________ is to ________________.

10. Milk is to glass as ________________ is to ________________.

WHAT'S COMMON? (III)

▼▼

Draw a ring around the things all the shapes in each box have in common.

Example:

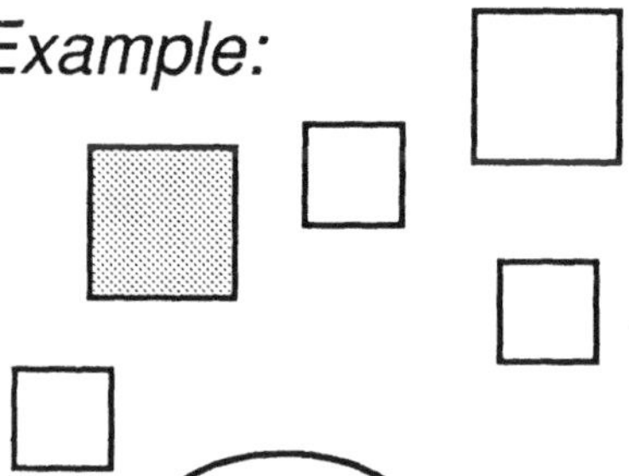

same shape (circled)
same size
same color

1.

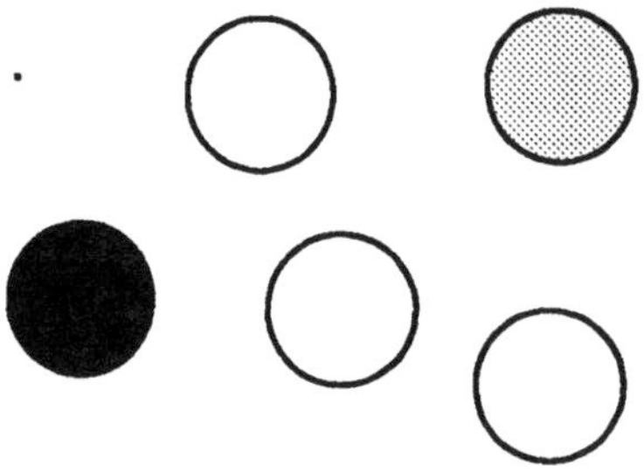

same shape
same size
same color

2.

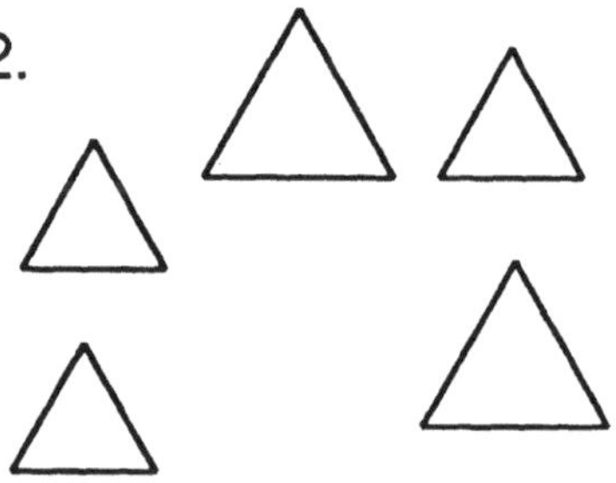

same shape
same size
same color

3.

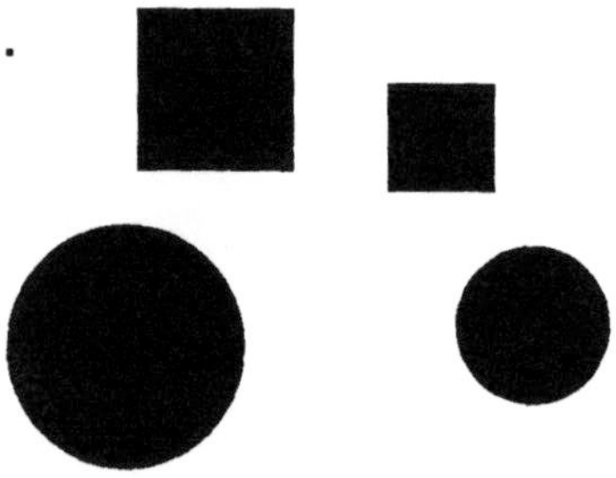

same shape
same size
same color

4.

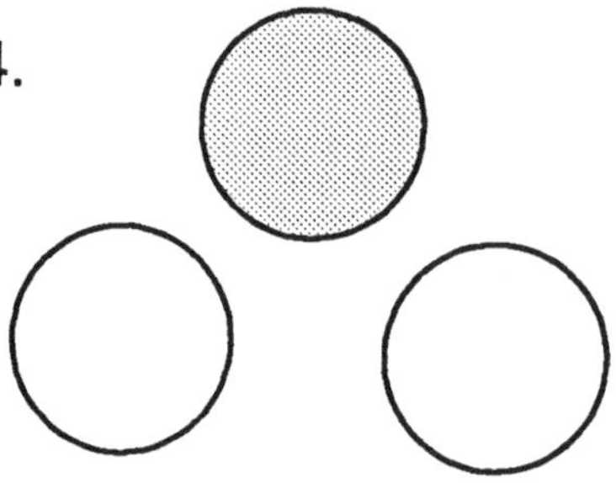

same shape
same size
same color

5.

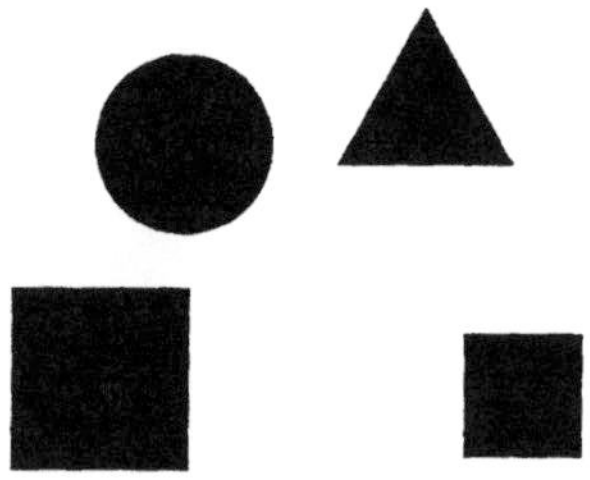

same shape
same size
same color

6.

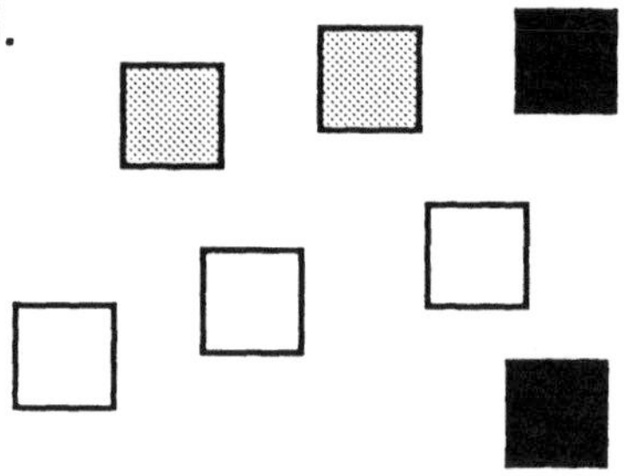

same shape
same size
same color

7.

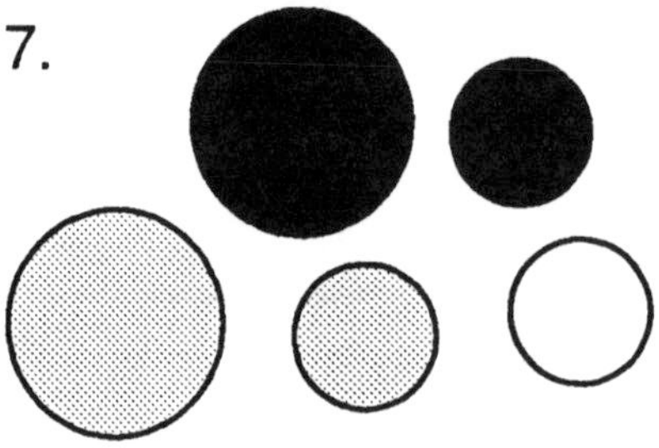

same shape
same size
same color

8.

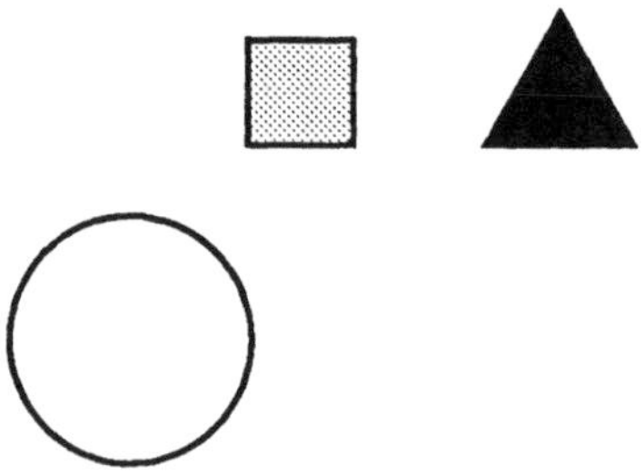

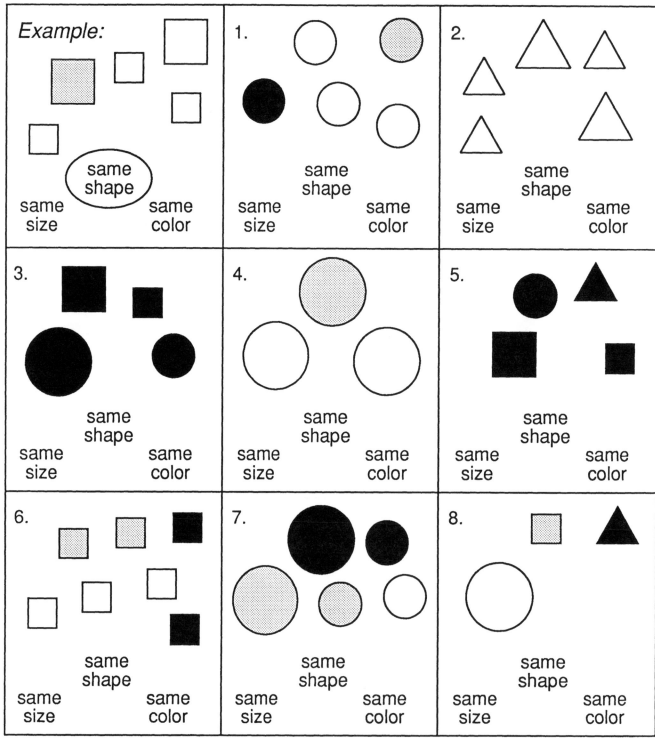

same shape
same size
same color

SAME OR DIFFERENT?

▼▼

For each pair of statements, decide whether they say the same thing or are different.

Example: All people like a sunny day.

Everyone likes a sunny day.

(Same) Different

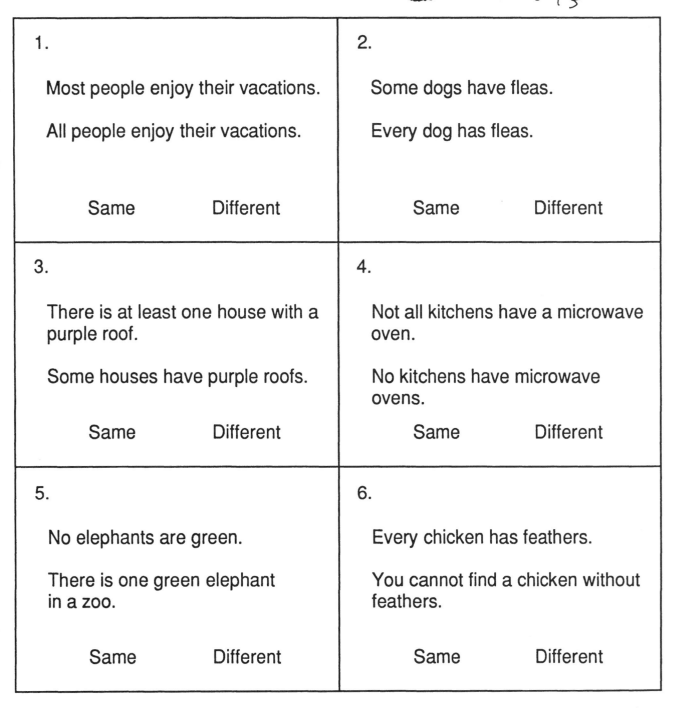

1. Most people enjoy their vacations. All people enjoy their vacations. Same Different	2. Some dogs have fleas. Every dog has fleas. Same Different
3. There is at least one house with a purple roof. Some houses have purple roofs. Same Different	4. Not all kitchens have a microwave oven. No kitchens have microwave ovens. Same Different
5. No elephants are green. There is one green elephant in a zoo. Same Different	6. Every chicken has feathers. You cannot find a chicken without feathers. Same Different

WHAT FIRST? (II) ▼▼

Read each task and the list of steps. Then write the steps in the right order to do the task.

STEPS: A. Sit and look at the TV set.
C. Turn on the TV set.
B. Hit a nail with a hammer.
D. Lift the hammer.

1. Hammering a nail

____

____

2. Watching TV

____

____

STEPS: A. Put water in a pan.
C. Take envelope to the post office.
B. Put letter in an envelope.
D. Put pan on a stove.

3. Boiling water

____

____

4. Sending a letter

THE PRESIDENT

____

____

STEPS: A. Pay bill.
C. Get on the school bus.
E. Order food.
B. Get off the school bus.
D. Read menu.
F. Ride on the school bus.

5. Going to school

School

____

____

____

6. Eating at a restaurant

____

____

____

OPEN BOOK

Decide where to open the book for each problem.

Example: You have a 400-page book. You want to turn to page 365. Do you open the book at the front? the middle? or the back? (Answer: Page 365 is near the back.)

Your book has 400 pages.

1. Page 195, open to the:	front	middle	back
2. Page 87, open to the:	front	middle	back
3. Page 237, open to the:	front	middle	back

Your book has 175 pages.

4. Page 37, open to the:	front	middle	back
5. Page 160, open to the:	front	middle	back
6. Page 95, open to the:	front	middle	back

Your book has 680 pages.

7. Page 101, open to the:	front	middle	back
8. Page 401, open to the:	front	middle	back
9. Page 319, open to the:	front	middle	back
10. Page 577, open to the:	front	middle	back

NUMBER LOGIC (I)

▼▼▼

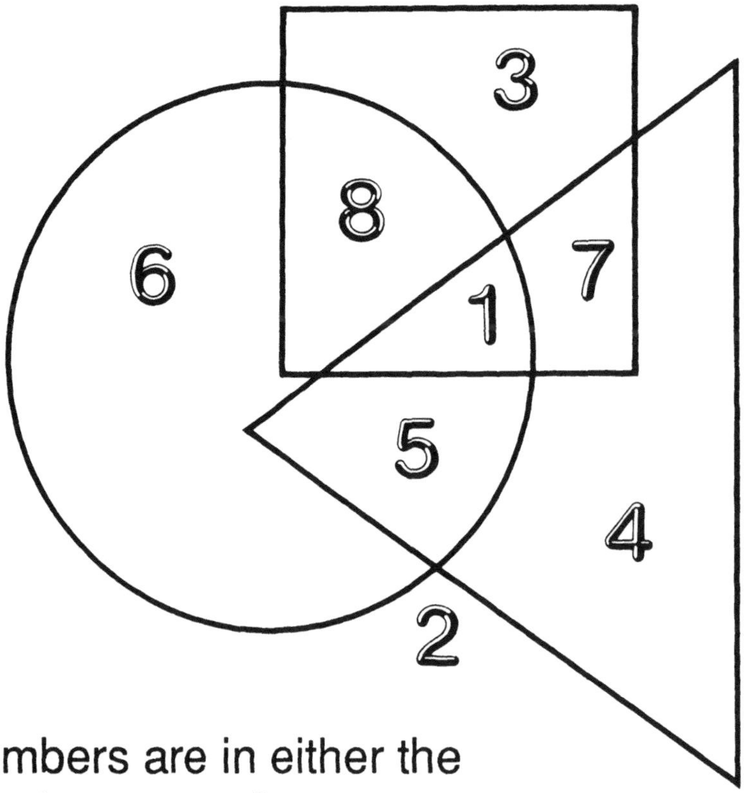
3
8
6
7
1
5
4
2

1. Which numbers are in either the triangle or the square? 1, 3, 4, 5, 7, 8
2. Which triangles are in both the triangle and the square? 1, 7
3. Which numbers are in both the square and the circle? ______
4. Which numbers are in either the circle or the triangle? ______
5. Which number is in all three shapes? ______
6. Which number is not in any shape? ______
7. Which numbers are in neither the circle nor the triangle? ______
8. Which numbers are in neither the circle nor the square? ______

SHELL GAME

▼▼▼

Find what number belongs under each shell.

1.
5
\+ 
12

 = ___

2.
17
− 
9

 = ___

3.
2
3
\+ 
11

 = ___

4.
8
4
\+ 
18

 = ___

5.
2
5

\+6
16

 = ___

6.

−8
5

 = ___

7. 9 + 1 +  = 14    = ___

WHAT'S COMMON? (IV)

Draw a ring around the things all the shapes in each box have in common.

Example:

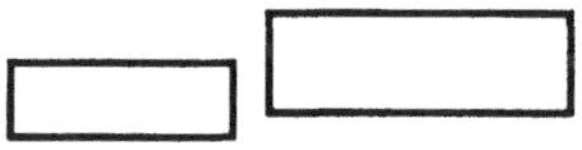

same shape (circled)
same size
same color (circled)

1.

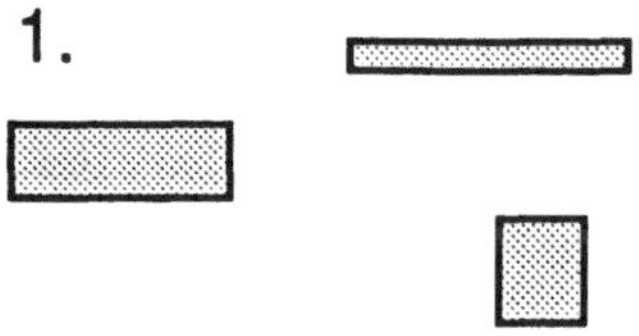

same shape
same size
same color

2.

same shape
same size
same color

3.

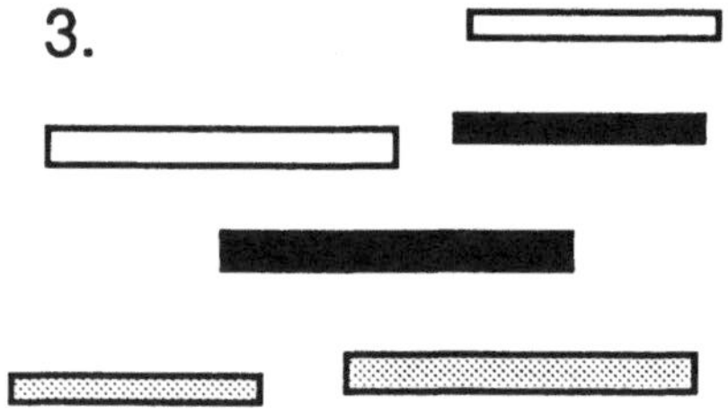

same shape
same size
same color

4.

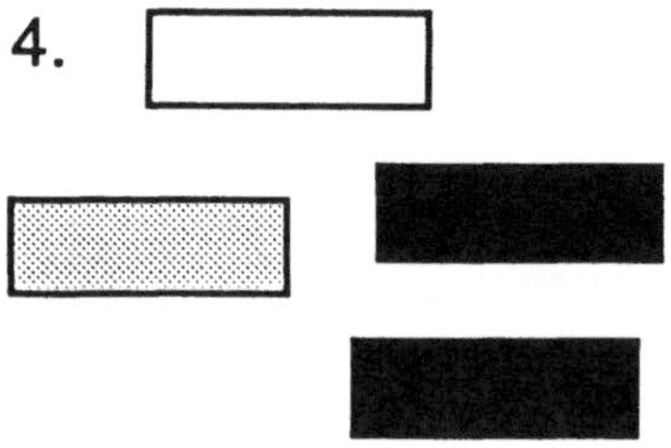

same shape
same size
same color

5.

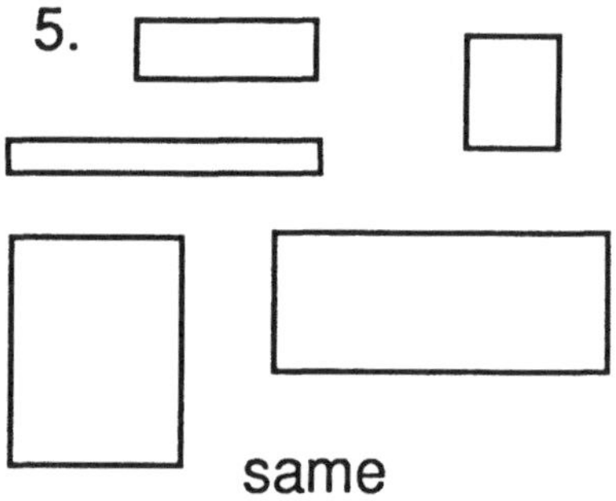

same shape
same size
same color

6.

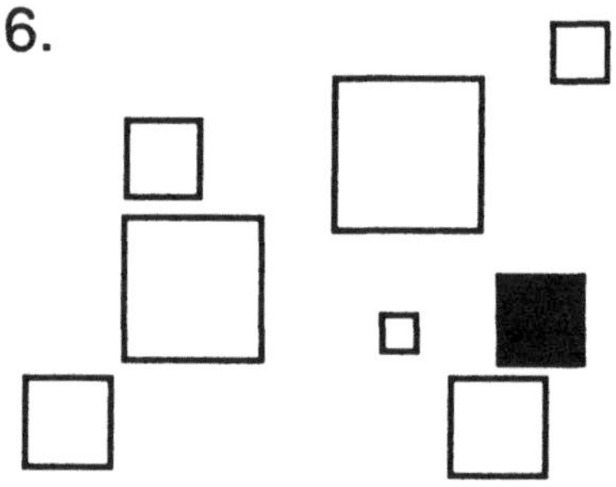

same shape
same size
same color

7.

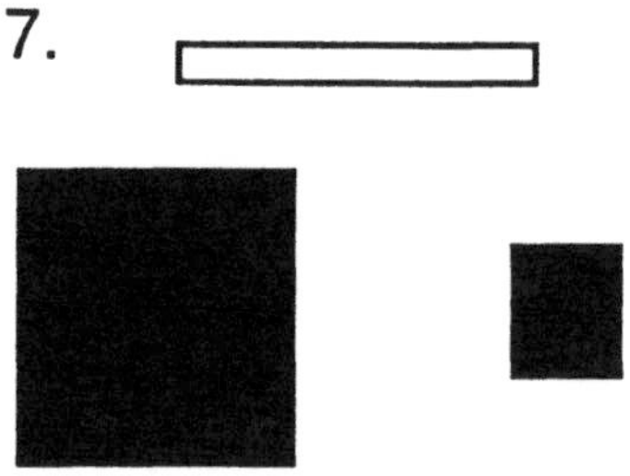

same shape
same size
same color

8.

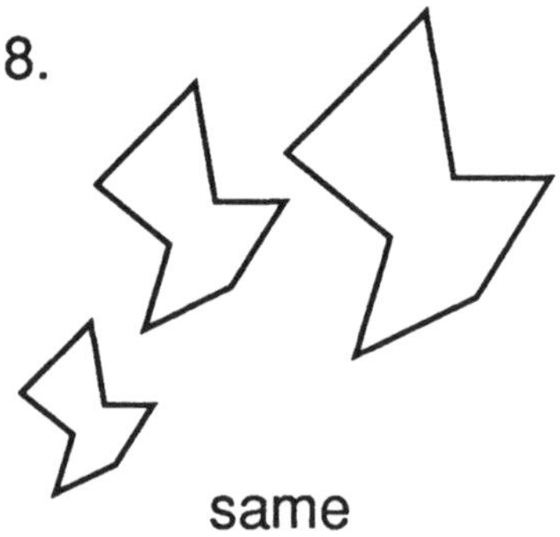

same shape
same size
same color

NUMBER LOGIC (II)

▼▼▼

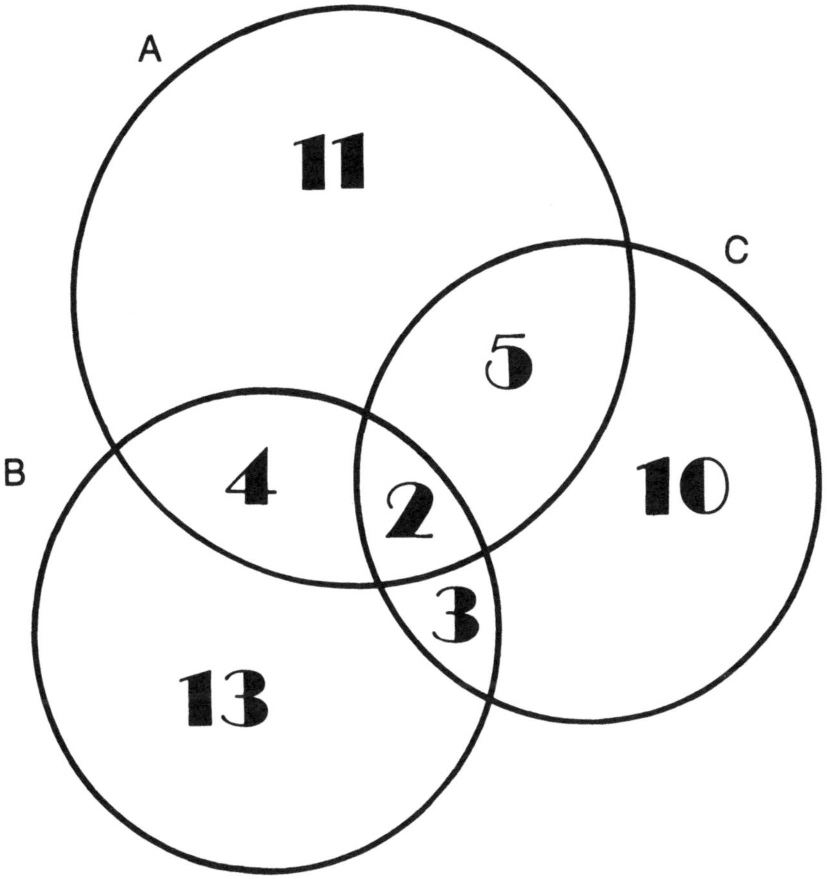
A
11
C
5
B
4
2
10
3
13

Find the sum of the numbers:

1. in circle C. _____
2. in circle B. _____
3. in both circle A and circle B. _____
4. in both circle B and circle C. _____
5. in both circle A and circle C. _____
6. not in circle B. _____
7. not in circle C. _____

JUGGLING NUMBERS

▼▼▼

Make the number sentences true. Write 2, 3, or 4 in each circle.

4
3
2

1. ◯ + ◯ + ◯ = 9

2. ◯ + ◯ − ◯ = 1

3. ◯ + ◯ − ◯ = 5

4. ◯ + ◯ − ◯ = 3

Make the number sentences true. Write 1, 3, or 4 in each circle.

4
3
1

5. ◯ + ◯ + ◯ = 8

6. ◯ + ◯ − ◯ = 6

7. ◯ + ◯ − ◯ = 2

8. ◯ + ◯ − ◯ = 0

BIGGER AND BIGGER

Which is bigger? Draw a ring around your choice in each problem.

1.	2.	3.	4.	5.
9 – 2	8 – 3	13 – 9	23 – 14	43 – 29
9 – 5	8 – 6	13 – 4	23 – 18	43 – 24

6. If the first numbers are the same in a subtraction problem, the difference is bigger when the second number is

____
(larger or smaller?)

7.	8.	9.	10.	11.
8 – 3	12 – 5	16 – 7	33 – 15	87 – 39
5 – 3	14 – 5	12 – 7	49 – 15	53 – 39

12. If the second numbers are the same in a subtraction problem, the difference is bigger when the first number is

____
(larger or smaller?)

MATH GROUP PROBLEM

▼▼▼

There are eight members of the math group. Each member is given a number. The numbers are 1, 2, 3, 4, 5, 6, 7, and 8. Draw a ring around each correct answer.

Anna is given a number greater than 5.

1. Could Anna's number be 7? yes no
2. Could Anna's number be 3? yes no
3. Could Anna's number be 5? yes no

Dal is not given 2, 4, 6, or 8.

4. Could Dal's number be 4? yes no
5. Could Dal's number be greater than 7? yes no
6. Could Dal's number be 7? yes no

Terry is given a number greater than 3 but less than 7.

7. Could Terry's number be 2? yes no
8. Could Terry's number be 6? yes no
9. Could Terry's number be 3? yes no
10. Could Terry's number be 5 or 6? yes no

2
5

WHAT IS MY NUMBER?

Draw a ring around each correct answer.

1. My number is greater than 5.
   So, my number could be 4. true false

2. My number is 2 more than yours.
   So, your number is less than mine. true false

3. Our numbers cannot be the same.
   So, our numbers cannot both be 5. true false

4. Laurie's number is half as great as Simon's number.
   So, Simon's number is greater than Laurie's. true false

5. My number is greater than yours.
   So, your number could equal mine. true false

6. Jesse's number is 11.
   My number is less than Jesse's number.
   So, my number is less than 11. true false

Your number is 3.
No, that's your number

WHAT'S NOT HERE? ▼▼▼

Draw a ring around the word on each list that is *not* on the grid.

1.

FOUR
SIX
FIVE
HOUR
TIME
FIRST

A	F	I	R	S	T
H	O	U	R	I	I
F	U	V	E	X	M
T	R	V	A	C	E

2.

NINE
EIGHT
SIX
FOUR
FIVE
ONE
TWO
TEN

C	F	O	U	R	A
S	I	X	T	N	S
O	V	N	E	P	C
D	E	I	G	H	T
T	E	N	F	I	W
G	K	E	J	H	O

3.

TWENTY
NINE
FOOT
TWO
EVEN
YARD
NINETY
THIRTY
LESS

T	W	E	N	T	Y	P
W	Y	V	I	H	A	L
O	A	E	N	I	N	E
D	R	N	E	R	D	S
F	O	O	T	T	Y	S
A	R	D	Y	Y	A	R

MISSING ANSWERS

▼▼▼

One answer is missing in each window. Write the missing answers.

Example:

1 + 2 (6) 4 − 2
( ) 5 + 1 (3)

1 + 2 = 3
5 + 1 = 6
4 − 2 = 2

2 is missing

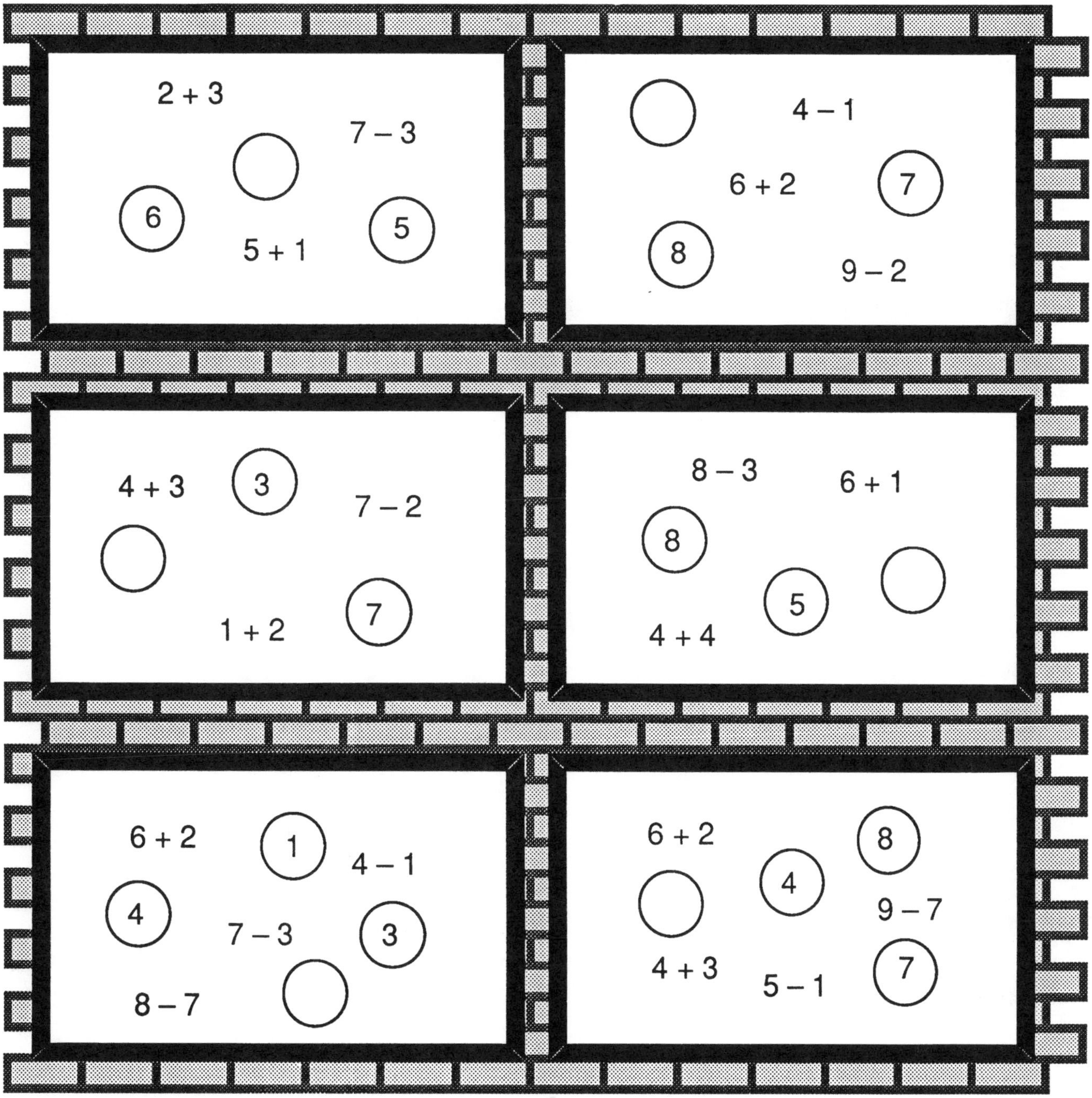

2 + 3
7 − 3
6
5 + 1
5
4 − 1
6 + 2
7
8
9 − 2
4 + 3
3
7 − 2
1 + 2
7
8 − 3
6 + 1
8
5
4 + 4
6 + 2
1
4 − 1
4
7 − 3
3
8 − 7
6 + 2
8
4
9 − 7
4 + 3
5 − 1
7

NUMBER PROBLEMS ▼▼▼

What value of ■ and ● make a number problem?
Remember: There can be more than one right answer.

1.

```
   ■
   2
+  ●
----
  10
```

■ = ____

● = ____

2.

```
   5
   ●
+  3
----
   ■
```

● = ____

■ = ____

3.

```
  16
+  ■
----
   ●
```

■ = ____

● = ____

4.

```
   2
   2
   ■
   2
+  ●
----
  10
```

■ = ____

● = ____

5.

```
  15
+ 1■
----
   ●
```

■ = ____

● = ____

6.

■ + ● = 17

■ = ____ ● = ____

7.

```
  15
+ 24
----
  ■●
```

■ = ____

● = ____

8.

```
  ■3
+ 2●
----
  49
```

■ = ____

● = ____

SMALLEST AND LARGEST ▼▼▼

For each box choose the smallest and write it in the chart below. Then choose the largest and write it below. Add your answers and compare.

1.	2.
7 + 5, 3 + 4, 8 + 2	6 – 1, 2 + 5, 9 – 3

3.	4.
4 – 1, 9 – 2, 3 + 8	11 – 5, 11 – 8, 11 – 3

5.	6.
13 + 3, 9 + 4, 17 – 11	18 – 5, 13 – 5, 15 – 5

7. SMALLEST

(1) ____________ = ______

(2) ____________ = ______

(3) ____________ = ______

(4) ____________ = ______

(5) ____________ = ______

(6) ____________ = ______

SUM = 32

8. LARGEST

(1) ____________ = ______

(2) ____________ = ______

(3) ____________ = ______

(4) ____________ = ______

(5) ____________ = ______

(6) ____________ = ______

SUM = 67

PICK A NUMBER

▼▼▼

Pick any number. Write this number in both boxes. Then do the steps from left to right. Pick a different number for each problem.

Example: [5] + 6 − 1 + 5 − 2 − [5] + 2 = (10)

1.	☐ + 6 − 1 + 5 − 2 − ☐ + 2 = ◯
2.	☐ + 6 − 1 + 5 − 2 − ☐ + 2 = ◯
3.	☐ + 6 − 1 + 5 − 2 − ☐ + 2 = ◯
4.	☐ + 12 − 3 + 4 − 11 − ☐ + 4 − 6 = ◯
5.	☐ + 12 − 3 + 4 − 11 − ☐ + 4 − 6 = ◯
6.	☐ + 12 − 3 + 4 − 11 − ☐ + 4 − 6 = ◯

Explain your answers to problems 4, 5, and 6: ____________________

____

____

CHANGE A WORD

▼▼▼

Add ⊕ or subtract ⊖ letters from the words to get a new word.

Example: FOUR ⊖ OUR ⊕ HIVE ⊖ H → ________
= F = FHIVE = FIVE

1.	TWO ⊖ O ⊕ E ⊖ W ⊕ N → ________
2.	NINTH ⊕ E ⊖ TH ⊕ TY → ________
3.	THINK ⊖ IN ⊖ K ⊕ R ⊕ EE → ________
4.	TWELVE ⊖ L ⊖ V ⊖ E ⊕ NTY → ________
5.	FOUR ⊖ U ⊕ T ⊕ Y → ________
6.	MILE ⊖ L ⊖ E ⊕ N ⊕ US → ________
7.	FOOT ⊖ T ⊖ O ⊕ U ⊕ R → ________
8.	SEVEN ⊕ IX ⊖ EVEN ⊕ TY → ________

ANSWERS

PART 1: PATTERNS

Page 2, Pattern Trains

1
2
3
4
5

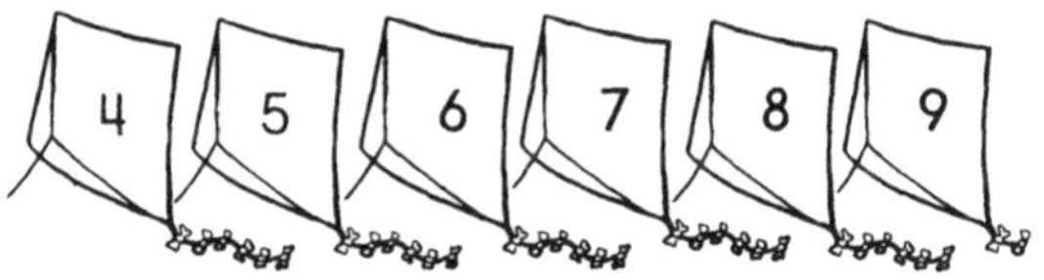
4
5
6
7
8
9

1
2
3
4
5
6
7

5
4
3
2
1

Page 3, Pattern Match

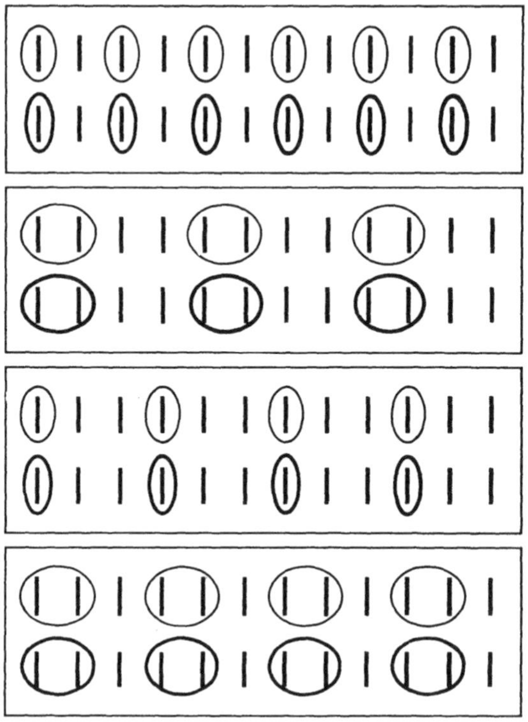

Page 4, One Hundred Apples

1	2	3	4	**5**	6	7	8	9	10
11	12	13	14	15	**16**	17	18	19	20
21	22	23	24	25	26	**27**	28	29	30
31	32	33	34	35	36	37	**38**	39	40
41	42	43	44	45	46	47	48	**49**	50
51	**52**	53	54	55	56	57	58	59	**60**
61	62	**63**	64	65	66	67	68	69	70
71	72	73	**74**	75	76	77	78	79	80
81	82	83	84	**85**	86	87	88	89	90
91	92	93	94	95	**96**	97	98	99	100

Page 5, Counting Circles (I)

There are 43 circles in all.

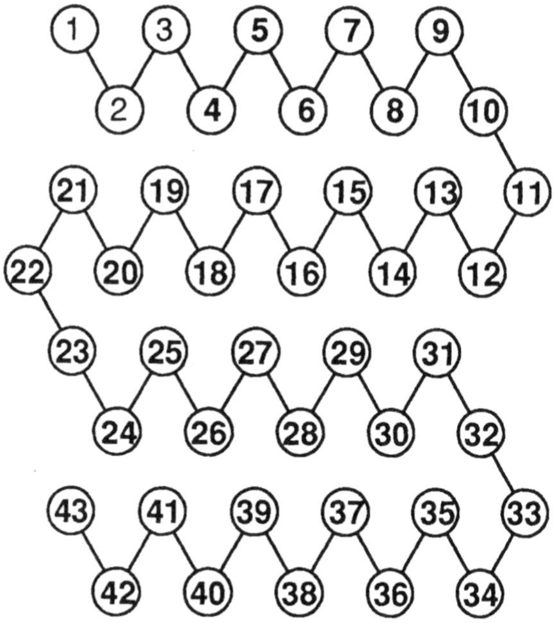
1 2 3 4 5 6 7 8 9 10
11 12 13 14 15 16 17 18 19 20 21
22 23 24 25 26 27 28 29 30 31 32
33 34 35 36 37 38 39 40 41 42 43

Page 6, Line Patterns

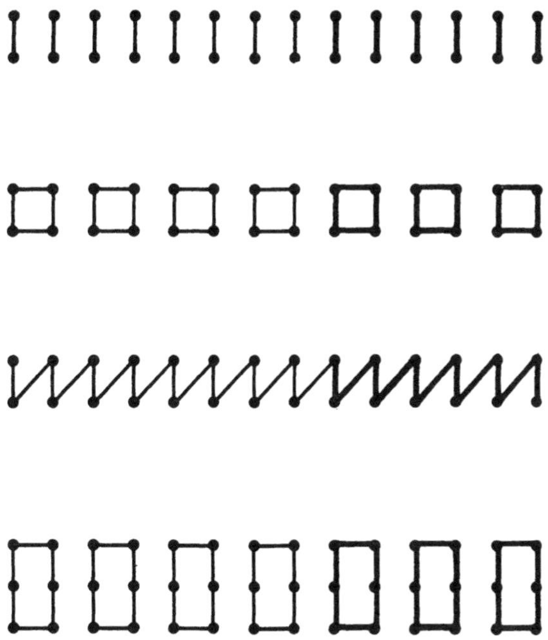

Page 7, More Line Patterns

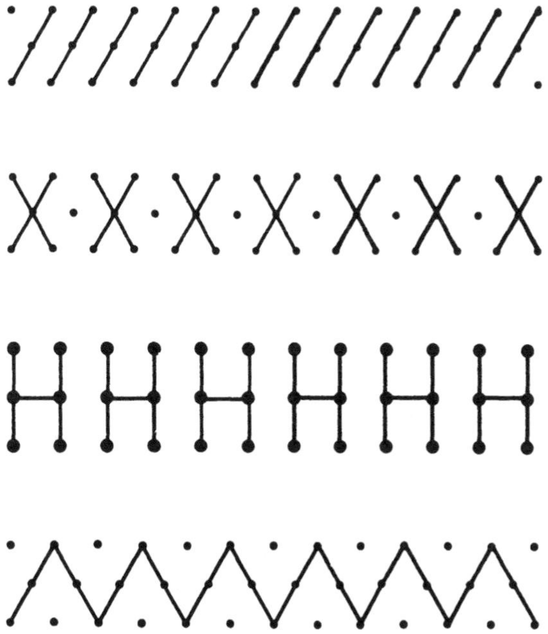

Page 8, Make a Match

1.
2.
3.
4.
5.
6.

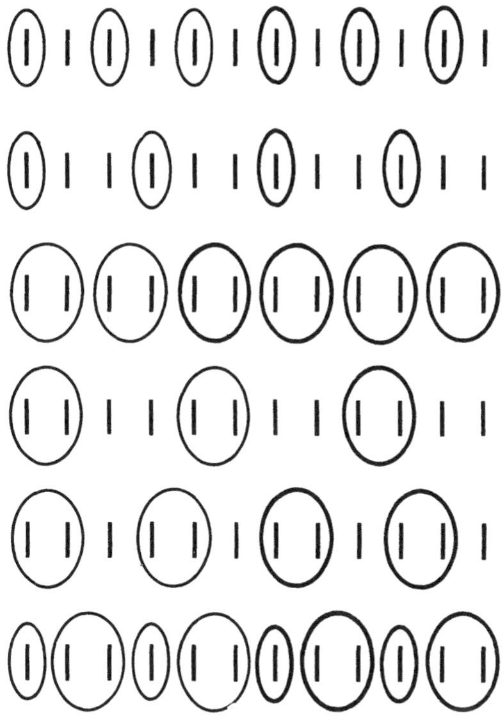

Page 9, Teddy's Chart

1.

1	2	3	4	5	6	7	8	9	10
11	12	13	14	15	16	17	18	19	20
21	22	23	24	25	26	27	28	29	30
31	32	33	34	35	36	37	38	39	40
41	42	43	44	45	46	47	48	49	50

2.

51	52	53	54	55	56	57	58	59	60
61	62	63	64	65	66	67	68	69	70
71	72	73	74	75	76	77	78	79	80
81	82	83	84	85	86	87	88	89	90
91	92	93	94	95	96	97	98	99	100

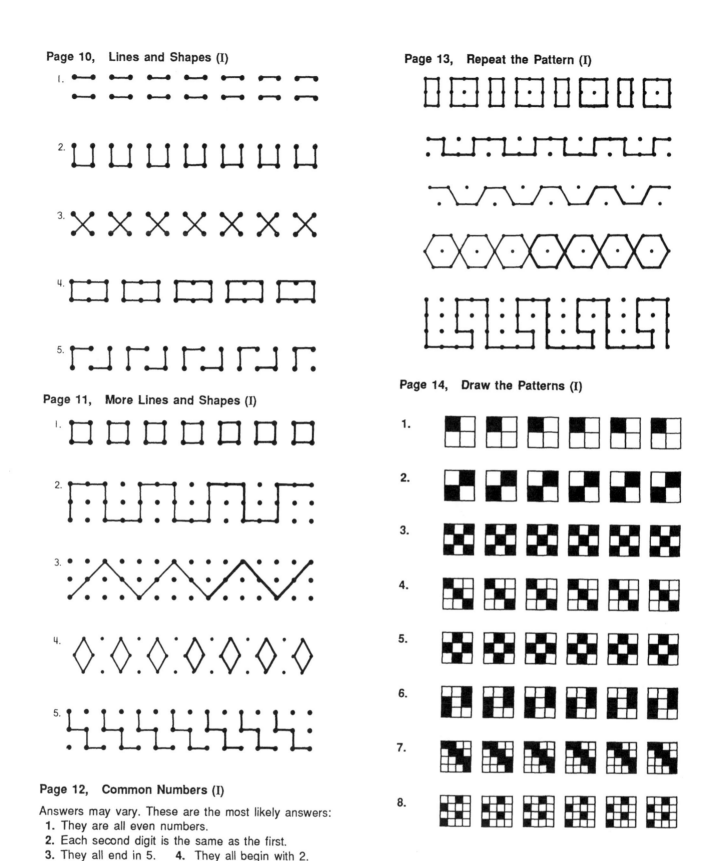

Page 10, Lines and Shapes (I)

1. 

2. 

3. 

4. 

5. 

Page 11, More Lines and Shapes (I)

1. 

2. 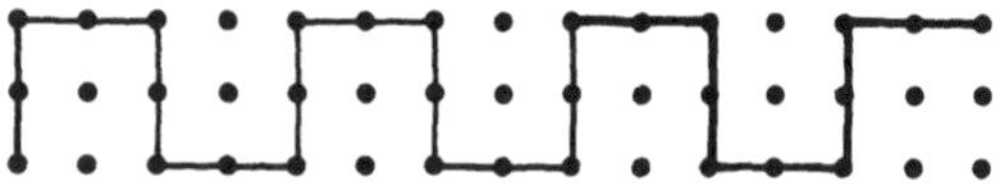

3. 

4. 

5. 

Page 12, Common Numbers (I)

Answers may vary. These are the most likely answers:

1. They are all even numbers.
2. Each second digit is the same as the first.
3. They all end in 5. **4.** They all begin with 2.

Page 13, Repeat the Pattern (I)

Page 14, Draw the Patterns (I)

1. 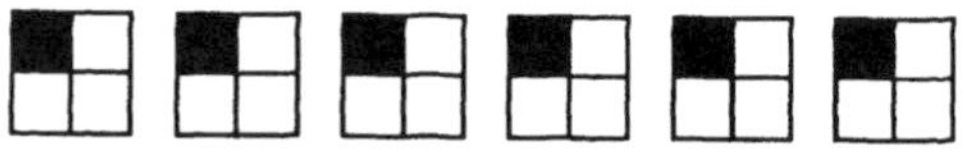

2. 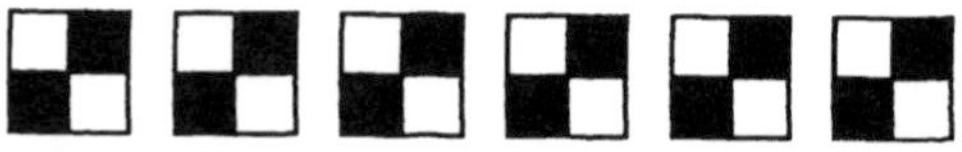

3. 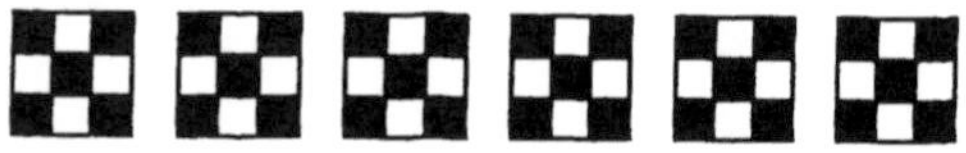

4. 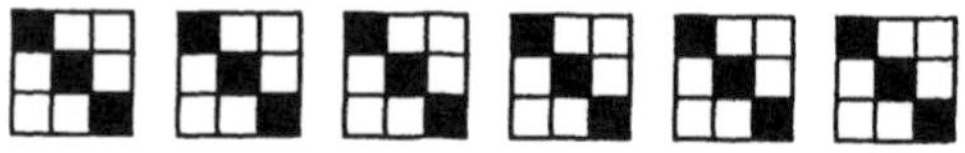

5. 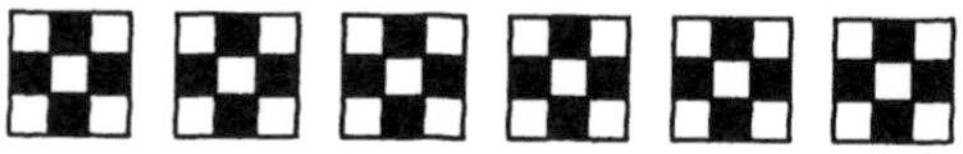

6. 

7. 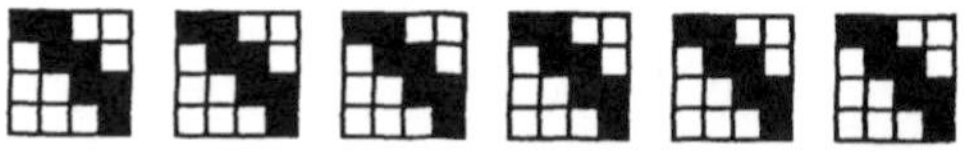

8. 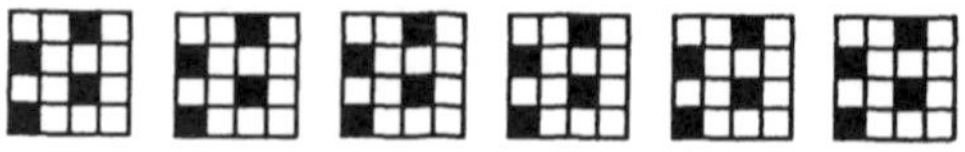

Page 16, One Hundred Hearts

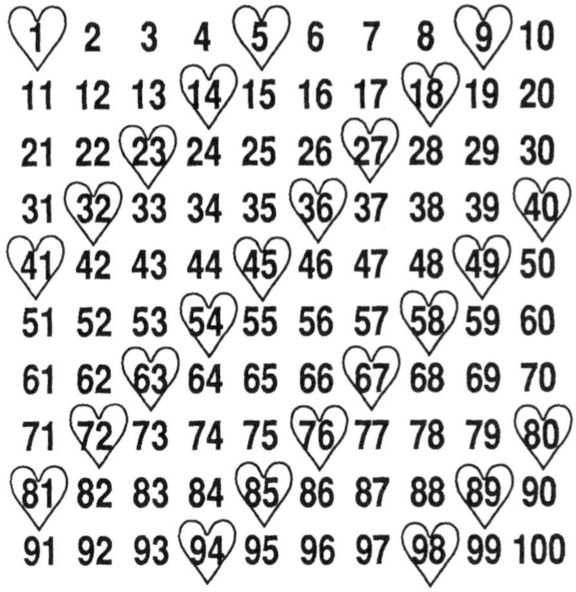
1 2 3 4 5 6 7 8 9 10
11 12 13 14 15 16 17 18 19 20
21 22 23 24 25 26 27 28 29 30
31 32 33 34 35 36 37 38 39 40
41 42 43 44 45 46 47 48 49 50
51 52 53 54 55 56 57 58 59 60
61 62 63 64 65 66 67 68 69 70
71 72 73 74 75 76 77 78 79 80
81 82 83 84 85 86 87 88 89 90
91 92 93 94 95 96 97 98 99 100

Page 17, Pattern Trains (II)

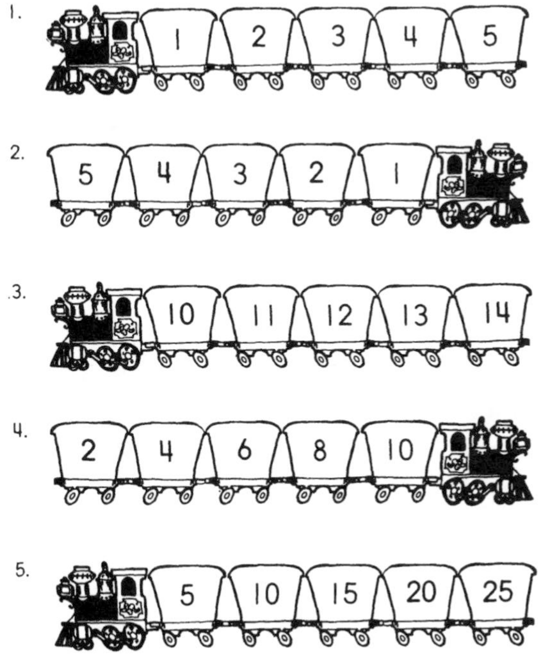
1.
1 2 3 4 5
2.
5 4 3 2 1
3.
10 11 12 13 14
4.
2 4 6 8 10
5.
5 10 15 20 25

Page 18, Lines and Shapes (II)

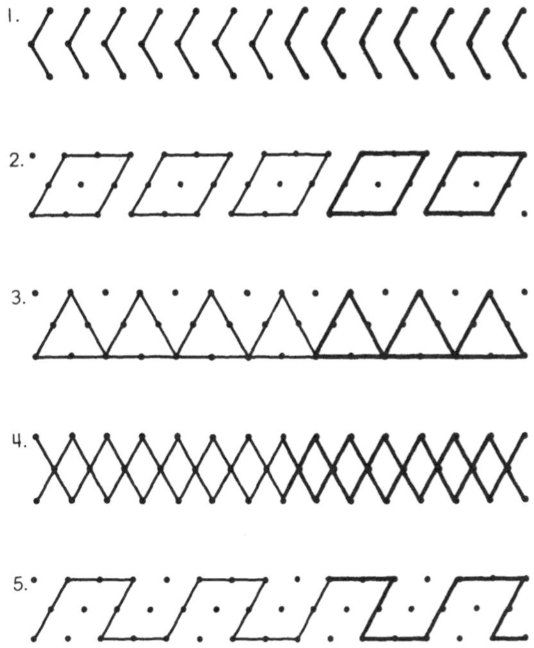
1.
2.
3.
4.
5.

Page 19, Mix and Match

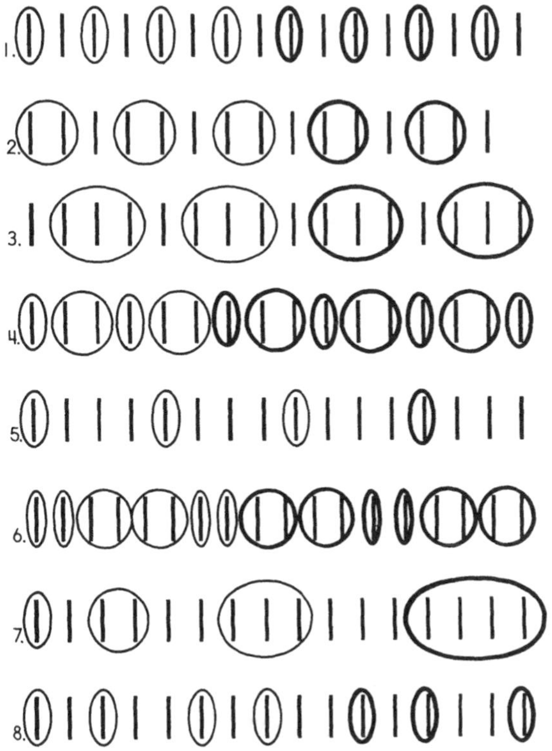
1.
2.
3.
4.
5.
6.
7.
8.

Page 20, Freddy's Chart

1.

1	2	3	4	5	6	7	8	9	10
11	12	13	14	15	16	17	18	19	20
21	22	23	24	25	26	27	28	29	30
31	32	33	34	35	36	37	38	39	40
41	42	43	44	45	46	47	48	49	50

The numbers show counting by fives.

2.

1	2	3	4	5	6	7	8	9	10
11	12	13	14	15	16	17	18	19	20
21	22	23	24	25	26	27	28	29	30
31	32	33	34	35	36	37	38	39	40
41	42	43	44	45	46	47	48	49	50

The numbers show counting by twos.

Page 21, More Lines and Shapes (II)

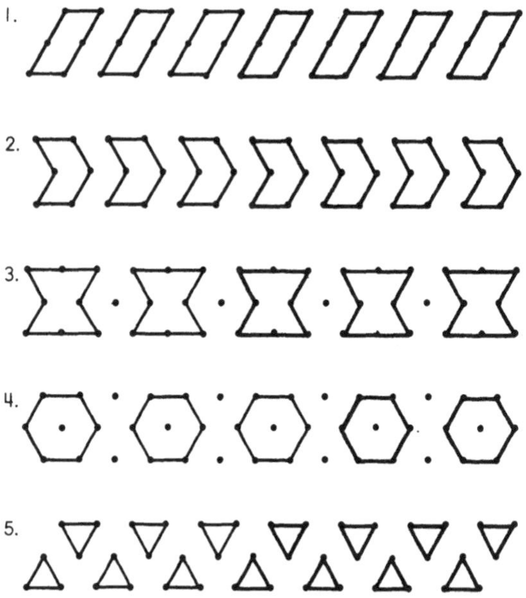
1.
2.
3.
4.
5.

Page 22, Trains and Chains (I)

1.

1 2 3 4 5 6 7

2.

10 9 8 7 6 5 4 3

3.
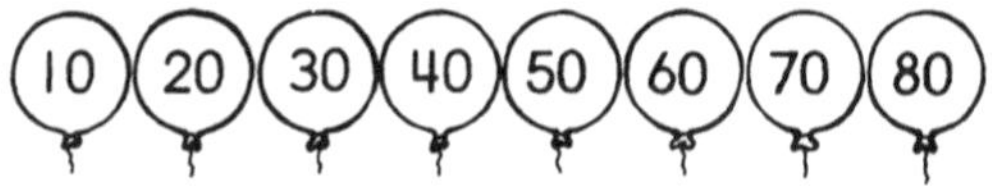
10 20 30 40 50 60 70 80

4.

11 12 13 14 15 16 17

5.

16 14 12 10 8 6 4 2

6.

5 10 15 20 25 30 35 40

Page 23, Counting Circles (II)

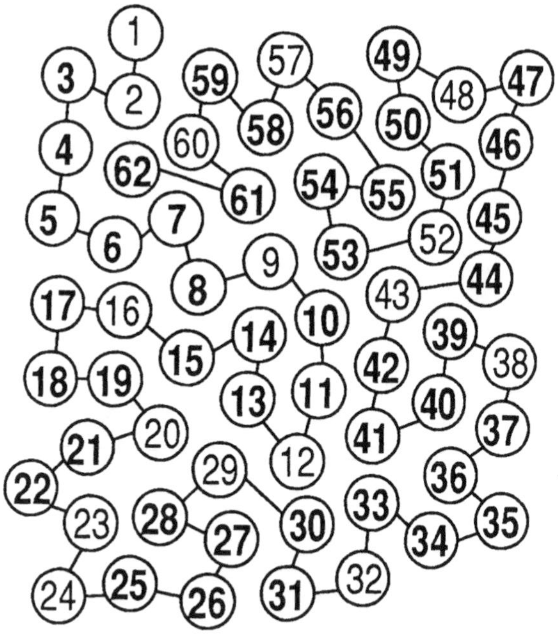

Page 24, Repeat the Pattern (II)

1. 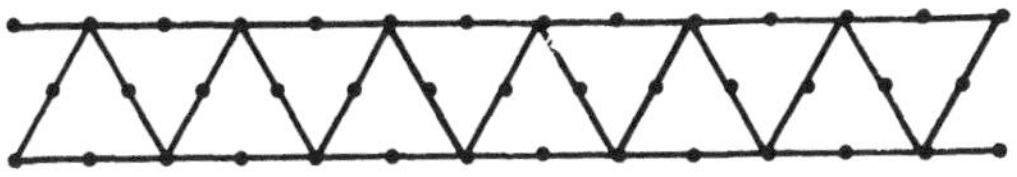

2. 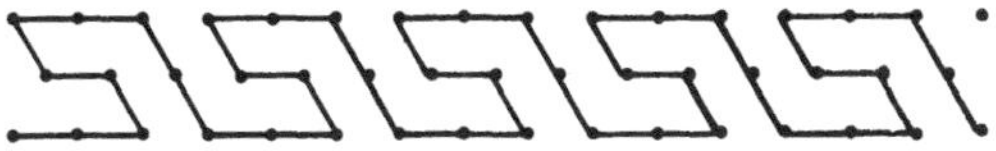

3. 

4. 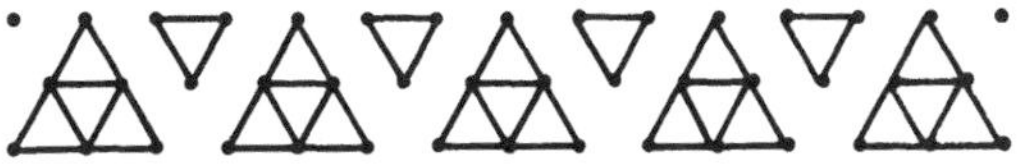

Page 25, Repeat the Pattern (III)

1. 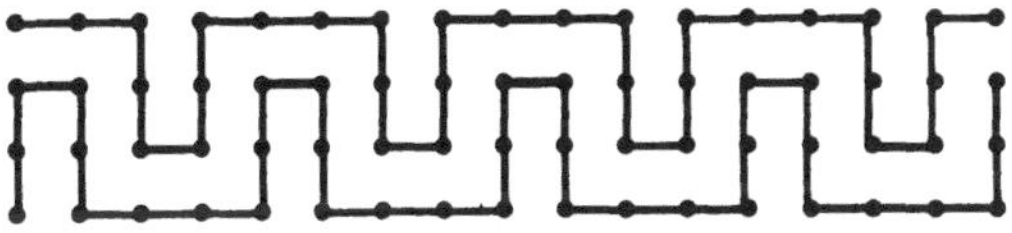

2. 

3. 

4. 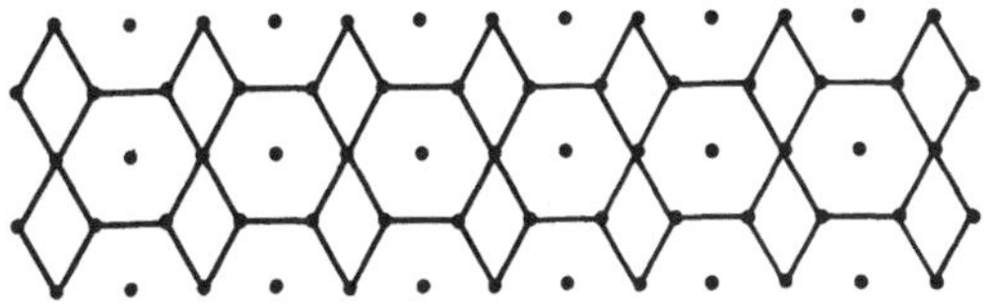

Page 26, Triangle Windows

1. 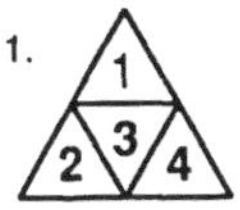
1
2 3 4

2. 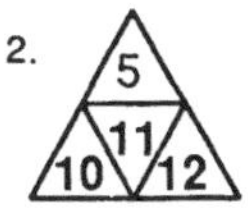
5
10 11 12

3. 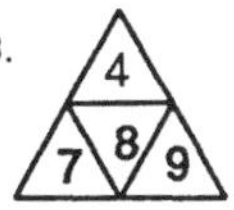
4
7 8 9

4. 
7
12 13 14

5. 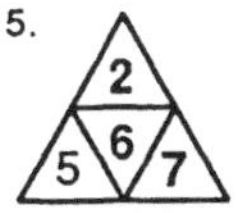
2
5 6 7

6. 
5 6 7

7. 
13 14 15

8. 
2 3 4
6 7 8

9. 
7 8 9
13 14 15

10. 
5 6 7
11 12 13

Page 27, Two at a Time

1. 5, 8, 13, 21 **2.** 6, 10, 16, 26, 42
3. 7, 11, 18, 29, 47 **4.** 9, 14, 23, 37, 60
5. 5, 8, 13, 21, 34, 55 **6.** 7, 12, 19, 31, 50, 81
7. 6, 10, 16, 26, 42, 68 **8.** 3, 5, 8, 13, 21, 34
9. 5, 10, 15, 25, 40, 65 **10.** Answers will vary.

Page 28, Dice Patterns

1. 

2. 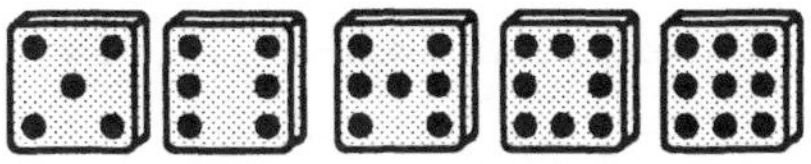

3. 

4. 

5. 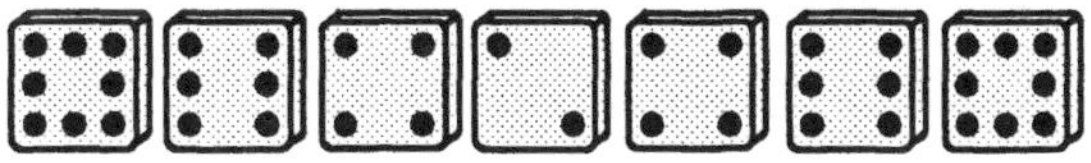

6. Answers will vary.

Page 29, Draw the Patterns (II)

1. 

2. 

3. 

4. 

5. 

6. 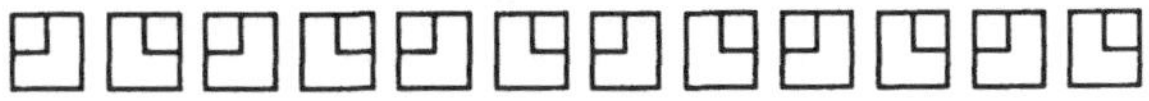

7. 

8. 

9. 

10. 

Page 30, Pattern Block

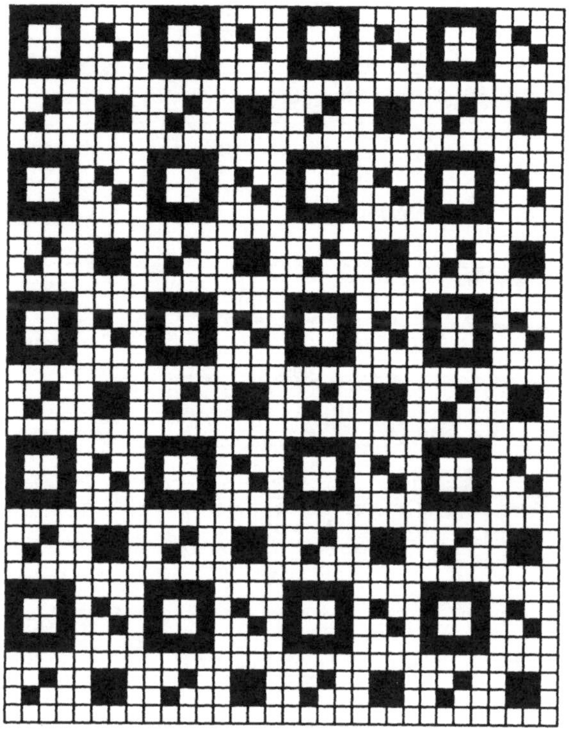

Page 32, One Hundred Suns

1	**2**	**3**	**4**	**5**	6	7	8	9	10
11	**12**	13	14	**15**	16	17	18	19	20
21	**22**	23	24	**25**	26	27	28	29	30
31	**32**	**33**	**34**	**35**	36	37	38	39	40
41	42	43	44	45	46	47	48	49	50
51	52	53	54	55	56	57	58	59	60
61	62	63	64	65	**66**	**67**	**68**	**69**	70
71	72	73	74	75	**76**	77	78	**79**	80
81	82	83	84	85	**86**	87	88	**89**	90
91	92	93	94	95	**96**	**97**	**98**	**99**	100

Explain the patterns you notice:

Answers will vary. One likely answer is: The numbers in the suns that go down increase by ten.

Page 33, Zeddy's Chart

1.

1	2	3	4	5	6	7	8	9	10
11	12	13	14	15	16	17	18	19	20
21	22	23	24	25	26	27	28	29	30
31	32	33	34	35	36	37	38	39	40
41	42	43	44	45	46	47	48	49	50

2.

1	2	3	4	5	6	7	8	9	10
11	12	13	14	15	16	17	18	19	20
21	22	23	24	25	26	27	28	29	30
31	32	33	34	35	36	37	38	39	40
41	42	43	44	45	46	47	48	49	50

What is the pattern of the missing numbers in chart 2?

They are multiples of 3.

Page 34, Trains and Chains (II)

1.

23 24 25 26 27 28 29 30

2.

73 74 75 76 77 78 79 80 81

3.

3 6 9 12 15 18 21

4.

1 1 2 2 3 3 4 4

5.

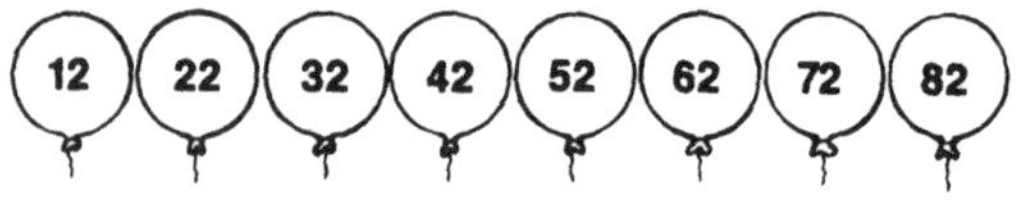
12 22 32 42 52 62 72 82

6.

10 20 30 40 50 60 70

Page 35, Number Chain

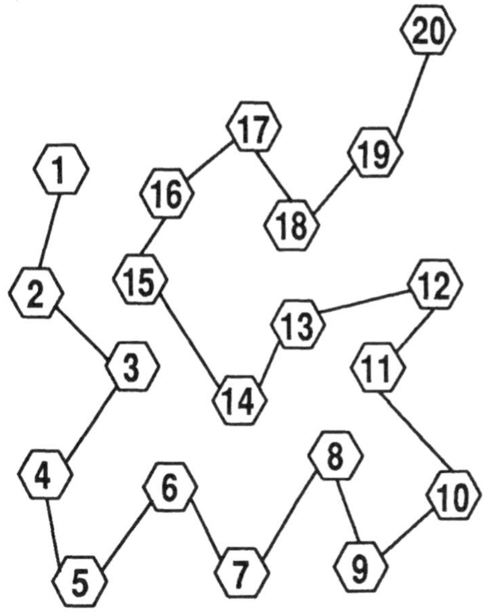

Page 36, Number Patterns

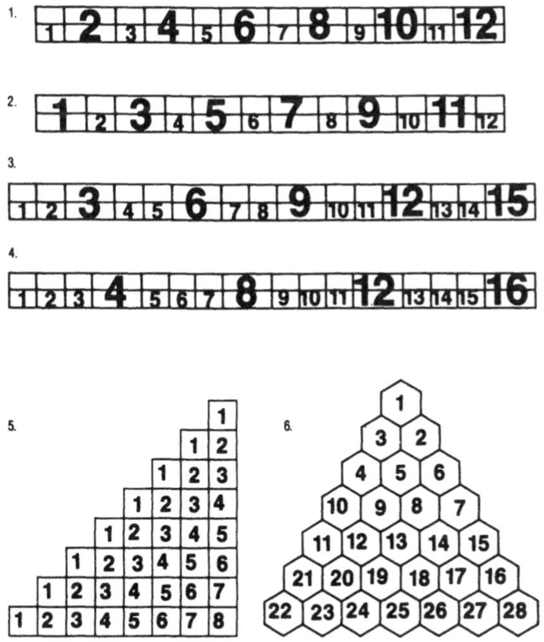

Page 37, Common Numbers (II)

Answers may vary. These are the most likely answers:

1. They are all even numbers.
2. They are all odd numbers.
3. The two digits in each number total 10.
4. Each first digit is two times the second.

Page 38, Shape Patterns

Answers may vary. The most likely answers are:

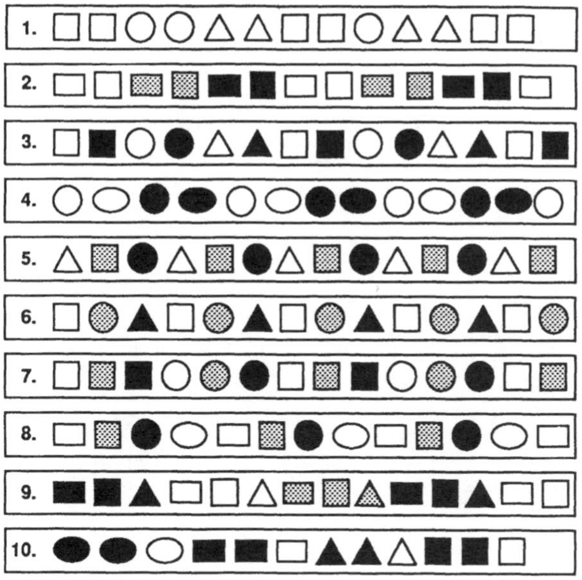

Explain one of the patterns here:

Answers will vary. For example: In problem 3, there are two of every shape, and the second shape of each pair is black. Also, the sequence of shapes runs squares, circles, triangles.

Page 39, Number Triangles

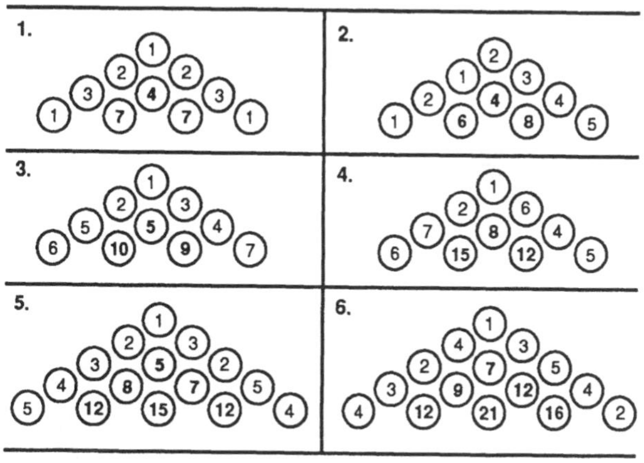

7. Answers will vary.

Page 40, Mailbox Patterns

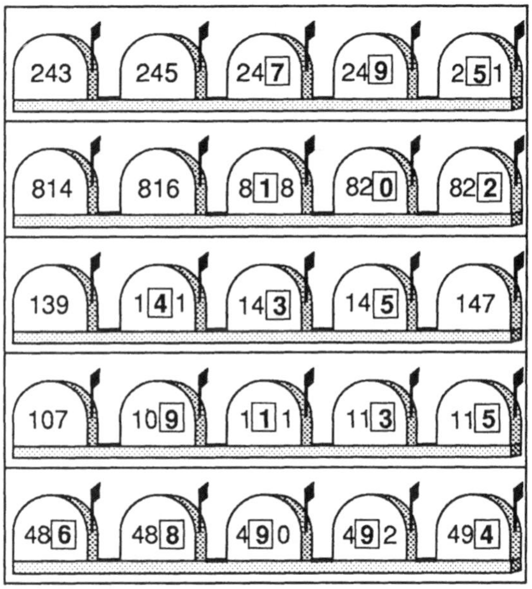
243 245 247 249 251
814 816 818 820 822
139 141 143 145 147
107 109 111 113 115
486 488 490 492 494

Page 41, Square Windows

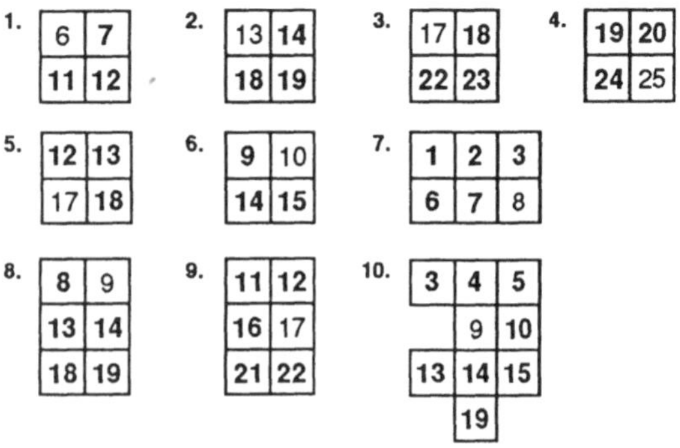
1. 6 7 / 11 12
2. 13 14 / 18 19
3. 17 18 / 22 23
4. 19 20 / 24 25
5. 12 13 / 17 18
6. 9 10 / 14 15
7. 1 2 3 / 6 7 8
8. 8 9 / 13 14 / 18 19
9. 11 12 / 16 17 / 21 22
10. 3 4 5 / 9 10 / 13 14 15 / 19

Page 42, Count and Check

Answers may vary. The most likely answers are:

1.	1 2 3 1 2 3 1 2 3 1 2 3 1 2 3 1 2 3 1
2.	1 2 1 1 2 1 1 1 2 1 1 1 1 2 1 1 1 1 1 2
3.	5 1 5 5 1 5 5 5 1 5 5 5 5 1 5 5 5 5
4.	3 6 4 5 3 6 4 5 3 6 4 5 3 6 4 5 3 6 4 5
5.	0 1 0 0 2 0 0 0 3 0 0 0 0 4 0 0 0 0 0 5
6.	3 9 3 3 8 3 3 3 7 3 3 3 3 6 3 3 3 3 3
7.	1 2 3 1 3 4 1 4 5 1 5 6 1 6 7 1 7 8 1 8
8.	0 9 1 1 8 2 2 2 7 3 3 3 3 6 4 4 4 4 4
9.	9 0 8 8 1 7 7 7 2 6 6 6 6 3 5 5 5 5 5
10.	1 1 2 1 2 3 1 2 3 4 2 2 3 2 3 4 2 3 4

Page 43, The Same Difference

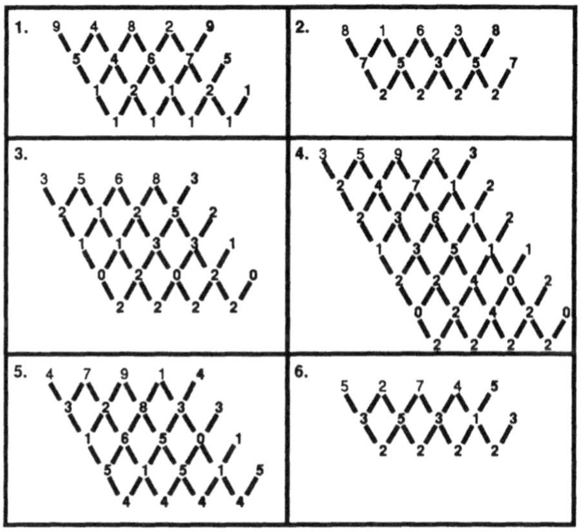

Page 44, What Next?

1. 9, 8, 13 **2.** 7, 9, 10 **3.** 3, 4, 6 **4.** 7, 16, 27
5. 36, 40, 60 **6.** 5, 7, 8 **7.** Answers will vary.

Page 45, Follow the Arrows

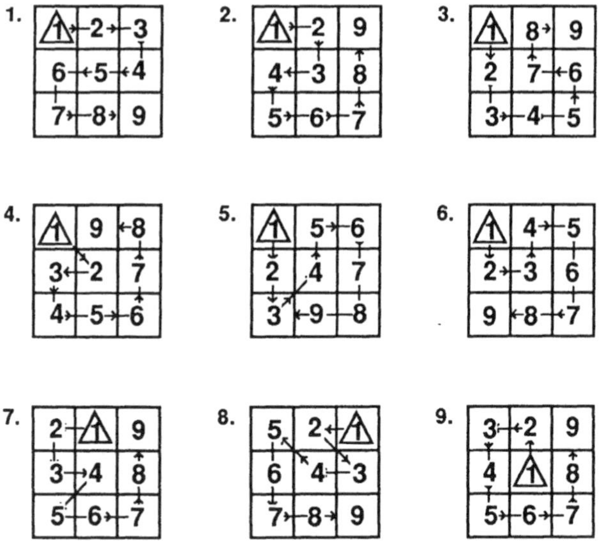

Page 46, Same Sum?

The numbers students draw a ring around will vary. But the sums for each row will be the same.

1. 24 **2.** 24 **3.** 24 **4.** 33 **5.** 33 **6.** 33
7. 39 **8.** 39 **9.** 39

Page 47, Draw the Patterns (III)

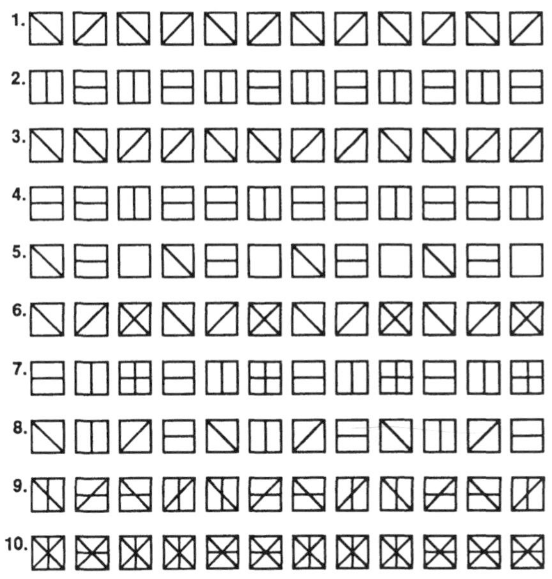
1.
2.
3.
4.
5.
6.
7.
8.
9.
10.

PART 2: IMAGERY

Page 52, Same Shapes

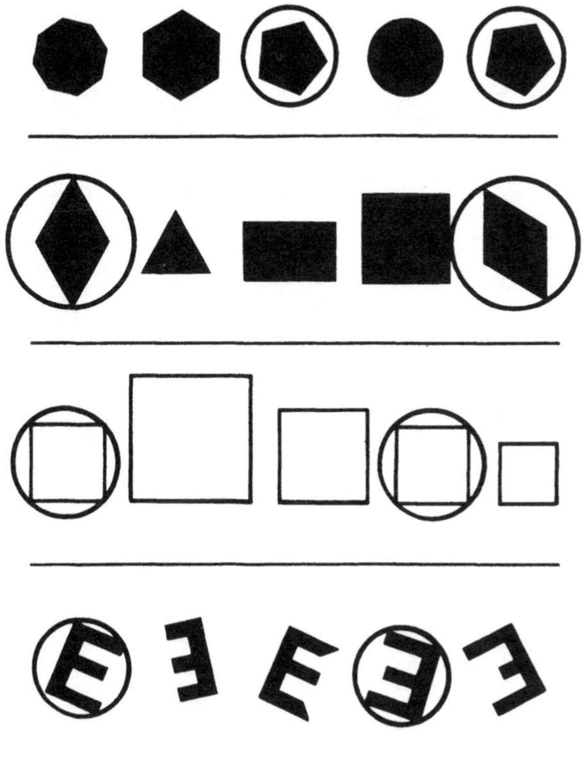

Page 53, Different Shapes

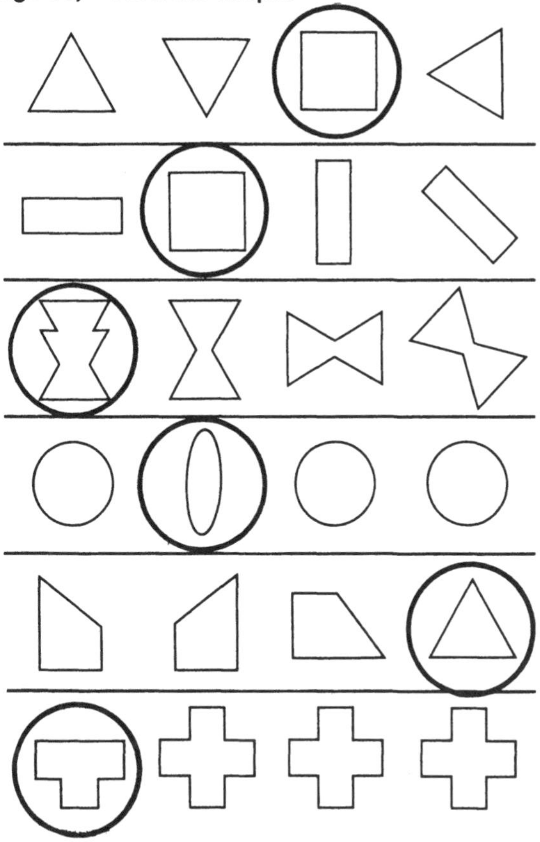

Page 54, Cat Match

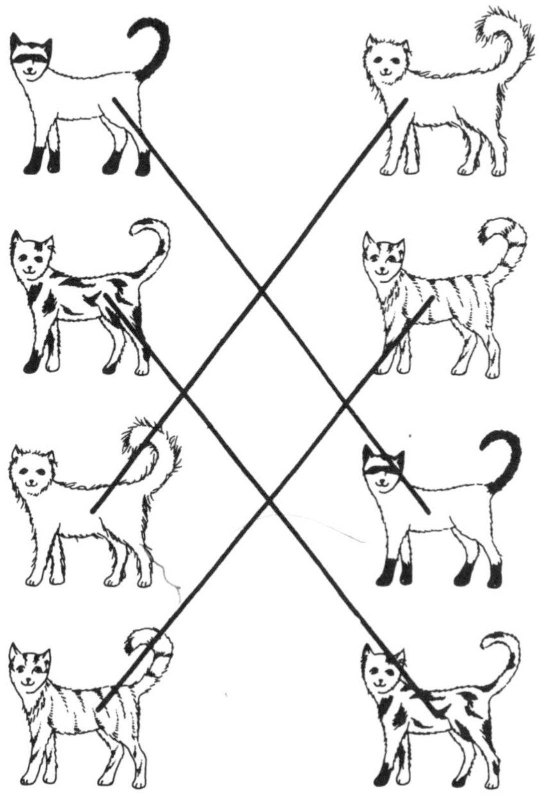

Page 55, **The Best Fit**

Page 57, **Dot Design (I)**

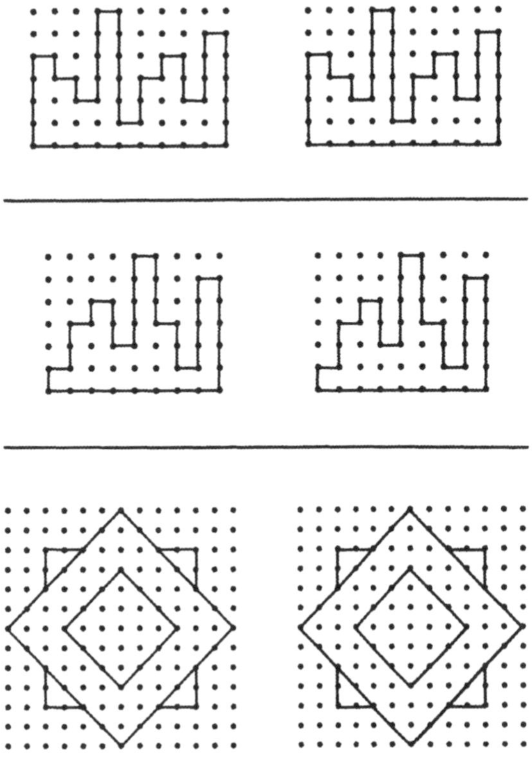

Page 58, **Dots Right**

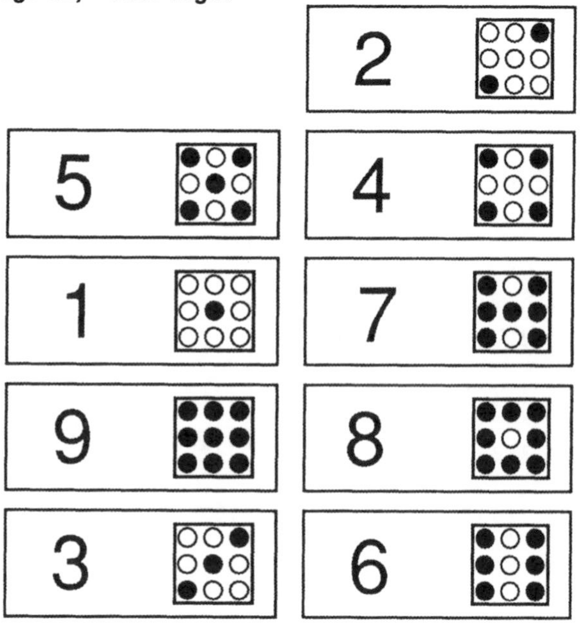
2
5
4
1
7
9
8
3
6

Page 59, **Color the Shapes (I)**

Page 60, What's the Same?

1. A, C **2.** B, E **3.** E

4.

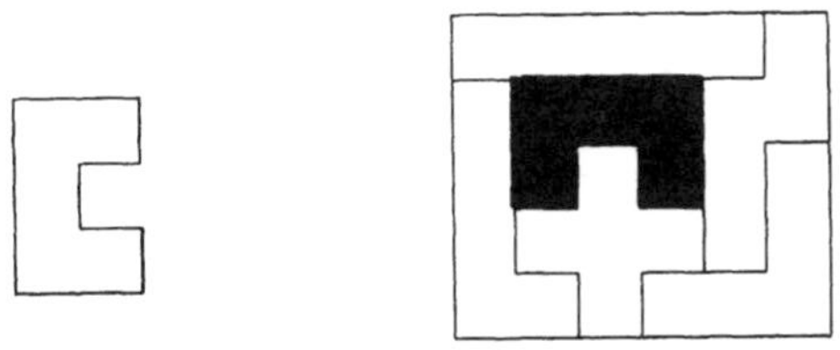

Page 62, Circle Match

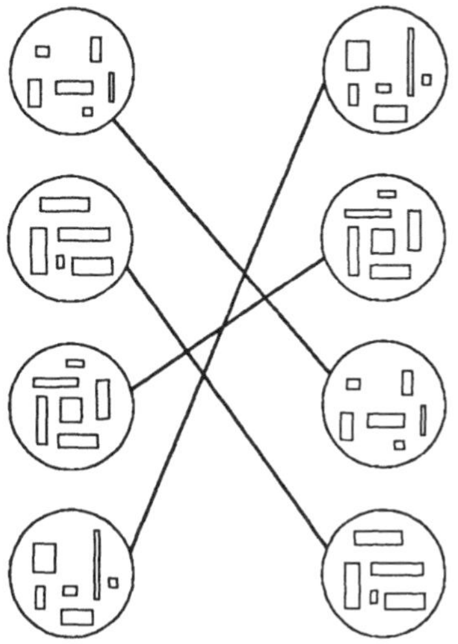

Page 63, Dot Design (II)

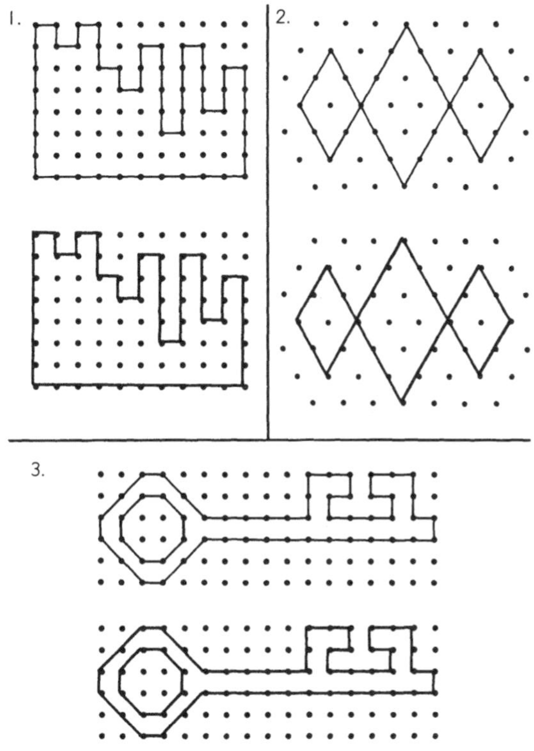
1.
2.
3.

Page 64, Color Each Shape

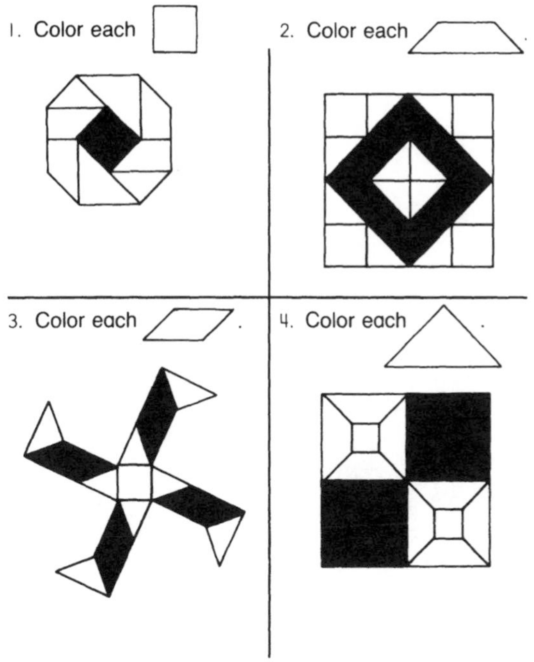
1. Color each
2. Color each
3. Color each
4. Color each

Page 65, Missing Piece (I)

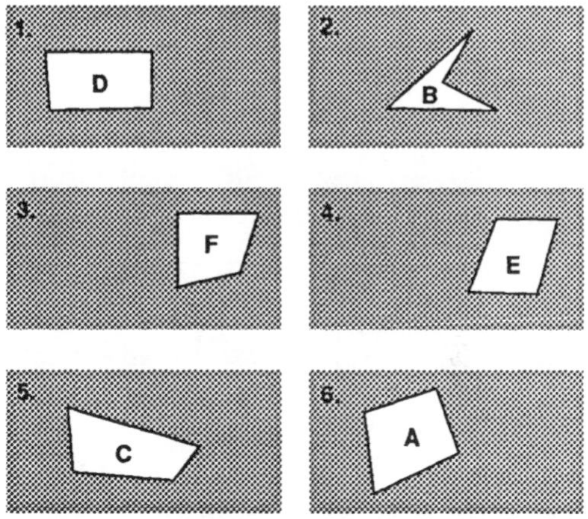
1.
D
2.
B
3.
F
4.
E
5.
C
6.
A

Page 66, Rectangle Match

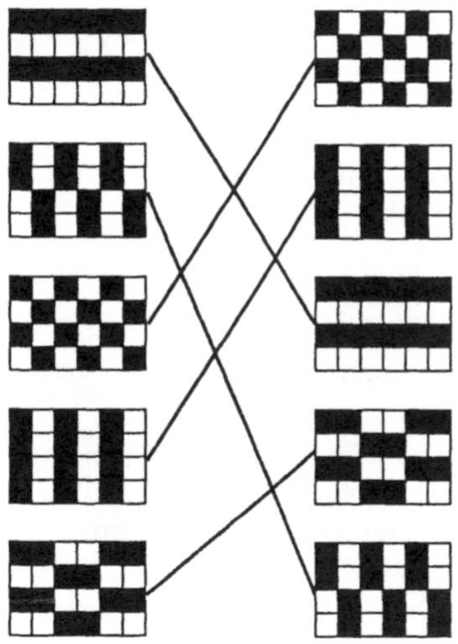

Page 67, Color the Shapes (II)

Page 68, What's Different?

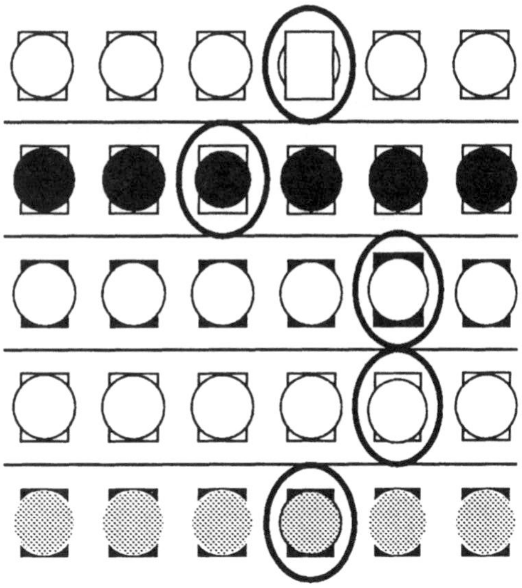

Page 69, Surprise Packages

The order of the answers may vary: A and F, B and H, C and G, D and E.

Page 70, Cartoon Pairs

1. One can is larger. The fish is shaded on one label.
2. One is a pair of sunglasses.
3. One fish bowl has a castle and sand at the bottom.
4. The times are different on the watches.
5. The puppets face different directions.
6. One hippo has no teeth.
7. The laces on one rollerskate are dark.
8. There is an extra pocket on one jacket.

Page 71, More Dot Designs (I)

Page 72, Match the Shapes

1. A, C **2.** A, E **3.** B

4.

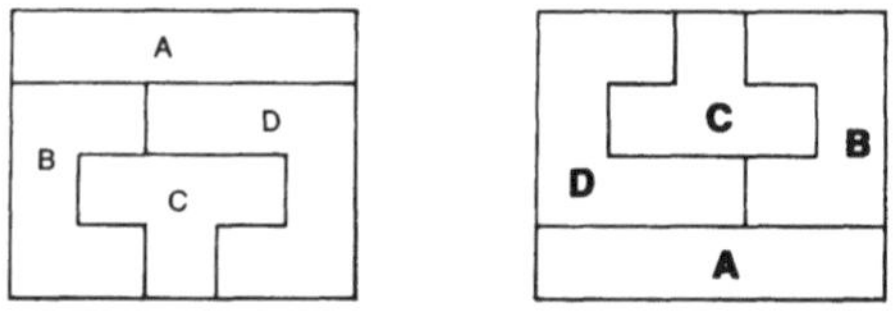
A
B
C
D
C
D
B
A

Page 73, Find the Shape

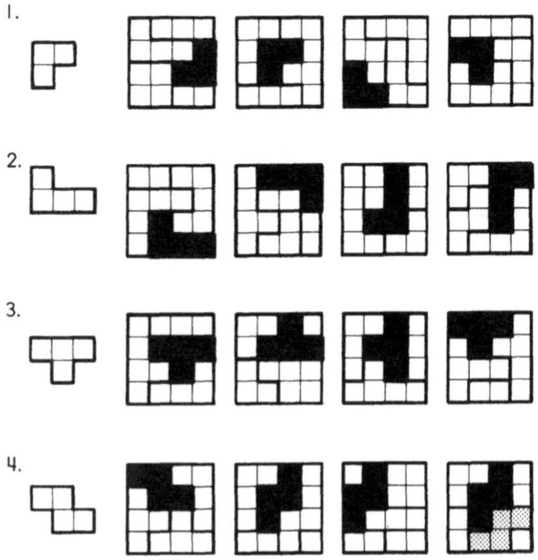
1.
2.
3.
4.

Page 76, Turned Shapes (I)

C
E
G
B
D
A
F

Page 77, Turned Shapes (II)

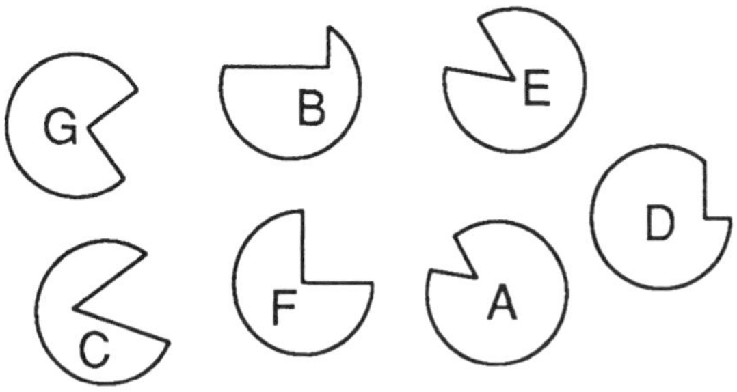
G
B
E
D
C
F
A

Page 78, What's My Design?

1.

A B C D E F

2.

3.

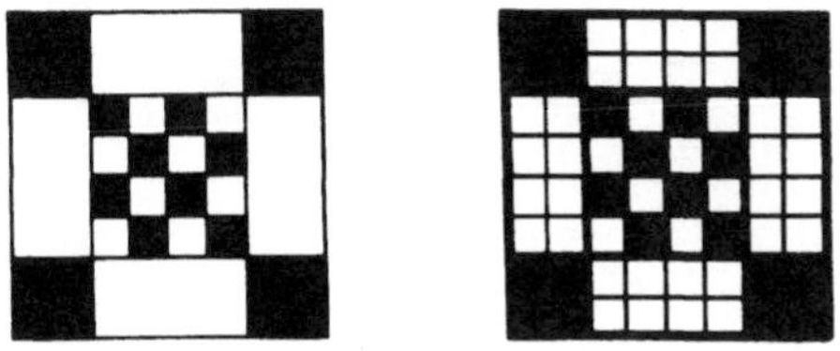

Page 79, Connect the Dots

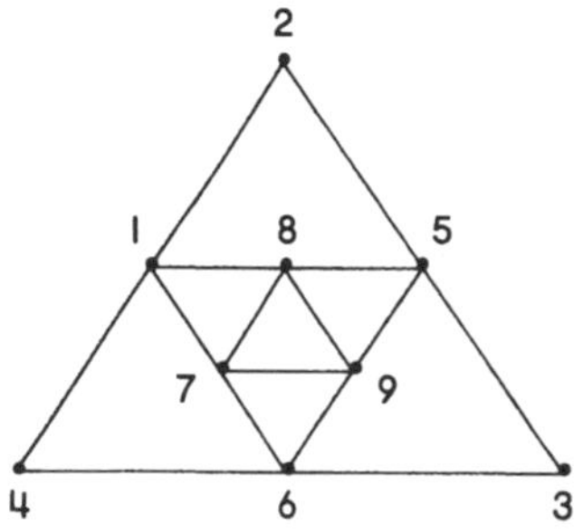
2
1
8
5
7
9
4
6
3

There are nine triangles in all.
(Accept any answers that state from four to nine triangles.)

Page 80, Different Strokes

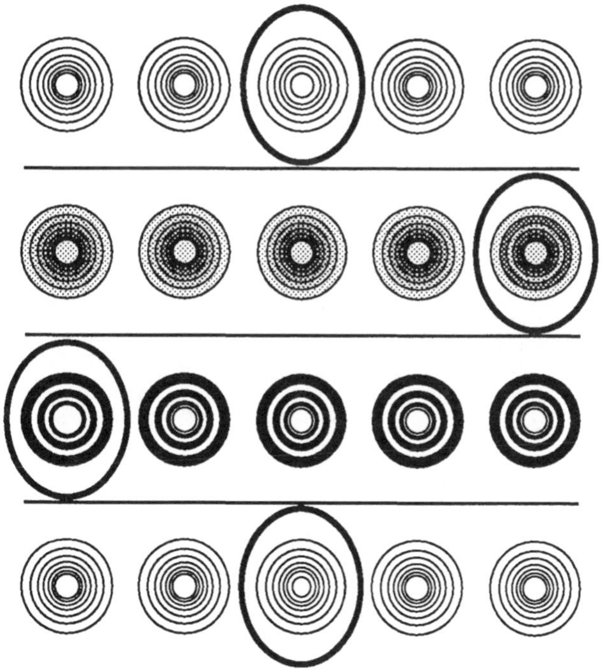

Page 81, Missing Piece (II)

1. E and F **2.** A and B **3.** D and D
4. F and C **5.** C and B **6.** E and A

Page 82, Triangle Match

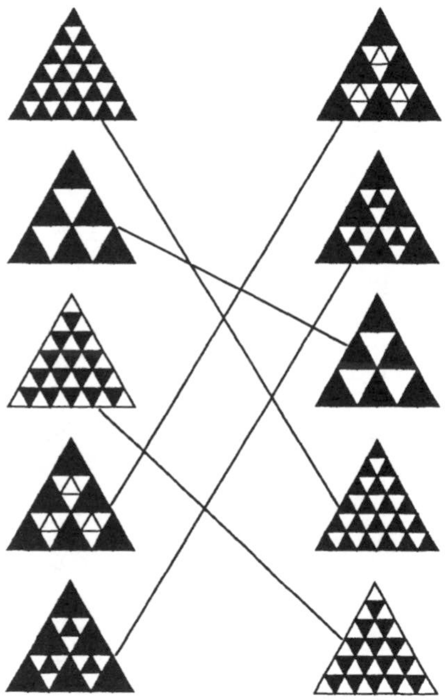

Page 83, Calculator Numbers

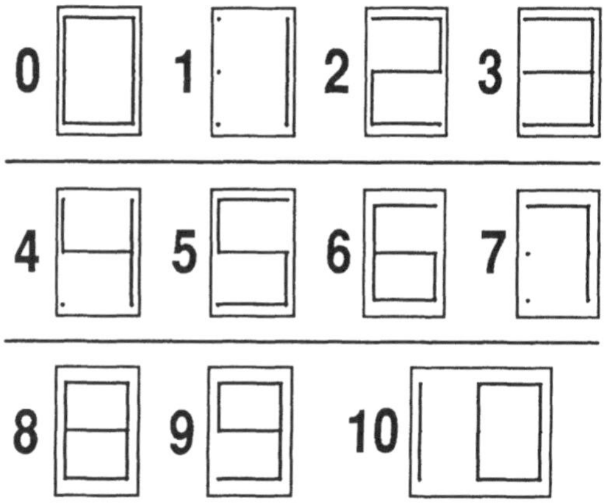
0
1
2
3
4
5
6
7
8
9
10

Page 84, Map Paths (I)

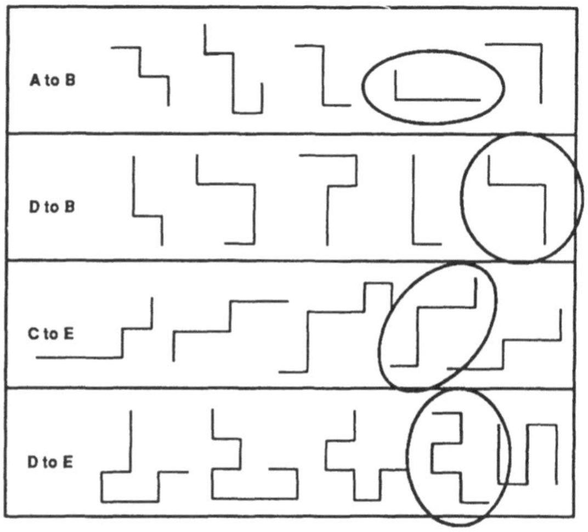
A to B
D to B
C to E
D to E

Page 86, Hexagon Match

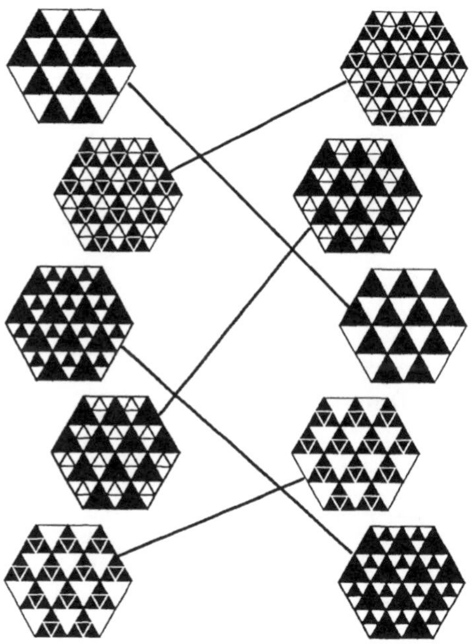

Page 87, Different Designs

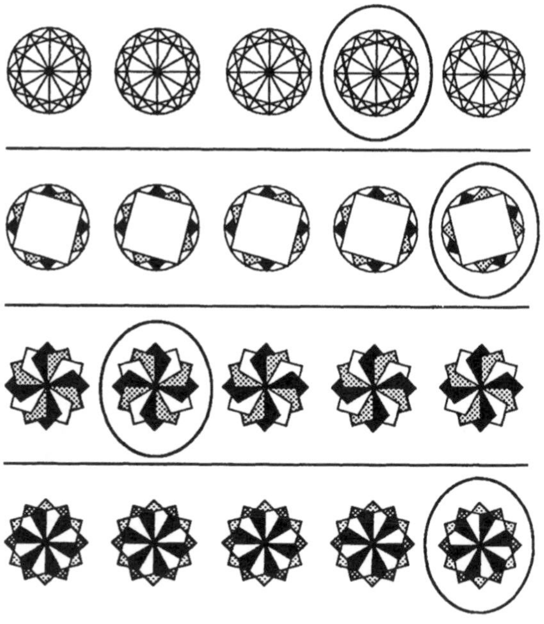

Page 88, More Dot Designs (II)

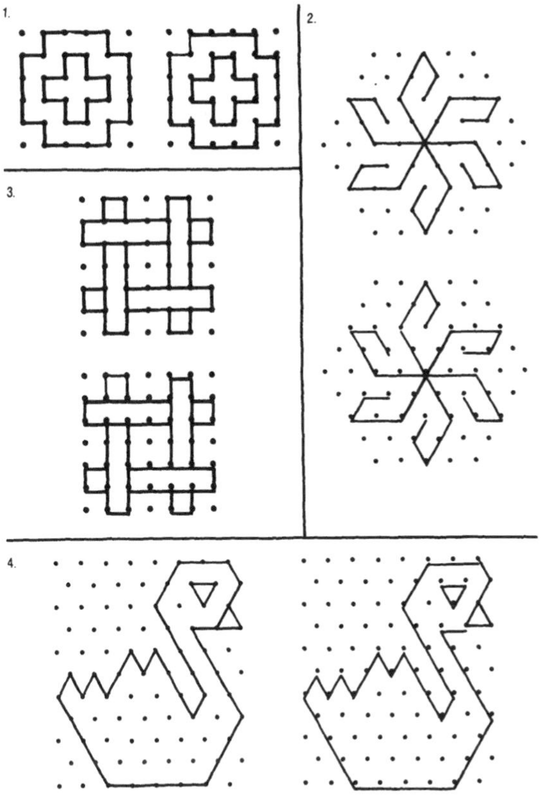
1.
2.
3.
4.

Page 89, Color the Design

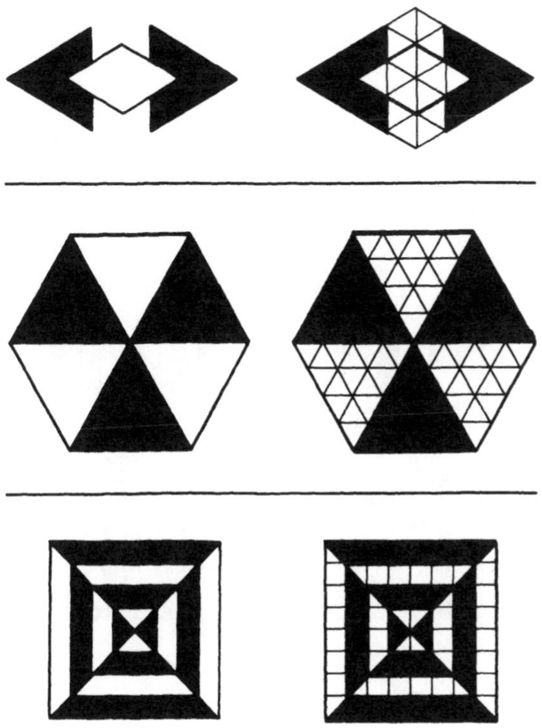

Page 90, Shape Match

1. A **2.** B **3.** C **4.** B

Page 92, Divided Shapes

1.

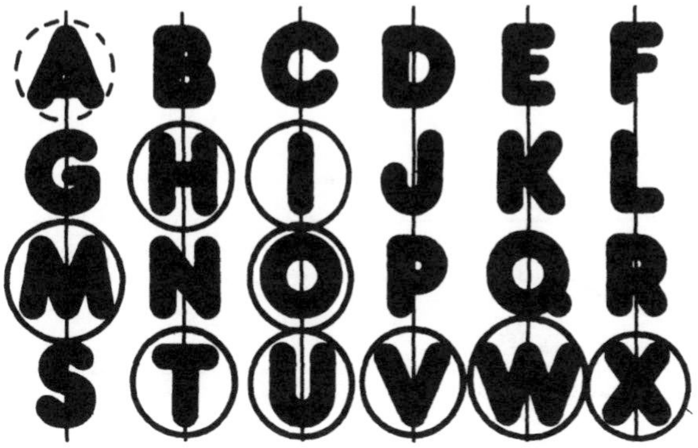
A B C D E F
G H I J K L
M N O P Q R
S T U V W X

2.

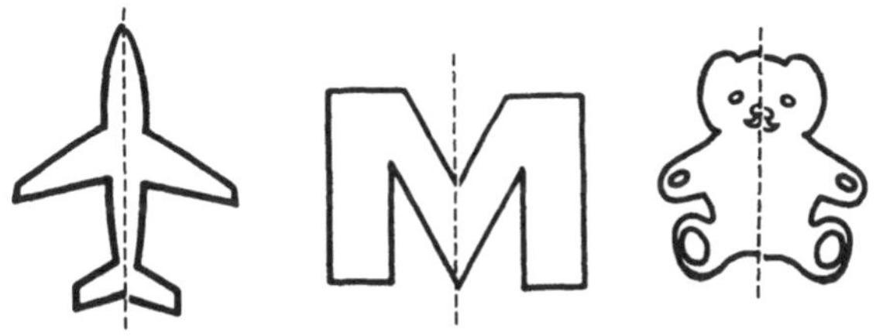
M

3.

Page 93, The Same Design

1. D **2.** E, H
3.

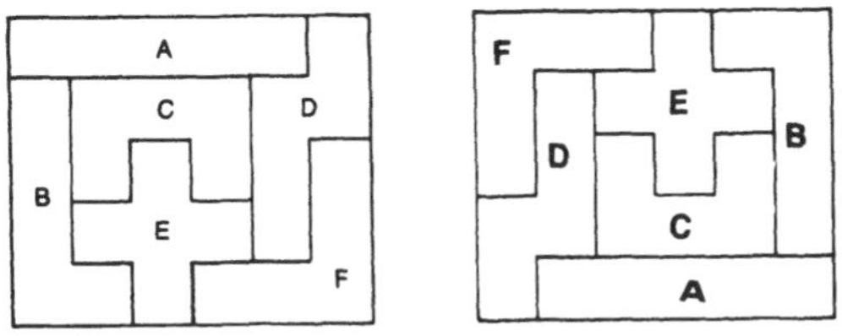
A
C
D
B
E
F
F
E
B
D
C
A

Page 94, Missing Piece (III)

1. E and F **2.** D and A **3.** A and D
4. C and E **5.** B and C **6.** F and B

Page 95, How Many Shapes?

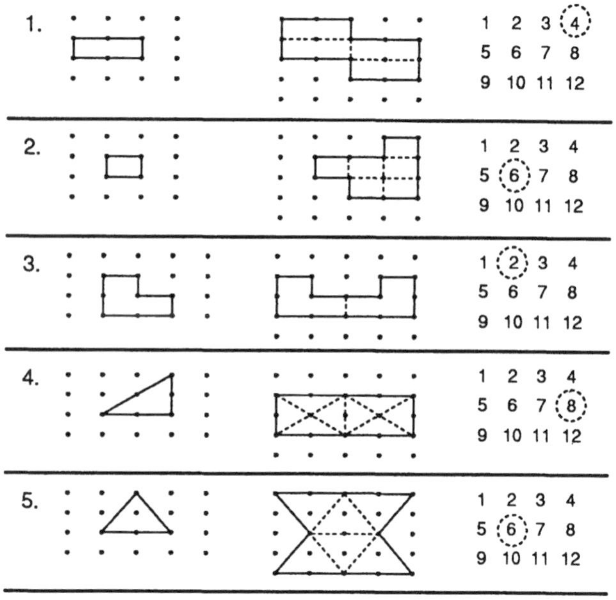
1.
1 2 3 4
5 6 7 8
9 10 11 12
2.
1 2 3 4
5 6 7 8
9 10 11 12
3.
1 2 3 4
5 6 7 8
9 10 11 12
4.
1 2 3 4
5 6 7 8
9 10 11 12
5.
1 2 3 4
5 6 7 8
9 10 11 12

Page 96, Letter Perfect

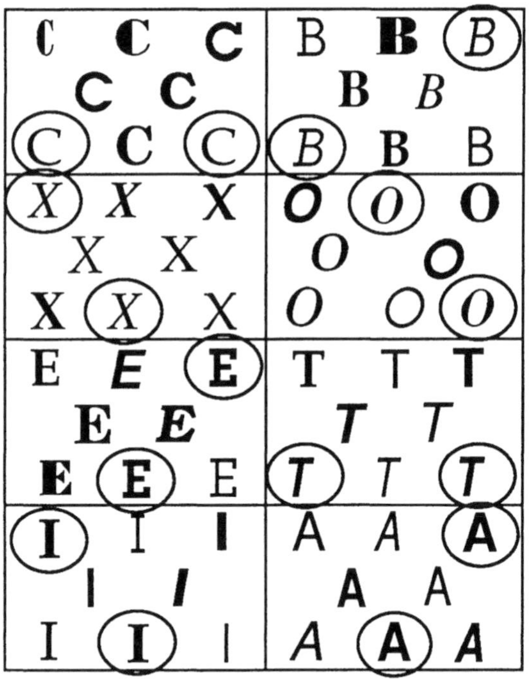

Page 97, Match Up

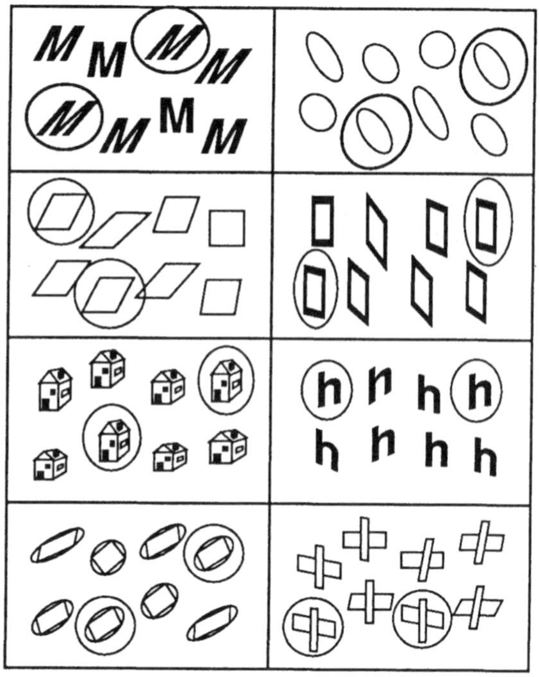

Page 99, Shortest Book

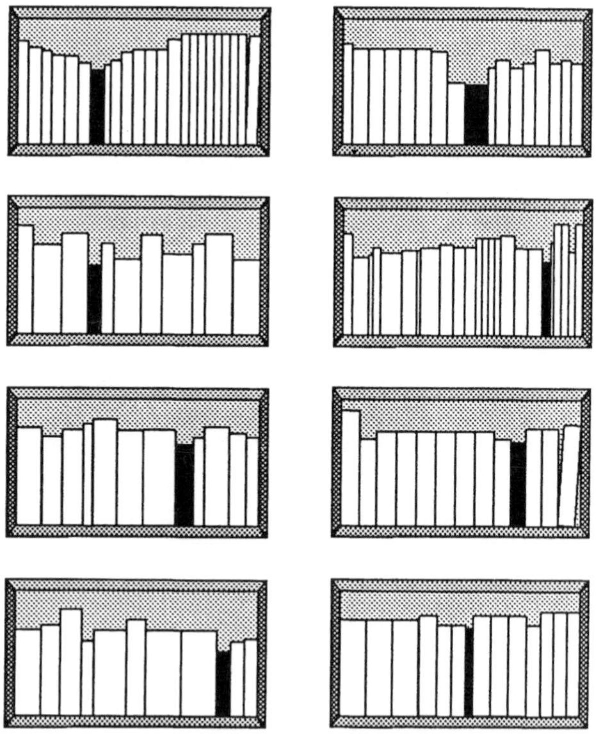

Page 100, Map Routes

1. School to Park	11 → 23 → 82 → 57	19 → 57
	11 → 23	19 → 23 → 82
2. School to Library	11 → 23 → 19	19 → 23 → 82
	19 → 57	19
3. Farm to Park	19 → 11	19 → 23
	57 → 82	57
4. Farm to School	57 → 82 → 23	19
	57 → 5	19 → 23

Page 101, Map Paths (II)

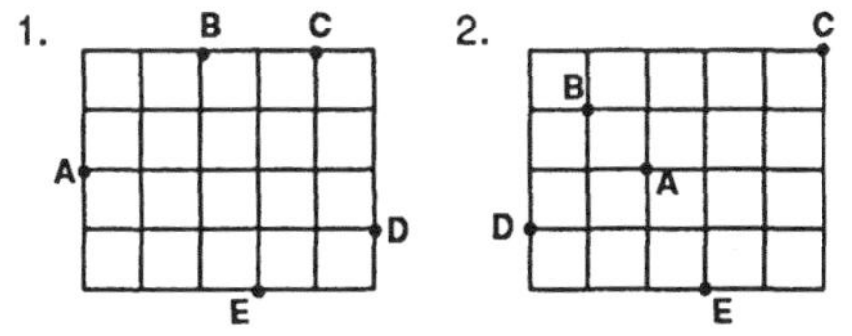
1.
B
C
A
D
E
2.
C
B
A
D
E

Page 105, Picture Logic

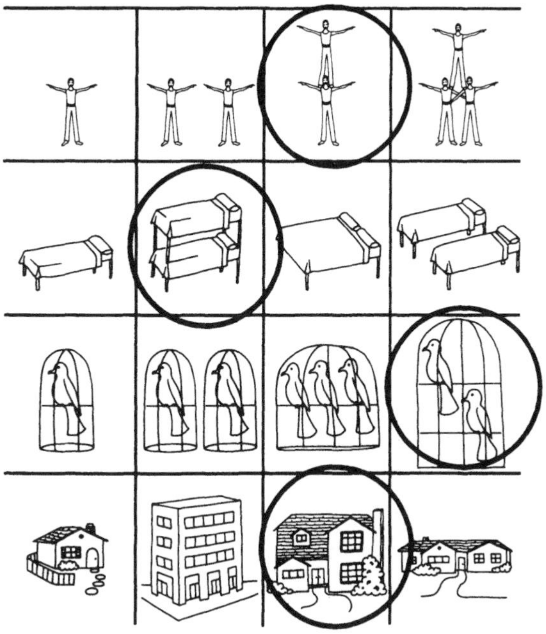

PART 3: LOGIC

Page 104, Dog and Puppy

Page 106, Lions, Horses, and Bears

B. 1 **C.** 4 **D.** 2 **E.** 3

Page 107, A Dog's Logic

A. 5 **B.** 4 **C.** 1 **D.** 8

Page 108, Logic Butterflies

A. 4 **B.** 3 **C.** 3 **D.** 2 **E.** 6

Page 109, Flowers and Snowflakes

A. 4 **B.** 2 **C.** 3 **D.** 2 **E.** 9

Page 110, Tree Logic Chart

	Tally	Number
How many trees are in the small circle?	II	2
How many trees are in the big circle?	III	3
How many trees are *not* in a circle?	II	2
How many trees are there in all?	~~IIII~~ II	7

Page 111, Leaf Logic Chart

	Tally	Number
How many leaves are in the circle?	卌	5
How many leaves are in the triangle?	III	3
How many leaves are there in all?	卌 卌	10
How many leaves are in both the circle and the square?	II	2
How many leaves are in both the square and the triangle?	I	1

Page 112, Cats and Dogs

	Tally	Number
How many cats are in the big circle?	I	1
How many dogs are in the square?	III	3
How many cats are in the small circle?	II	2
How many animals are in the square only?	III	3
How many animals are in the small circle only?	II	2

Page 113, Boys and Girls

	Tally	Number
How many children are inside the circle?	IIII	4
How many children are outside the circle?	卌	5
How many boys are inside the circle?	III	3
How many girls are outside the circle?	II	2
How many children are there in all?	卌IIII	9

Page 114, Square Logic

	Tally	Number
Squares in the big circle	卌 I	6
Squares in the small circle	III	3
Squares in the middle circle	卌 I	6
Squares in both big and middle circles	II	2
Squares in both small and middle circles	I	1

Page 115, Animal Logic

	Tally	Number
Frogs in the circle	I	1
Frogs in the square	II	2
Fish in the circle	III	3
Fish in the circle only	II	2
Frogs in the square only	I	1
Turtles in the square		0
Turtles in the circle	I	1

Page 116, What's Common? (I)

1. same shape **2.** same shape and size
3. same color **4.** same shape **5.** same color
6. same shape and size **7.** same shape and size
8. same shape, size, and color

Page 117, What's First?

1. A **2.** B **3.** B **4.** A **5.** B **6.** A **7.** B **8.** C

Note: The answers for problems 3, 7, and 8 may vary. It's possible students might go to sleep before turning out the light—or put bread in before plugging in the toaster. They might also read a book (while in the library) before they borrow it.

Page 118, Bird Logic

	Number
Birds in the square	11
Birds in the square only	6
Birds in the circle	9
Birds in both the circle and the square	5
Birds in both the circle and the triangle	2
Birds in the triangle only	3
Birds in the circle, the triangle, and the square	1

Page 119, Jet Logic

	Number
Jets not in a rectangle	1
Jets in all	15
Jets in rectangle 1	9
Jets in rectangle 2	7
Jets in rectangle 3	9
Jets in both rectangles 1 and 3	4
Jets in both rectangles 2 and 3	5
Jets in all three rectangles	2

Page 120, Shape Logic

	Number
▲ in the rectangle	3
▲ in the circle	2
■ in the circle	1
■ in the rectangle	2
■ not in any shape	2
▲ in all	4
■ in all	5

Page 121, Count the Cones

1. 8 **2.** 9 **3.** 5 **4.** 5 **5.** 11 **6.** 9

Page 122, Squares and Circles

	Number
Circles in the big circle	3
Squares in the big square	3
Circles in the big circle only	2
Squares in the big square only	1
Squares in both big shapes	2
Circles in both big shapes	1
Circles in the big square only	2
Squares in the big circle only	1

Page 123, Logic Leaves

	Number
Leaves in the circle only	5
Leaves in the square only	3
Leaves in the triangle only	2
Leaves in both the circle and the square	2
Leaves in both the square and the triangle	3
Leaves in neither the circle nor the triangle	6
Leaves in the rectangle only	3
Leaves in the rectangle	18

Page 124, What's Common? (II)

1. same shape and size **2.** same color
3. same shape and color **4.** same shape and size
5. same shape, size, and color **6.** same color
7. same shape and color **8.** same shape and size

Page 125, Missing Words

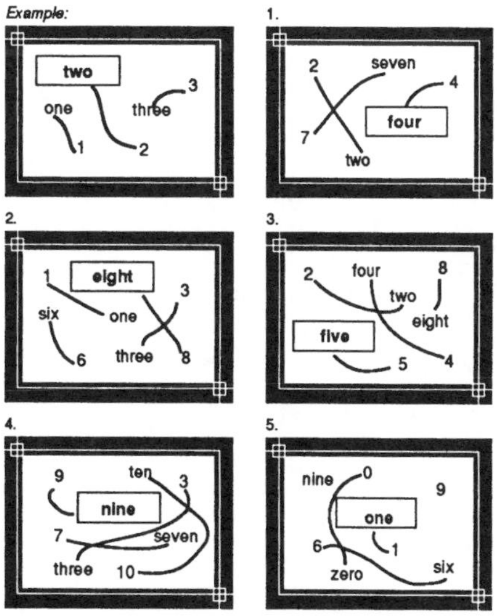
Example:
two
one
three
1
2
3
1.
2
seven
4
four
7
two
2.
1
eight
3
six
one
6
three
8
3.
2
four
8
two
eight
five
5
4
4.
9
ten
3
nine
7
seven
three
10
5.
nine
0
9
one
6
1
zero
six

Page 126, Number Names

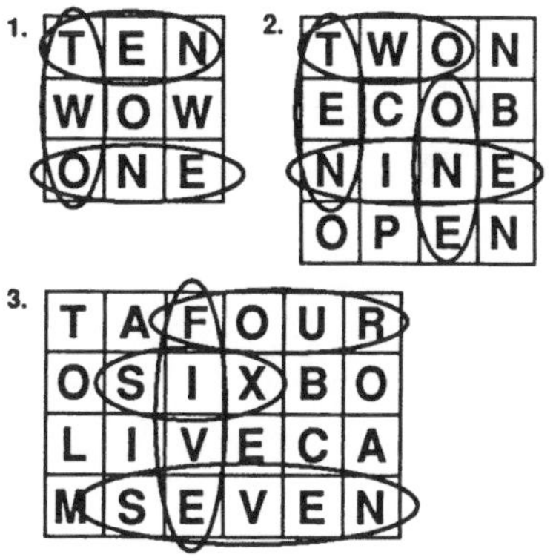
1.
T E N
W O W
O N E
2.
T W O N
E C O B
N I N E
O P E N
3.
T A F O U R
O S I X B O
L I V E C A
M S E V E N

Page 127, Relationships

1. puppy **2.** lake **3.** hand **4.** foot **5.** egg
6. air **7.** go **8.** painter **9.** peacock, bird
10. cookie, plate
Note: Some of these answers, particularly those for problems 9 and 10, may vary.

Page 128, What's Common? (III)

1. same shape and size **2.** same shape and color
3. same color **4.** same shape and size **5.** same color
6. same shape and size **7.** same shape
8. None of these attributes are in common.

Page 129, Same or Different?

1. Different **2.** Different **3.** Same **4.** Different
5. Different **6.** Same

Page 130, What First? (II)

1. D, B **2.** C, A **3.** A, D **4.** B, C **5.** C, F, B
6. D, E, A
Note: The order of some of the answers may vary, particularly for problems 2 and 4.

Page 131, Open Book

1. middle **2.** front **3.** middle **4.** front
5. back **6.** middle **7.** front **8.** middle
9. middle **10.** back

Page 132, Number Logic (I)

3. 1, 8 **4.** 1, 4, 5, 6, 7, 8 **5.** 1 **6.** 2 **7.** 2, 3
8. 2, 4

Page 133, Shell Game

1. 7 **2.** 8 **3.** 6 **4.** 6 **5.** 3 **6.** 13 **7.** 4

Page 134, What's Common? (IV)

1. same color **2.** same shape **3.** same shape
4. same shape and size **5.** same color **6.** same shape
7. None of these attributes are in common.
8. same shape and color

Page 135, Number Logic (II)

1. 20 **2.** 22 **3.** 6 **4.** 5 **5.** 7 **6.** 26 **7.** 28

Page 136, Juggling Numbers

1. 2 + 3 + 4 **2.** 2 + 3 − 4 **3.** 4 + 3 − 2
4. 4 + 2 − 3 **5.** 1 + 3 + 4 **6.** 4 + 3 − 1
7. 4 + 1 − 3 **8.** 3 + 1 − 4

Page 137, Bigger and Bigger

1. 9 − 2 **2.** 8 − 3 **3.** 13 − 4 **4.** 23 − 14
5. 43 − 24 **6.** smaller **7.** 8 − 3 **8.** 14 − 5
9. 16 − 7 **10.** 49 − 15 **11.** 87 − 39 **12.** larger

Page 138, Math Group Problem

1. yes **2.** no **3.** no **4.** no **5.** no **6.** yes
7. no **8.** yes **9.** no **10.** yes

Page 139, What Is My Number?

1. false **2.** true **3.** true **4.** true **5.** false
6. true

Page 140, What's Not Here?

1. FIVE **2.** ONE **3.** YARD

Page 141, Missing Answers

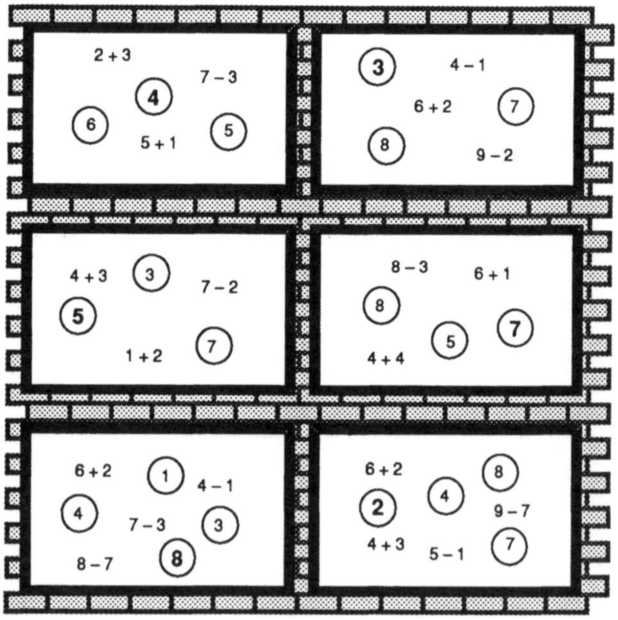

2 + 3
7 − 3
4
6
5 + 1
5
3
4 − 1
6 + 2
7
8
9 − 2
4 + 3
3
7 − 2
5
1 + 2
7
8 − 3
6 + 1
8
7
5
4 + 4
6 + 2
1
4 − 1
4
7 − 3
3
8 − 7
8
6 + 2
8
4
2
9 − 7
4 + 3
5 − 1
7

Page 142, Number Problems

Answers will vary (except in problems 7 and 8). Some possible answers are:

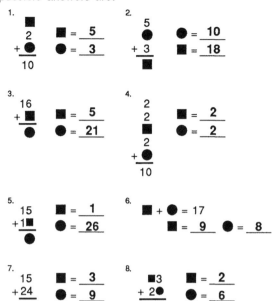

1.
```
   ■
   2
 + ●
 ---
  10
```
■ = 5
● = 3

2.
```
   5
   ●
 + 3
 ---
   ■
```
● = 10
■ = 18

3.
```
  16
 + ■
 ---
   ●
```
■ = 5
● = 21

4.
```
   2
   2
   ■
   2
 + ●
 ---
  10
```
■ = 2
● = 2

5.
```
  15
 +1■
 ---
   ●
```
■ = 1
● = 26

6. ■ + ● = 17

■ = 9 ● = 8

7.
```
  15
 +24
 ---
  ■●
```
■ = 3
● = 9

8.
```
  ■3
 +2●
 ---
  49
```
■ = 2
● = 6

Page 143, Smallest and Largest

SMALLEST

1. 3 + 4 = 7 2. 6 − 1 = 5 3. 4 − 1 = 3
4. 11 − 8 = 3 5. 17 − 11 = 6 6. 13 − 5 = 8

LARGEST

1. 7 + 5 = 12 2. 2 + 5 =7 3. 3 + 8 = 11
4. 11 − 3 = 8 5. 13 + 3 = 16 6. 18 − 5 = 13

Page 144, Pick a Number

1. [10] + 6 − 1 + 5 − 2 − [10] + 2 = (10)
2. [2] + 6 − 1 + 5 − 2 − [2] + 2 = (10)
3. [100] + 6 − 1 + 5 − 2 − [100] + 2 = (10)
4. [17] + 12 − 3 + 4 − 11 − [17] + 4 − 6 = (0)
5. [20] + 12 − 3 + 4 − 11 − [20] + 4 − 6 = (0)
6. [3] + 12 − 3 + 4 − 11 − [3] + 4 − 6 = (0)

Explain your answers to problems 4, 5, and 6: **The answers are all zero. You subtract your starting numbers, and the other operations result in zero.**

The numbers chosen for each problem will vary. Some possibilities are shown above. However, the outcome of problems 1–3 should be 10—and that of problems 4–6 should be 0.

Page 145, Change a Word

1. TEN 2. NINETY 3. THREE 4. TWENTY
5. FORTY 6. MINUS 7. FOUR 8. SIXTY